Greenhill Books

FIGHTING THE
BOMBERS

WORLD WAR II GERMAN DEBRIEFS
PUBLISHED BY GREENHILL BOOKS

THE ANVIL OF WAR
German Generalship in Defence on the Eastern Front

THE BATTLE OF THE BULGE: THE GERMAN VIEW
Perspectives from Hitler's High Command

FIGHTING IN HELL
The German Ordeal on the Eastern Front

HITLER'S ARDENNES OFFENSIVE
The German View of the Battle of the Bulge

THE LUFTWAFFE FIGHTER FORCE
The View from the Cockpit

SPEARHEAD FOR BLITZKRIEG
Luftwaffe Operations in Support of the Army, 1939–1945

INSIDE THE AFRIKA KORPS
The Crusader Battles, 1941–1942

FIGHTING THE INVASION
The German Army at D-Day

FIGHTING IN NORMANDY
The German Army from D-Day to Villers-Bocage

FIGHTING THE BOMBERS

The Luftwaffe's Struggle
Against the Allied Bomber Offensive

AS SEEN BY ITS COMMANDERS

by
General der Flieger Josef Kammhuber, Generalleutnant
Josef "Beppo" Schmid, Generalmajor Hans-Detlef
Herhuth von Rohden, Dr. Willi Messerschmitt,
Generalleutnant Adolf Galland, Generaloberst Hubert
Weise, General der Flieger Wolfgang Martini, Major
Heinz-Wolfgang Schnaufer, Major Heinrich Ruppel,
Major G. S. Sandmann, Major Josef Scholls

Edited by
David C. Isby

Greenhill Books, London
Stackpole Books, Pennsylvania

Fighting the Bombers:
The Luftwaffe's Struggle against the Allied Bomber Offensive
First published 2003 by
Greenhill Books, Lionel Leventhal Limited,
Park House, 1 Russell Gardens, London NW11 9NN
and
Stackpole Books, 5067 Ritter Road,
Mechanicsburg, PA 17055, USA

British Library Cataloguing in Publication Data
Fighting the bombers:
the Luftwaffe's struggle against the Allied bomber offensive
1. Germany. Luftwaffe – Drill and tactics   2. World War,
1939–1945 – Aerial operations, British   3. World War,
1939–1945 – Aerial operations, American
4. Bombing, Aerial – Germany
I. Kammhuber, Josef II. Isby, David C.
940.5′44941

ISBN 1-85367-532-6

Library of Congress Cataloging-in-Publication Data available

Designed and typeset by Roger Chesneau
Printed and bound in Great Britain

Contents

Introduction

This book is a collection of Luftwaffe leaders' views of the Defense of the Reich against the Allied combined bomber offensive. The accounts give their version of the course of the battle against the bombers, how technology was developed and deployed—or not—in the increasingly sophisticated operations, and how the technology was employed in combat by fighter leaders and controllers. The longest and largest air campaign in history has certainly attracted its share of historians. However, the German accounts provided here give some unique insights.

The authors compiled most of these documents as prisoners of war, under the authority of the US Army Air Forces (although some of the interrogations on nightfighting were conducted by RAF specialists, themselves veterans of the bomber offensive). These documents represent the command "debrief" of many of the Luftwaffe's leaders, undertaken in 1945 or 1946. It is to our advantage that these debriefs were carried out while memories were fresh, for the prisoners were without most official documents. The exceptions were the von Rohden and Messerchmitt chapters, which were historical narratives requested by the USAAF and US Navy, respectively. These accounts are written by professionals, for other professionals. Much of the syntax and capitalization is non-standard and reflects that of the German original. The authors assume that those for whom they are writing know the abbreviations, equipment, and references they use freely (which has required the provision of a glossary).

The accounts include matters often overlooked, such as the development of German fighter control capabilities and tactics. They are, quite literally, the first draft of the history of the Luftwaffe fighter force, and make up in immediacy what they may lack in reflection and opportunities for archival research. Each of the authors was interrogated on subjects about which he had direct personal knowledge: the intense internal secrecy of the German war effort makes claims to knowledge that did not come from such hands-on experience suspect.

These accounts are earlier and less refined than the better-known series of historical studies written by former Luftwaffe officers (some volumes of which have been reprinted by publishers such as Greenhill Books and Garland) and collectively referred to as the Karlshrue Studies. However, the chapters by von Rohden—who went on to manage the Karlshrue Studies—may be seen as being the first of the series of studies. These chapters written done as a collaborative effort with a number of other Luftwaffe officers, including at least two of the authors of this volume, Adolf Galland and "Beppo" Schmid.

This book is in many ways complementary to *The Luftwaffe Fighter Force: The View From the Cockpit*, published by Greenhill in 1998. That was the history of an air force—that part of the Luftwaffe which flew fighters—from organization to ultimate defeat; *Fighting the Bombers* is the story of that force's greatest battle. Thus, it begins with historical narratives (those of von Rohden, Weise and Kammhuber) to set out the overall context. Then the technologies involved are introduced in more detail. Finally, there is consideration of the manner in which these technologies were applied by the fighter controllers and fighter pilots involved in the Defense of the Reich. *Fighting the Bombers* also stresses the technology of radio and radar and the night battle whereas the earlier book put more emphasis on covering the daylight battles. This reflected the role of Adolf Galland—whose concern was daylight air fighting—as the unifying voice in that book. In this book, although Galland reappears, there is a greater range of authors and concerns. The current volume could be subtitled "The View From the Ops Room," because that is where the authors did most of their fighting, leading and directing the fighters. While this volume's contributors include Major Schnaufer, the highest-scoring nightfighter ace (with 121 victories), the emphasis is on the system itself rather than the pilots who were at its "sharp end."

The narratives are all highly personal to the authors and certainly do not represent a more nuanced view taking a broader range of sources into account; some of the authors—most notably Kammhuber and Schmid—took this wider view in the 1950s when they prepared volumes in the Karlshrue studies. Others, like Schnaufer (killed in a post-war accident), never got to tell their story again. There has been no attempt to correct the accounts, even where the authors get things wrong, or to insert more recent or superior knowledge. Whenever possible, the original spellings and terminology have been maintained, including even such elementary things as capitalization and the rendering of umlauts into English, which have been placed without consistency in the original documents. The translation has been edited to bring specific terminology, but not necessarily grammar and syntax, into line with standard English-language usage. But the alterations have been kept to a minimum.

David C. Isby
Washington, March 2002

The Contributors

Galland, Generalleutnant Adolf Ace with 103 victories. Served as *Waffengeneral* (*General der Jagdflieger*) 1941–45, when relieved and put in command of Me 2629equipped JV 44. Widely known author postwar.

Kammhuber, General der Flieger Josef Bomber *Geschwader* commander at the start of the war, shot down by the French. Given command of *Fliegerkorps XII* against early RAF night raids. Built up night-fighter force but was relieved after Hamburg raids in 1943, after which he commanded in Denmark and Norway (in command of *Luftflotte 5*). Put in charge of jet- and rocket-powered aircraft programs in 1945. Worked on Karlshrue studies. Returned to *Luftwaffe* service in 1950s, becoming first *Inspekteur* (1956–62).

Martini, Generalmajor Wolfgang Chief of *Luftwaffe* Signal Troops (including radar) from September 1941 until the end of the war.

Messerschmitt, Dr Willi German aircraft designer from the First World War through to end of the Second. Responsible for many outstanding wartime combat aircraft designs, first with the Bayerische Flugzeugwerke A.G. and then with his own company. Postwar, also worked in automotive industry.

Rohden, Generalmajor Hans-Detlef Herhuth von Head of *Abteilung 8*—the Historical Section of the OKL—during the Second World War. Also held staff positions with operational formations (including six months each as chief of staff of IV Fliegerkorps and Luftflotte 4 on the eastern front). Post-war went to work for USAAF. Helped organize German logistical support for Berlin Airlift, 1948. In the 1950s, based at Karlsruhe, produced a series of studies written by former Luftwaffe officers for the USAF.

Ruppel, Major Heinrich First World War pilot and reserve officer. Sector controller at Darmstadt. Served as Ia, JaFu Mi Helrhein, at the end of the war. Considered by Schmid to be the best fighter controller in the *Luftwaffe*.

Sandmann, Major G. S.   Air Tactics Officer, Air Defense Section, OKL, at the end of the war. Previously served as Fighter Controller, *3. Jagddivision*.

Schmid, Generalleutnant Joseph "Beppo"   Intelligence chief of the *Luftwaffe* from January 1938 to November 1942. Given command of *I. Jagdkorps* from September 1943 until November 1944, despite being a non-aviator. *Luftwaffe West* commander for remainder of war. Worked on Karlshrue studies postwar.

Schnaufer, Major Heinz-Wolfgang   Highest-ranking *Luftwaffe* night-fighter ace, with 121 victories (almost all with Fritz Rumpelhardt, his radar operator throughout the war). Commanded *NJG 4* at the end of the war. Killed in road accident in 1950.

Scholls, Major Josef   Night-fighter pilot. Served with *NJG 6* at the end of the war.

Weise, Generaloberst Hubert   Senior flak officer who commanded *Befehlshaber Mitte* (and later *Luftflotte Reich*) from 1940 to 1944, when he was replaced by Stumpff. Later became head of Germany's missile defense program (preparing defenses against Allied copies of the V-1 and V-2).

PART ONE

THE DEFENSE OF THE REICH

This section provides the historical context and describes the course of events relevant to this book. The first chapter is a survey of the Defense of the Reich, compiled in 1946 by von Rohden; its later date than the other chapters is evident from the fact that it includes quotations from postwar US publications. The other chapters provide historical accounts by two of the senior Luftwaffe commanders who were in charge of defending the Reich in the earlier years of the bomber offensive—Generals Kammhuber and Weise.

The German air defense effort was largely an improvisation, and little "Prussian efficiency" is apparent in these accounts. This was especially pronounced in night-fighting, where extensive prewar experience was unavailable and the combat experience of the opening battles of the war was less transferable than to daylight operations.

Also apparent in these accounts are the limitations of the authors when writing about subjects in which they lacked personal knowledge, as shown by von Rohder's assertion that the Me 262 could have been operational much earlier than it was—which recent studies have contradicted.

D.C.I.

Chapter 1

Reich Air Defense in World War II
A strategic-tactical survey

Compiled by Generalmajor Hans-Detlef Herhuth von Rohden, August 1946

I. Pre-war Interpretation of
the Strategic Employment of Modern Air Forces

Even before 1939 certain ideas concerning an extensive air war had been accepted by military experts and authorities. Concrete conceptions as to the conduction of this new type of war had, however, not yet been built up. In spite of all technical performances, the planes and weapons needed for successful accomplishment were still wanting.

The numerical strength of the air arm was inferior to that of the armies and navies. These "old branches" of the armed forces could still maintain their predominance, but there seemed no doubt that a modern war would shift military operations into the air to a great extent. The more the air forces would augment their numerical strength, the more they would extend the combat ranges and increase the efficiency of their weapons, that much more would the air war gain a global scale.

It was presumed that the war in the air might in itself influence land and sea war activities. The air forces were not dependent upon the geographic conditions established by continents and oceans. In addition to that, the air forces were able virtually to outflank the army battle lines and the combat areas of the navies. Effecting the methods of independent air warfare, the "sky wings" could break through to the enemy's sources of power. Moreover, the air forces were considered an indispensable battle instrument, very decisively supporting the ground troops and the naval units. In the opinion already prevailing before the war, the struggle which the respective air forces would have to get through over the entire territories of the belligerent states was calculated to be of prime importance in the initial operations of all the armed forces fighting on both sides.

Air superiority, if possible air supremacy, should be the final goal. However, an air power inferior at the beginning of the war might have the faculty of equalizing the enemy's advantage during the following operations. The home front, of course, must ward off the first assault sufficiently to guarantee war production to an extent necessary for steady reinforcement of the armed forces.

In case of war, it was Germany's top task to hold free her skies and thus to prevent the air menace to which she was subjected because of her central geographic situation in Europe. The most essential reasons for her susceptibility to air attack are quoted below:

1. A large population living in overcrowded terms and other settlements.
2. The accumulation of industrial plants depending upon the natural distribution of raw materials.
3. The very complicated and interwoven power supply system.
4. A centralized communication net aggravating the difficult conditions which passive air defense already had overcome.

The following composition will give a short survey of the question, whether the organization and strategic conduct of the Reich Air Defense, as well as its tactical achievements, were placed in line with the real requisites induced by the actual course of the war in the air—or not!

II. The Offensive-Mindedness of the German Wehrmacht Delayed the Establishment of a Powerful Air Defense over the Reich, 1939–1941

In adaption to the leading political ideas, the German High Command was guided by a strategic concept of aiming to smash the respective adversaries separately by annihilating their armed forces in short campaigns. A war of attrition, as well as decisive campaigns in the two or even three theaters at one time, was to be avoided.

The Luftwaffe (GAF), too, was thinking offensively. The striking power should be used to break down the enemy's resistance on the very battle field and to wrest from him the freedom of action for strategic defense or new offensive operations by raiding his rear installations.

But at the same time training and combat doctrine should adjust the GAF to the task of a strategic and independent air war. The objective of those activities was to set out of action the opponent's sources of power. However, in conformity with the "Blitz-campaigns" planned, such air warfare did not seem very probable, at least not in the initial operations.

The sooner and the more efficiently the enemy could be driven from the bases used by his bombing forces, the less it would be necessary to provide major units for Air Defense of the Reich. In no case was offensive power to be weakened. Germany's military-historical tradition always regarded "the offensive the best defense." Besides that, the German forces were insufficient to establish a strong offensive and defensive at the same time. For that reason the air-war policy and the accomplishment of the overall strategic concept planned by Germany seemed to be coordinated to the conditions which the GAF wanted after an evolution spell of only 6 years. Its striking power was not yet adapted to sustain a longer war.

Therefore we do not wonder that the German High Command relied upon each and every means guaranteeing the offensive strategy.

In 1939 the order of battle and the operational objective of the German Air Defense forces had been set up according to the conception that the well-fortified "Western Zone of Air Defense" (Luftverteidigungs-zone West) would have the power to repulse even heavier air raids which the British-French Allies might undertake.

The available AA forces were distributed over Germany from the West up to the Elbe area. They were fixed to protect a series of special objects most important within the "Western Zone of Air Defense" stretching behind the "Westwall" to the east of Germany's western boundaries.

The dayfighter groups allocated to battle in the Reich proper were also concentrated around some definite objects to be protected.

Criticizing these measures, we must come to the conclusion that the German command authorities had virtually retrogressed to use the experiences gained in the Spanish Campaign, which were based on a tactical rather than on an air-strategical viewpoint. These events had not developed the concept of a grand strategy, neither in offense or defense. Besides that, the technical capacities of air defense were underestimated in regard to own offensive successes expected. They were overrated in view of enemy attack possibilities; the *future* development of fighter, bomber, and AA techniques had not been taken into full enough consideration.

In the same respect it is conceivable that the GAF had ignored opportunities to increase emphasis on the nightfighter arm. Before the war there existed some test units. Nightfighter actions were not supposed to reach such a peak as they did later. This opinion seemed to be proved by the fact that in the beginning of the war, until spring 1940, the British-French Allies did not achieve large scale night raids either. Night operations were restricted to occasional harassing attacks. Combat planes had primarily to drop propaganda publications. The activities spread over the Reich's western provinces; they reached the north-western coast district too.

On 13 December 1939, the RAF launched a strong daylight bombing raid on navy installations in the north-western German coast areas. The bombers suffered heavy losses from timely counter-attacks launched by a German fighter command post, utilizing radar sets (by way of trial) for the first time.

The "Battle in the German Bay" had proved that daylight penetrations into inner Germany could not be made without escort cover. German daylight air control over the Reich was assured . . . further attacks did not take place.

This success, however, did not introduce large scale employment of these modern air-war instruments. Technical consequences were not drawn immediately. The German fighters used radar detection sets on a larger scale only from 1941 and 1942 on. AA units applied them since 1940 to detect approaching enemy planes and to control effective gunfire.

An earlier introduction was handicapped by production difficulties and, perhaps, by the fact that the High Command had not recognized in time the future importance these implements would have for air-war tactics, as well as for the whole air strategy.

Since the battle of France was opened, the first night attacks on a larger scale were launched by the British against targets situated in the northern part of Germany. After the ground operations in France had come to an end, the RAF intensified the night raids in the northwestern German areas and on Berlin.

The hopes on which Germany's war concept was based had been realized only partially. Great Britain continued to fight. The plans for the invasion of the UK were relinquished because of the doubtful successes expected. Moreover, the German High Command began to plan the Russian Campaign; it was very probable that the war in the East would tie up extraordinarily strong GAF forces.

Despite this, the GAF launched the "Blitz." Germany considered her power strong enough to lame Great Britain from the air. Again the offensive concept predominated, although even in the first days of the Battle of Britain the RAF air defensive proved its decisive importance.

These offensive objectives of overall German strategy (Gesamtkriegs-führung) and the underrating of the British adversary make conceivable why improvised means were used to strengthen the active Air Defense of the Reich, virtually up to the last episodes of the war. The High Command also hoped for decisive interception of the Allied air forces *beyond* Germany's boundaries. In the East no dangerous air raids were expected.

Up to 1941 the Reich Air Defense forces were controlled only by the respective "Air Region Commands" (Luftgaukommandos). The AA units bore the main burden of the defense. The bulk of the dayfighters operated in the ground-front areas. Until the end of 1940 the whole strength of the nightfighters amounted to three groups located in the Netherlands.

From the fall of 1941 on, the idea to combine the air defense system as a whole under the supreme command of a high-level authority was slowly strengthened. In April 1941 the "Air Force Command Center" (Luftwaffenbefehlahaber Mitte) was activated. The newly built-up nightfighter division was put under the direct control of the AFCC. The "Air Region Commands" (Luftgaukommandos), also subordinate to the AFCC, commanded the AA units, as well as the respective auxiliary services (signal units, aircraft warning system, passive aerial defense, etc.).

Although the Battle of Britain had been lost, the strategic concept to induce decision by offensive operations was maintained. For that reason a powerful Reich Air Defense had been established: A FUNDAMENTAL EXPANSION OF ITS ARMAMENT WAS NOT EFFECTED!

Anyway, the night penetrations achieved by the British in 1940 had called for a change of air defense tactics. Two nightfighting methods were built up:

1. Non-controlled *object*-fixed nightfighter defense (Wilde Sau).
2. Controlled *object*-fixed nightfighter defense (Zahme Sau).

The first type fixed the nightfighters at one particular object to be protected. The units had to work in close cooperation with the AA. The other system represented special nightfighter operations separated from the AA activities. The fighters were controlled by radar ground stations.

Further development brought about 'light' (helle) and 'dark' (dunkle) nightfighting. The lightened one was supported by a large number of searchlight batteries distributed over a determined area, e.g. the Hamburg–Bremen area. Limited combat sectors, in accordance with the main attack directions the RAF used to take, were set up. Within the limits of 'dark nightfighting' the AA searchlights were replaced by radar-control sets. In the two latter systems the nightfighter engagements had absolute priority.

From 1941/42 on General Kammhuber (C.G. of the nightfighter arm of the GAF) intensified the nightfighter operations. The "controlled *area*-fixed nightfighter defense" (Himmelbettverfahren) was established.

In 1941, as well as before, the RAF was not able to attain the initiative by launching a powerful air offensive, although Great Britain exhibited a considerable recuperative power after the Battle of Britain; but she could strengthen her own air defense very successfully. Directly in front of the UK's gateways the Germans possessed the advance air-bases in France, in Belgium, and in the Netherlands. There the German dayfighter wings operated and their losses did not increase sharply. The capacity of German aircraft production rose to such an output that the number of fighter planes ready for action could still be kept up sufficiently. Both contestants conducted daylight operations cautiously.

In opposition to this limited strategy, British night-bombing increased. As it was supposed in Germany, these raids had the goal to train crews, as well as to improve attack methods. Besides that, the RAF hoped for adequate effects.

In the meantime the big German air offensive had been stopped because of the Russian Campaign. After this fatal war was opened, there remained in France only two fighter wings of Luftflotte 3. One fighter group at a time stayed in Holland and in the coast area of the German Sea (Nordsea). Moreover, at the Western Air Front (Luftflotte 3), there remained the training groups of all given fighter wings. Although they had little value for battle, they might pretend a greater fighter strength in the West, at least for a limited period. Each of these groups set up special "combat-squadrons"(Einsatzstaffeln). These prevented the unescorted British day-bombing raids into areas otherwise stripped of German fighters from being carried out without losses.

Now, after the greater part of the German fighter wings had left the western battle zone for Russia, the RAF carried out daylight operations. Considering the strength of forces, the combat range, and the respective targets, we must presume that the strategic objective was to tie up German air units in the West, and to influence the Russians politically. The area attacked did not exceed the range of fighter escort, i.e. about up to the line Antwerp–Brussels–St Quentin–-Amiens—Le Mans—Nantes.

In 1941, with the exception of one fighter group operating in the Bay of Heligoland, there were no pursuit forces at hand in Reich territory. The GAF fighters restricted their activities to the advance battle area in Western Europe.

On the whole, RAF night-bombing had a harassing character in 1941. Methods of navigation, target-finding, and bombing techniques had not yet reached a peak; consequently, no effective "area bombing" took place. The RAF night operations were flown in extended formation. They were carried out on a widely dispersed front. Turning back the RAF bomber streams even enlarged the intervals.

In the face of these tactics the "controlled area-fixed nightfighter defense" (Himmelbettverfahren) proved itself very appropriate and efficient within the range of the radar ground sets, which determined the extent of the nightfighting area. The further increase of successes seemed to depend only upon:

1. Adequate augmentation of nightfighter units operating in the respective areas. The goal must be to "cover" THE ENTIRE AREA and to meet every enemy bomber approaching the target-area.
2. Improvements in training and experience both of radar ground crews and flying crews.

Criticising the events of the year 1941, we recognize the following important facts, as far as the problem of Air Defense of the Reich is concerned:

1. The German *daylight* air *control* over the Reich territory did exist; but the British had not contended for it!
2. The German *night* air control over the Reich was in question; *superiority* just barely existed.
3. In the East and in the South the German armies started offensive operations. However, serious setbacks were going on. Strong GAF units formed the backbone for the frequent crucial situations.
4. The German sources of power (Kraftquellen), the heart of a successful overall strategy (Gesamtkriegsführung), were not absolutely assured.
5. Decisive measures to strengthen Reich air defense radically were not stepped up.
6. The German High Command underestimated the British and Russian war potential, as well as the armament and military performance to be expected of the USA.
7. Germany's industrial and technical capacity for building a powerful air defense existed, but was not utilized sufficiently.

III. Air Defense over the Reich not Strong Enough—the Wehrmacht did not Gain Decisively at the Outer Fronts, but Suffered Reverses

1942   By the beginning of 1942 the OKL (High Command of the Air Forces) had decided to activate two air defense dayfighter wings. These were composed of several combat squadrons (Einsatzstaffeln). For a long time their value in combat was low because of the want of experienced pilots.

On the other hand, the RAF daylight operations lacked strategic effect. It must be admitted, however, that there were certain signs heralding the rising strategic air war. Harassing attacks in bad weather and long-range daylight recce flights by Mosquitoes, noteworthy merely because of their concept and arrangement, prepared for the coming large-scale air strategy.

In this respect one daylight operation deserves our notice. Twelve Lancasters of Bomber Command were launched against the MAN U-boat diesel engine plants in Augsburg on 17 April 1942. Of these, eight aircraft pushed into the target-area. Seven bombers were shot down by AA and fighters. These defense actions, however, were successful because of favorable circumstances: good weather conditions, lack of fighter escort for the bombers, report in time by the German air warning system, and complete readiness for action of the defense units.

Thus it was understandable that GAF command authorities fostered an erroneous opinion concerning the efficiency of German air defense strength. It was thought that the interceptor units (Alarmeinheiten) sent up by the fighter training schools could successfully deal with daylight operations in the inner German territory. Apparently, the High Command aimed to avoid any measure which would necessitate the building up of new formations, which would decrease the effective strength of units operating in the front areas. The GAF had insufficient reserves.

Attempts to ward off the Mosquito reconnaissance planes were unsuccessful for the following reason:

1. Unsatisfactory performance of:
   The aircraft warning service (Flugmeldedienst).
   The radar detection system (Funkmessdienst).
   The radar fighter control (Jägerleitsystem).
2. The speed of the German fighter planes was little if any greater than that of the Mosquitoes.
3. The crews sent up by the interceptor units lacked combat experience.
4. The Mosquitoes flew too high and too fast for effective AA fire.

From the middle of 1942 on the German High Command recognized the activation of the American Eighth Air Force in the UK. Good data existed concerning armament and the other equipment, indicating that daylight operations were planned. In October 1942 the combat strength of the USAAF bombers striking in France mounted to more than 100 aircraft. However, the opening of the strategic daylight offensive against the Reich proper had been retarded because considerable forces were transferred from the English bases to the North Africa theater (probably four fighter groups and two heavy bomber groups). The German command authorities recognized the long-range capabilities of the USAAF fighter escort units.

As far as German defense activities were concerned, in many respects the German fighters showed some noticeably weak spots. The USAAF bombers took advantage of their strong defensive armament and their solid structural strength, making them hardly vulnerable to gun hits. At this stage of the air war the German fighters had not yet mastered the combat tactics of launching concentrated attacks by several planes at a time. This method was very necessary to split the bomber defense fire. Perhaps the German fighters overrated the defense power of the "Flying Fortresses" and their susceptibility to gun fire too much.

Besides this, in 1942 the RAF night-bombing increased seriously. The number of planes participating in the big attacks and the devastating effect of area bombing went beyond the extent reached by the Germans in the Battle of Coventry in November 1940. The RAF raids were achieved from higher altitudes. The speeds increased.

The efficiency of German nightfighter operations still improved because the defense radar sets and the radar communication systems were not interfered with. The British bomber units flew widely dispersed. The individual planes could be tracked and were knocked down. The RAF defensive weapons had a very low rate of fire. British long-range nightfighters had not yet appeared. The successes pleased the German command authorities. However, they did not foresee that the RAF would develop new tactics and modernized technical equipment to overcome German defense methods and instruments.

Despite the fact that the German "controlled area-fixed nightfighter defense" (Himmelbettverfahren) began to prove too inflexible, due to the continually changing enemy attack procedures, new tactical methods were not considered to be urgently and immediately necessary. The reasons for the system's failure were:

1. Once established, it was impossible to move the installations rapidly into other areas in accordance with the objectives newly chosen by enemy bomber units.
2. The tactics of the RAF bomber stream considerably shortened the attack time and grouped the flying components. They did not allow a sufficient number of pursuit planes to be brought into successful engagement.
3. The system concerned did not permit building any effective resistance against harassing operations spread out over *larger areas beyond* the *fixed* radar ranges, let alone against activities expanding over the entire Reich.
4. Therefore, German fighters could not engage in wide-spread pursuit operations.

The air defense did not yet perform modern patterns of nightfighting, e.g. pursuit activities over long distances, long-range nightfighting over enemy airbases (forbidden by Hitler himself), a powerful fixed air defense system to keep a particular locality completely clear by means of reformed material equipment. Only the number of fighter planes and radar stations employed in the "Himmelbett" areas were augmented. The command authorities hoped that applying these measures would bring further success.

In consideration of these developments, the year 1942 must be regarded as the starting point of a real modern air war. More and more, but still hardly perceptible, the center of combat gravity passed over from land strategy to air strategy. This shifting was the result of the fact that in the western war zones the air forces governed the situation, influencing naval operations as well. The global scale of the entire war had been developed when the USA effectively entered this real world war. Improving their technical means and strengthening their striking forces, the Western Allies had recognized—earlier than the Axis—that the final success would depend, above all, on a tremendous air superiority enabling the air forces to knock out the German industrial war potential and morale.

On the other hand, at this stage the Axis probably saw their air war strategy as a delaying one. The decisive operations were to be reactivated when Russia was downed. To land strategy in the east absorbed a lot of forces—and therefore almost the bulk of the GAF—to smash Soviet power. In this theater the ground war elements dominated, even though they were unsuccessful. Thus, in view of the serious realities in the West, it is true that this strategy fogged the clear thinking of the German war leaders.

But the German air armament did not increase in time, either technically or in numbers; the performances of German air defense were not placed in line with the requisites of a mighty strategic scale. Besides that, German strategic bombing had already come to a deadlock. The efforts made in the east to lame or even to destroy important parts of Russian war production were wasted indeed. Great Britain strengthened her defense power, and struck back effectively enough. The US armed forces and the British battered the Axis in the Mediterranean. The USAAF attacked the German perimeter—air forces in the German-held western territories, in Italy, and in the Balkans. Allied shipping, up to this time lamed by the German U-boat raids and the air attacks, now began to recuperate by warding off the German sea and land activities.

It must be admitted, however, that there were not yet very clear signs that the final victory might be accomplished, or at least would be prepared decisively by the air forces alone. Following its landminded concept, the German High Command trusted more than ever before in the hope that the German armies would be able to outweigh Russian resistance at the end of 1942, as well as gain the victory in the Mediterranean!

Was that logical thinking? Why did not the German High Command draw the conclusion that just the GAF had constituted the initial successes by covering and supporting the extended army battle zones in all theaters? The Luftwaffe had interrupted the enemy supply lines; it had facilitated the armies' advances; the GAF had overcome crucial moments in which the army had suffered in the East as well as in the South; the GAF had weakened the Allied air and ground

MAJOR TARGETS:
The Strategic Bombing
Offensive

troops; the GAF had provided German forces with "air supply goods"; the Luftwaffe represented the element combining air, sea, and land warfare in the Mediterranean!

Now the Luftwaffe was going to decay, and there was nobody indeed who asserted himself valiantly and unconditionally in order to enforce *fundamental* efforts to *strengthen the German air defense radically*! It could not be denied that the course of events in all theaters, last but not least over the Reich itself, were going to herald a possible defeat!

But the German High Command was tied up in the would-be victories at Stalingrad and El Alamein. The GAF Commander-in-Chief, too, did not fully comprehend what was going to happen. So, the pace of German air defense has not been sufficiently stepped up in time. The rising giant of the Allied strategic air war was considered as not existing, even though the preliminary performances were notorious!

That was the situation at the end of the fateful year of 1942. Just this period represented the moment urgently calling for radical improvements and still promising successes. But the declaration of "total war" remained to be a vain attempt.

IV.The Struggle for Air Control over Germany: 1943–1944 up to D-Day.

The year 1943 was the base for the final result of World War II. In consideration of the Allied air warfare, in 1943 the following milestones are remarkable:

1. The USAAF headed stronger air offensive operations against the German war potential targets in the Reich territory.
2. The setting up of long range fighter escorts.
3. The number of Allied combat planes fighting over Germany was increased.
4. The demolishing effects were emphasized by "carpet-bombing" achieved by closely flying bomber units.
5. The air raids were carried out over a larger range.
6. The British night-bombing increased considerably.
7. The Casablanca Directive.

The main objectives were:

1. The U-boat bases, U-boat building yards, and repair installations.
2. The ball-bearing factories.
3. Air industry plants (air-frame production, assembly factories, and engine plants).
4. Oil supply.

The biggest daylight operations were flown by the English-based US Eighth Air Force. At the end of 1943 the 15th Air Force, taking off from bases in Italy (and to a smaller extent the Ninth Air Force), participated. Those latter Air Forces launched attacks against targets situated in Austria and in the Balkans.

The British efforts to destroy the dams of the Eder and Möhne rivers, as well as the battle of Hamburg, seriously sharpened the situation of German Air Defense. The dam attack operations (16 and 17 March, 24 and 25 June 1943) had been surprise blows because of their suddenness and the effect which the new, specialized bombs had produced. The strength of the AA defense was low; in the area of the Eder valley-barrage only a small number of light AA guns were in action. As a result of these blows, which had produced heavy damage and very high personnel casualties, the respective ground defense units were strengthened.

At the end of July 1943 the colossal three-night offensive against Hamburg devastated the city. For the first time the British used "Window" successfully.

The new type of warfare—the high-frequency war—emphasized its importance. The "Window" interfered with the airborne interception equipment, as well as jamming the radar ground stations. The nightfighter engagements and AA fire were at the point of losing their essential former effectiveness.

Moreover, now the RAF used concentrated "bomber-stream tactics'" insuring success of attack. The Reich air defense faced a situation completely altering the former combat conditions. The calculations made in respect to the strength of AA units needed for ground defense operations proved to be outstripped. The space of time required for mass attacks from now on was reduced so much that AA fire no longer achieved satisfactory results.

Modern types of night bombers (Lancaster and Halifax) were put in operation. They clearly expressed the momentary superiority of air offense over air defense, at least as far as the tactical and technical means both the belligerent sides employed at this stage of the war. While in May 1942 about 1,000 RAF bombers had battered Cologne and dropped 1,500 tons within a space of 1½ hours, in 1943 the same sort of blows were carried out by scarcely 400 planes during 15 minutes.

Nevertheless, the number of aircraft in question increased. But now the RAF bomber losses did not rise. The causes are quoted above.

As far as the daylight air war was concerned, the year 1943 is considered the decisive period too. After having accomplished their first tasks without constant escort cover, from May 1943 on the US bombers (Eighth Air Force) struck under the protection of Thunderbolts. They operated over Holland and Western Germany. One of the most decisive steps to build up a separate and far-reaching strategic air war was made.

Now, as before, the German High Command thought that the US daylight penetrations finally would not succeed. It guessed that the German fighter forces, even though inferior in numbers, could inflict such unbearably prohibitive losses that the USAAF might be compelled to cease larger operations. Although there was available very clear information regarding the long range those aircraft might be made to fly, the German High Command did not believe these performances. Perhaps it was expected that the USAAF would slip back into the old faults the Germans had made in the Battle of Britain. There they had carried out a daylight offensive neglecting its prerequisites, i.e. to attain and to hold air superiority, even air supremacy.

Despite the clear trend of development the war in the air was now taking, the German High Command did not accomplish an important reinforcement of air defense in the homeland proper. In Hitler's opinion each larger defensive strategy seemed to be a retrogression. Even when it was obviously recognized

A Bf-110, caught by a USAAF fighter, demonstrates its vulnerability in daylight. By 1944, the Bf-110 required an escort for daylight operations. (US National Archives)

that the US escort fighters absolutely could penetrate the Ruhr area, no decisive measures to neutralize this danger were introduced.

In 1943 the Mosquito activities rose to a larger scale. Special German fighter units, experienced in the Russian Campaign, were drawn back from the Eastern front and set in to battle the Mosquitoes. At this time the GAF did not possess any pursuit plane capable of fighting Mosquito reconnaissance successfully. All desperate efforts had no results. The GAF lacked forces to compensate this technical inferiority. If it would have been possible to establish a lot of special Mosquito defense fighters, and to distribute many, even small units over the entire Reich, then those forces might have engaged the Mosquitoes under favorable combat circumstances, everywhere, but pursuit engagements conducted over large distances were of no use.

This "west-bound" fighter strategy had aimed at battling the enemy bombers—at least with partial defense forces—just at the moment when they were entering the periphery of German-held territory. In no case—this was the plan—was any precious time and combat space to fight the enemy to be lost. Because of their location, however, only individual fighter groups, one after the other, were enabled to engage the bombers. The German pursuit units were split over a large area. The average number of planes ready for action in the various groups did not exceed about 20 aircraft. The group represented the "combat unit" fighting autonomously. From April 1943 on, auxiliary fuel tanks were introduced in order to enable the fighters to increase their combat range.

In the inner Reich the fighter schools, the fighter training groups, and even the factory test-flight services were ordered to set up small "alarm units" (Alarmeinheiten). They were to intercept enemy planes which had come through the western air wall. The successes were small.

In the meantime the Allied daylight operations had caused serious conditions in the Reich itself. The attacks launched at the end of July against the air industry plants and, in the middle of August against the ball bearing industry, accomplished remarkable reductions in the whole armament program. The accuracy in bombing, the area bombing and the well-planned Allied overall strategy began to lame the most important bottle-neck industrial plants. The German war potential, intensifying its capacity just at this stage of the war, would hardly absorb the demolishing results effected by those operations for any length of time.

On the other hand, good hopes were nourished because of Milch's self-supporting efforts to increase fighter production. We note the fact that these improvements were not challenged by the proper High Command. However, it must be admitted that the program was designed only to utilize to capacity those industrial and technical means which already existed. We cannot ascertain a radical shifting of the entire German armament in favor of developing a powerful air defense. Probably the German High Command believed that it would be possible to conduct the war in the air without such a change. Hitler argued that Europe was to be defended first in Tunisia, then in Sicily, and finally in Italy. In any case, had sufficient number of fighters been provided, the Allies would not have dared to operate over inner Germany without fighter cover at this stage of the war.

But the German fighter arm had to battle at the periphery of German-held Europe, according to the orders given. The units were worn out by the rising Allied air superiority; consequently, heavy combats "swallowed" instantly every sort of material supply; any remarkable alleviation, let alone any effective reinforcement, could not be materialized; the losses produced a rapid dwindling of the material and moral combat faculties.

Only in July 1943, when the attempts to break Allied air supremacy in the southern theater had fallen down, a couple of exhausted fighter groups were transferred into Reich territory. From Russia, too, two groups were withdrawn. The units did not receive any rest, neither for recuperation nor to become acquainted with the special combat conditions, existing in the battle fields of the strategic air war. They had to fight immediately because of the crucial hardships of the German air situation.

From spring 1943 on, for want of daylight fighters, the nightfighter units were put into daylight operation. They were equipped with Bf-110 (interceptors) and Ju-88 (bomber and reconnaissance planes). The crews concerned, however, did not master close-formation flying and the tactics of concentrated attack. The planes were too big and too sluggish. These dayfighter engagements sapped both the crews and the aircraft. Nevertheless, the result seemed to be positive as long as Allied escort cover did not operate. When this materialized, however, the German nightfighter losses rose rapidly and prohibitively. Their strength decreased severely; above all, the experienced crews were lost. In 1944 the employment of such units in daylight operations over Reich territory had to be relinquished.

The first combat operations by the strengthened German forces eased the crucial air situation within the Reich to a certain extent, although it was a belated effect. The Eighth Air Force escort fighters still hardly penetrated beyond Holland and the northern German coast district. In any case, German fighter activities were not essentially handicapped.

At the same time, the defense fighters equipped with 21 cm rockets gained transitory successes. Applying this method, they operated beyond effective bomber fire (about 880 m). On the other hand, the purpose of these weapons, to split the close bomber formations, was accomplished only in isolated instances. The escort cover later achieved by the USAAF largely nullified the operational effect of these weapons.

In spite of everything, the air struggle had reached a point at which German fighters engaged the USAAF penetrations into inner Germany effectively although weak in numbers. Examples were the air battles over Cassel (28 July 1943) and Schweinfurt (17 August 1943). The respective losses reached the following figures:

Cassel: 7 German fighters, 35 USAAF bombers.
Schweinfurt: 25 German fighters, 60 USAAF bombers.

The Schweinfurt battle was a "shuttle" operation. The successes raised the self-confidence of the German fighter crews. It almost seemed possible to repeat such defense engagements at any chosen time, and to improve the results if the fighter forces would be strengthened; but they ought to have operated in a still more concentrated manner.

This successful period of the German air war gradually came to an end. The P-47 extended its range to 325 miles by using droppable auxiliary tanks. A well organized and executed relay fighter escort system was built up. However, it must be stated that the escort fighter efficiency could not be estimated too highly as long as they operated defensively, i.e. as long as they were bound to close protection of the bomber components. Notwithstanding, the technical data on expected P-51 performances made it evident that the fighter-escort range had not reached its peak.

The USAAF did not intend to repeat the faults the Germans had made in 1940. There the Germans had believed it would be possible to gain air supremacy over the UK using an escort range of about 250 km. The USAAF daylight operations, too, would have failed if they had missed the long-range fighter cover so urgently needed for the fulfillment of the overall concept.

By this time the USAAF-activities fell into two groups:

1. Fighter-escorted raids launched against nearer targets (north German coast area, Holland, Belgium and France).
2. Several attack operations carried out against inner Germany targets. Fighter escort was used only to accompany the bombers up to the German boundaries; returning, the bombers were met in the same area.

The latter mentioned undertakings were very hazardous ones. There would have been heavy losses in bomber planes if the German fighters had been withdrawn into the depths of the Reich itself.

Facing the USAAF fighter-escorted penetrations, the Germans resumed their former mistakes: the German pursuit planes had to attack only the Allied bombers; the fighter escort should be ignored, as far as that might be possible. Attack tactics, plane equipment, training, and armament were exclusively adapted for fighting the bombers. Surely, the decision to engage escort-cover and bomber components simultaneously was hard to make, because the ratio of the defense forces became more

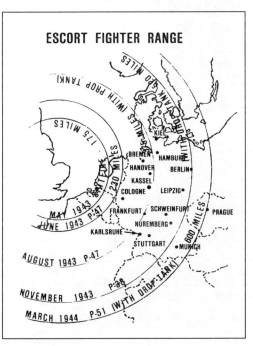

ESCORT FIGHTER RANGE

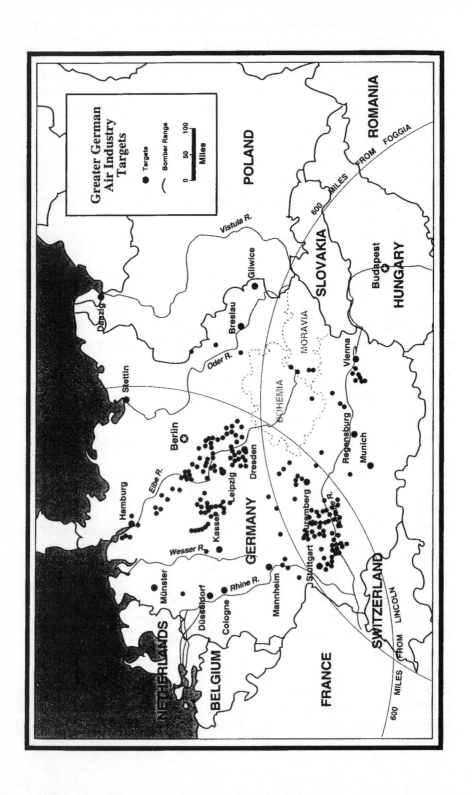

Greater German
Air Industry
Targets

● Targets

⌒ Bomber Range

Miles

0   50   100

and more unfavorable. Consequently, it would have been necessary to induce by force a series of 'fighter-battles', and to ignore the bombers, perhaps absolutely. Only the knockout of the escort fighters could accomplish the annihilation of the bombers and then the resurrection of German air supremacy.

On the other hand, the USAAF had not yet obtained the decisive prerequisites of any successful strategic bombing, air control, at least not at this stage of operations over the Reich. But the German High Command had not decided soon enough to draw back the fighter forces from the advance western airbases into the Reich. Due to this fact the US Eighth Air Force had not sustained far heavier losses in their attacks on eastern Germany.

But the aerial pincers complicated the situation on the whole. On 13 August 1943, North-Africa based Ninth Air Force units (61 B-24s) attacked the Messerschmitt plants in Wiener-Neustadt. The Allies had set up the "Second Air Front."

Hardly any sufficient forces were available to ward off such an "air encirclement." The necessary preparations had to be effected very hastily. Near Vienna the "Fighter Command Ostmark" (Jägerführer Ostmark) was activated. Two pursuit and one interceptor group were put under its control. These units had to operate in Austria, in Hungary, and in southern Germany, according to the enemy activities; therefore it was necessary to subordinate the "Fighter Command Ostmark" to the 8th Fighter Division, Munich.

Undoubtedly, the attack operations of the Ninth Air Force and later of the 15th Air Force against targets in Hungary and southern Germany had split the German air defense, which was just now being strengthened. From the viewpoint of the US High Command, this result must be considered just as important as the enlargement of escort range.

In view of the fact that the USAAF fighters could not gain air control throughout Germany until the end of 1943, this did not prevent the launching of a strategic air war into the depth of the Reich. Despite the losses the USAAF suffered in the initial operations over western Germany, the fact that a large-scale daylight bomber offensive could be achieved had been proved. The *long-range fighter escort*, working over greatest distances, had made strategic bombing economical. *This* air-war instrument represented the clue to the decisive turn of the entire war. It seems, however, that the USAAF High Command had decided to base the "attrition air war" on the massed employment of escort fighters only during the course of the air operations in 1943. Otherwise it would be difficult to comprehend why, in 1943, the USAAF at first flew unescorted raids and thereby sustained losses, and why they did not wait long enough for the moment from which sufficient escort fighters were available, both in numbers and in

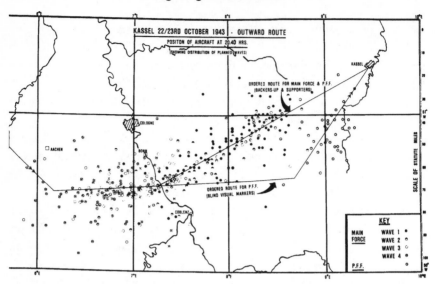

KASSEL 22/23RD OCTOBER 1943 · OUTWARD ROUTE
POSITON OF AIRCRAFT AT 20.40 HRS.
(SHOWING DISTRIBUTION OF PLANNED WAVES)

ORDERED ROUTE FOR MAIN FORCE & P.F.F.
(BACKERS-UP & SUPPORTERS)

ORDERED ROUTE FOR P.F.F.
(BLIND VISUAL MARKERS)

KEY
MAIN   WAVE 1 •
FORCE   WAVE 2 ◦
             WAVE 3 ○
             WAVE 4 ◉
P.F.F.   ○

technique. This fact might possibly be explained by underestimation of German defense capacity, and by the wish to finish the war as quickly as possibly and by means of the air war alone.

On 27 September 1943, 300 B-17s escorted by fighters attacked Emden. "Overcast bombing" (H2X) was used for the first time. On 9 October 1943, the Eighth Air Force launched a very hazardous assault against Gdynia, Danzig, Marienburg, and Anklam. The assembly plants of the Focke-Wulf factories were hit in Marienburg and Anklam. Generally, in the summer of 1943, about 14 aircraft industries were attacked.

It was clearly recognizable that the USAAF operations aimed to weaken the German air defense by destroying fighter production. Indeed, in the last four months, a considerable under-production occurred. As a result, German hopes to intensify this important part of war potential were prevented, at least temporarily.

As far as the production of air armament was concerned, the crucial situation over Germany caused the establishment of the "Fighter Staff Saur" (Jägerstab Saur) working in the Ministry of Armament and War Production. Fighter manufacture got a higher priority. But in no case did this fact induce the beginning of a fundamental rearmament for Reich air defense. The German High Command decided to continue bomber construction and requested fighter-planes only in the amount which circumstances would allow.

On 14 October 1943 Schweinfurt was attacked for the second time by 226 US bombers. But the Allied fighter escort penetrated only to the Eiffel mountains. The approach and return trip were accomplished in such a manner that almost all air defense fighters and interceptors, as well as a part of the fighters based in France (Luftflotte 3), could take part in the defense operation. This was the most important air battle of the year 1943. The German interceptors and a considerable part of the fighters were equipped with 21 cm rockets. They succeeded in splitting some bomber formations and in destroying them almost completely. The decisive fact was that the US escort could not participate in the battle. On the German side about 300 fighters, 40 interceptors and several nightfighters were engaged. Out of 228 bombers, 60 planes were shot down, 138 damaged (US data). The German losses mounted to 35 fighters and interceptors. "The United States Strategic Bombing Survey" stated:

> "Repeated losses of this magnitude could not be sustained; deep penetrations with escort, of which this was among the earliest, were suspended and attacks on Schweinfurt were not renewed for four months."

Undoubtedly, the German air defense had gained a good partial success. US information talked of their "previous loss of air supremacy." Surely, that was right only as long as these Allied strategic operations were carried out without escort. But there was still the consideration that the German nightfighters and interceptors could no longer be employed in daylight defense actions against Allied fighter-cover because of the technical inferiority those German planes exhibited.

Considering the German situation on the whole, we state the fact that the gallant fighting of all the German air defense forces could not make good the faults the German High Command had committed in the field of overall strategic concept (periphery-defense and insufficient strengthening of the defense forces), and of the air armament by delaying the production of jet-fighters. The decisive year 1943 passed along without producing fundamental and effective measures in favor of a powerful Air Defense of the Reich.

In 1944 the Allied air war was put into full-fledged action. The operations were based on the Casablanca Directive:

> "On 21 January 1943, the Combined Chiefs of Staff finally sanctioned continuance of bombing by day and issued the Casablanca Directive which called for the destruction and dislocation of the German military, industrial, and economic systems and the undermining of the morale of the German people to the point where their capacity for armed resistance is fatally weakened." (*Strategic Air Power: Fulfillment of a Concept, General Spaatz. Foreign Affairs, An American Quarterly Review*, April 1946, page 389).

Air control over Germany was the necessary condition on which effective fulfillment of such a concept had to be based. Air control over France had to be obtained in order that the German communication system could be neutralized. Furthermore, air supremacy represented the prerequisite the Allied ground forces and the navy needed to accomplish the landings and to break down the German resistance on the battlefield. The general assault on the "German fortress" could be charged only at the very moment when Allied air power was able to guarantee the successful operations of all the armed forces. Thereby the strategic air forces most convincingly demonstrated the decisive influence they were exerting in the final course of the entire war!

The German High Command only incompletely and hesitatingly adjusted its command organization to this wide and massed Allied air strategy. In the fall of 1943 the XII (Nightfighter) Corps was renamed I Fighter Corps (I Jagdkorps) and took over the command of the dayfighters, too; but the respective units continued to be located in the Netherlands and in the north-western part of Germany. Contemporarily, in France, the II Fighter Corps (II Jagdkorps) was activated, but it had to conduct defense operations on the orders of the 3rd Air Force (Luftflotte 3) in Paris. The periphery-defense strategy was kept. Pertaining to the real Reich's Air Defense too, there existed a deficiency. In the fall of 1943, the 30th Fighter Division (30th Jagdivision) had been built up. Nominally, the division was subordinate to the AFCC (Air Force Command Center; Luftwaffe Befehlstaber Mitte). However, the Commander (Colonel Herrmann) of the 30th Division received special orders from the GAF Commander in Chief, Göring, directly. This division was activated with the combat goal of getting the

The Luftwaffe's last great hope for daylight combat, the Me-262A. (US National Archives)

single engine dayfighter planes into night operation, as the RAF seemingly did so successfully. Because of the way the activation was made in opposition to the opinions of Generals Kammhuber and Galland (Commanding General of the Nightfighter Corps and Inspector General of the German fighter arm respectively), and because of the lack of fighters, these units later had to fight in daylight operations as well. The forces were worn out. In the spring of 1944 the division was inactivated.

At about the end of 1943, the AFCC was replaced by the Air Force Reich (Luftflotte Reich), commanding all the Reich air defense forces. The aircraft warning system was put under the control of the fighter divisions; radio intelligence interception operated under the orders of Air Force Reich (Luftflotte Reich) and Luftflotte 3 (France) respectively. This arrangement assured direct transmission of tactical and strategic air situation reports to the fighter command posts.

Already in March 1944 the numerical superiority of the Allied fighters had become so great that the number of combat engagements the German fighters encountered proved to be extremely heavy. The fighter units based in the west, as well as the interceptors, suffered considerable losses. In isolated cases the interceptors still engaged unescorted Allied bomber main streams. In general, the number of aircraft ready for action was below the average level. On the other hand, the range of Allied strategic bombing extended to the line Bremen–Hannover–Kassel–Frankfurt/M–Vienna–Munich. From the summer of 1944 on, the fighter escort operated over the entire Reich. Now the fact which the German Air Defense Authorities had prophesied since 1942—in opposition to the opinions of the High Command itself—had materialized.

All fighter and interceptor units of I. Fighter Corps were withdrawn toward the east in order that new and heavier losses should be avoided. They left the Netherlands because the Allied fighters attacked the Germans the very moment that the latter took off or assembled in the air. In German territory, several separate fighter units were combined; they formed two dayfighter wings.

In the spring of 1944 the German defense forces engaging the Allied escorted bomber groups had the following tactical tasks (according to OKL directives):

About one third of the fighters had to tie up the enemy escort. These engagements should give freedom of action to the rest of the fighters, as well as for the nightfighter planes and interceptors (used as dayfighters), to attack the bomber streams. Nightfighters and interceptors should attack bomber groups which were separated from their own fighter escort.

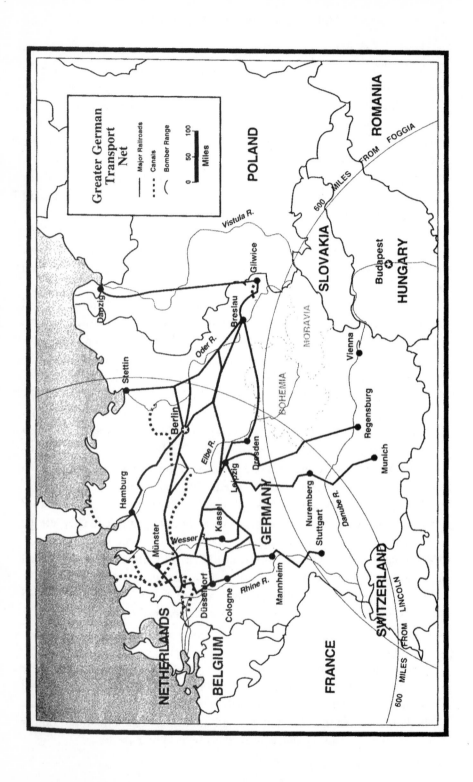

Greater German Transport Net

Major Railroads
Canals
Bomber Range

Miles
0   50   100

POLAND

Vistula R.

Gilwice

Breslau

Oder R.

Stettin

Berlin

Elbe R.

Dresden

Leipzig

Hamburg

Kassel

Nuremberg

Stuttgart

Wesser

Münster

Düsseldorf

Cologne

Rhine R.

Mannheim

Danube R.

GERMANY

Regensburg

Munich

Vienna

BOHEMIA

MORAVIA

SLOVAKIA

ROMANIA

600 MILES FROM FOGGIA

Budapest

HUNGARY

NETHERLANDS

BELGIUM

FRANCE

SWITZERLAND

600 MILES FROM LINCOLN

Danzig

This directive renewed the capital faults the Germans had made in the field of dayfighter tactics beginning in the fall of 1943.

In the spring of 1944 the first jet-fighter squadron (Me-262) was got in action to protect the chemical plant at Leuna. For the first time, a type of fighter aircraft that might have produced a fundamental improvement in the air-war situation, as concerned Reich's Air Defense, began to operate. However, the GAF was bitterly disappointed. Hitler ordered the jet planes to operate as fighter-bombers. The Reich's Air Defense was deprived of a new and effective weapon. The conflicting opinions did not come to any decision as to how the jet planes were to be employed, as bombers or as fighters. Again and again production was delayed. When it was absolutely too late Hitler agreed that the jet planes should be used as fighters. In the fall of 1944 the German war industry could no longer reach any sufficient output. We can state the fact that it would have been possible to get the jet fighters into successful operation as early as 1942, if the German High Command would have recognized their decisive value in good time!

From April 1944 on the tactical principles of fighter operations were changed. Now the idea to re-establish German air control over the Reich by conducting heavy blows against the USAAF and staging a series of several big battles, came into play. For this purpose very detailed preparations were made to build a powerful force of about 200 fighters. Later we will see that these accumulated reserves were wasted: they were annihilated in quite other operations.

The fighter forces withdrawn from the Netherlands and the western German territories were combined into three groups:

1. Hannover-Berlin
2. Frankfurt/Main *or* Westphalia ⎤ operating according to the
3. Nuremberg *or* Vienna ⎦ respective Allied penetrations.

The withdrawal of German fighter forces into the inner Reich accomplished tactical advantages, but no effective strategy materialized, i.e. no engagements of one single Allied bomber stream by concentrated and strong, possibly superior German fighter forces developed. With respect to the weakened fighter units (there were about 250 fighter planes ready for action), the formation of three widely dispersed groups must be considered a new and disadvantageous splitting. Furthermore, the High Command adhered to the idea to attack whenever possible *all* enemy groups flying into the German area, even if the defense forces were insufficient in numbers and the expected combat circumstances did not seem to be absolutely favorable for the German fighters.

It is very possible that the object of this strategy was to mitigate the anxiety of the German people, who seldom saw massed German forces over the homeland.

The German High Command (Hitler, Göring and their first advisors) had not had the nerve to stop the defense operations completely for a time for accumulating strong forces, and then to set them in action when big and decisive blows could be expected. The real events showed that these split attacks undertaken against the Allied air forces had not been successful. Steadily increasing losses impeded the activation of any powerful, massed fighter force. Undoubtedly however, the Allied operations would have been given a remarkable setback if *one* massed group of German fighters had attacked *one* individual USAAF bomber force, battering it completely. Had the Germans used such a strategic concept, they would have better succeeded in protecting the oil plants and the aircraft factories, as well as in overcoming the crucial period until the jet fighters could be set into action. But the real course of the air war precipitated the German defeat.

Until the beginning of the invasion of France the Allied air operations accomplished the following results:

1. Absolute air control over the invasion area.
2. Air supremacy over Germany.
3. Dangerous decrease of oil supply for the German air and ground forces.
4. The attacks on the German communication net had limited Reich military and economic freedom of action.
5. Fighter production decreased partially.
6. Weakening of the German war industry, above all of tank and U-boat production, as well as of other key-industry factories.

Germany had lost the struggle for Air Control. The collapse of German power had become unavoidable!

V. Defeat and Collapse, 1944–1945

6 June 1944 represented the decisive turning point of World War II. This milestone was a marker in Allied air warfare as well. Until D-Day the Allied efforts had had the object of preparing for and assuring the success of the big assault (Grosseinsatz). From this time on, its chief aim had to be the maintaining of the advantage gained, and of inducing Germany's final collapse by force.

The more the ground battle lines advanced towards the east, the more the intensified Allied air warfare shifted its center of gravity in the same direction. As a result, the German homeland was hit enormously, both by the strategic and later by the tactical air forces. The numerical strength of aircraft participating in the air raids, as well as the number of raids undertaken, reached a scale unknown up to this period.

In May 1944, during a time of good weather conditions, the air defense forces, both fighters and AA simultaneously, were worn out by uninterrupted Allied offensive operations. On 9 July 1944 the *first reserve* of about 900 fighters, accumulated by Milch's and Galland's efforts, had to be pushed into battle at the invasion front.

They suffered heavy losses the moment they flew into the battle area. Until the end of August both these forces and the *second fighter reserve* thrown into the invasion campaign were sapped. Allied air superiority was so complete that the German fighter units had no real successes.

In Reich territory a couple of single engine nightfighter groups remained. They were located widely dispersed (Berlin, Frankfurt, Bavaria, Vienna). Two groups of this type were also sent to France. During three months the single engine nightfighters conducted a gallant but inadequate daylight struggle against

The impact of the bombing. The destruction of the German transportation infrastructure was a key element in the final collapse of the country's war economy in the winter of 1944–45. (US National Archives)

the strongly (20 fold) superior opponent. Hardly fighting, the German units were worn out.

As early as July 1944 the German invasion front command recognized that the Allies dropped "Window" of a modernized type. The airborne radar apparatus SN II (Bordsuchgerät SN II) could no longer work accurately because of this new Allied jamming. The prudent use of Rotterdam sets and the very skilful radio-feints and jamming as well as the Allied system of directing bomber streams confused the German command posts and produced new troubles in obtaining a clear "air picture" of enemy activities. The feint operations and the diversionary attacks of Allied long-range fighters increased the uncertainty of German radio intelligence interception.

German progress in the field of radar techniques (Airborne detection set SN II, Bordsuchgerät AN II, Radar set type 218, radar ground station type "Panorama") were useless; they could not counteract Allied advantages in radar production and commitment.

The evacuation of France and Belgium had contributed to the failure of German radar interception (Funkherchaufklaerung) in the western battle zones. Before the invasion had begun, the net of radar ground stations erected in the area to the west of the line Cologne–Frankfurt/Main was hardly developed. Before the invasion the net existing at advanced airbases in the German occupied countries had seemingly been sufficient. The Eifel mountains were not favorable for building up a denser one. Consequently, a gap arose in the bearing system, preventing the accurate recognition of enemy operations in good time.

During the invasion period, the AA forces carried the burden of defense activities over the Reich. Moreover, considerable AA forces were transferred to the invasion front. Many AA units were tied up at the Eastern front. To be sure, the number of AA batteries operating in the Reich itself had been increased, but the personnel consisted mostly of Luftwaffehelfer (Air Force Auxiliaries), of foreigners (mostly Russians), and later of AA women. These measures had not accomplished any effective increase in combat power: virtually the contrary had occurred!

Until the summer of 1944, the mass employment of the latest AA weapons had not yet begun. Now, by order of Hitler, AA armament got a higher priority, but decisive results from the efforts made in these respects did not materialize even though very modern types of heavy and light AA guns etc. were introduced to a greater extent.

As pertains to the tactical principles, only in 1944 was the concept to concentrate a bulk of AA batteries around the most important targets (oil plants, aircraft industry and ball-bearing factories, railway systems) asserted.

Above all, it was the want of fuel that influenced the operations in favor of the Allies during the last episodes of the air war.

From September 1944 on, the total number of nightfighters ready for action had been reduced not only in respect to technical maintenance but also in terms of personnel strength. The want of fuel limited the test flights so necessary for the control of the complicated radar sets.

These apparatuses suffered heavily because the aircraft had to be parked in the open air as a result of the frequent air attacks. Condensation moisture appeared on the high-frequency instruments exposed to the damp air and cool nights. In addition to that, the want of fuel decreased the quality of training in the correct handling of the radar sets, especially in view of the new methods used in the intricate combat of modern aerial warfare.

The want of fuel hampered the operations of searchlights too. Since September 1944 the capacity of public power plants had diminished alarmingly. Without fuel the generators could not develop the electric current needed to set the radar ground stations in action.

On the other hand, until the fall of 1944, the Allied Air Forces considerably improved their facility in target-finding at night and in bad weather conditions. Although the Mosquito night operations did not produce any decisive damage, the extent of areas to be warned of air raids was enlarged by these activities. The harassing effect was remarkable. Production capacity of the factories in the path of aircraft diminished because of work hours lost.

Of the defense methods applied against these massed night raids, the "controlled area-fixed nightfighter defense" (Himmelbettverfahren) could not accomplish the effective results so urgently needed to neutralize these GAF operations.

In the fall of 1944 the German High Command considered two methods for the successful continuation of Air Defense of the Reich:

1. Concentration of all dayfighter forces within one single area of the Reich.
2. Systematic preparation of the fighters for a "big blow" against USAAF daylight penetrations (technical and personnel recuperation, reorganization, etc).

The recuperation was delayed because the forces had to ward off the airborne operation at Arnhem; moreover, the want of fuel and the slow flow of aircraft supply hampered carrying out the intentions. These could not be fulfilled in October 1944, as had been planned. They were postponed to December 1944. Then, however, the "big blow" could not be carried out. The fighters had to operate in the Battle of the Bulge in support of the ground forces. There the *third reserve* of fighters for Reich air defense accumulated in 1944 was wasted.

In October 1944 the tactical conceptions for the "big blow" were studied in a great "game of war." The idea to set whole fighter wings in action exclusively against Allied fighter escort occurred for the first time.

Despite all these intentions and preparations, German fighter activities were not to be weakened. Orders were given to attack all Allied forces, even in bad weather. Consequently the Germans suffered heavy losses. The successes gained were low in the face of strong Allied superiority. In addition to that, the casualties effected by bad weather were rising because the problem of de-icing cabin windows had not been resolved satisfactorily.

In September to October 1944, four fighter wings and the remnants of the single engine nightfighters were withdrawn from France. Their new task was to protect the industrial installations in central Germany, the factories located around Berlin, as well as the oil plants of central Germany, of Pölitz (Stettin) and Silesia, and in the northern part of Bohemia. The "big blow" was not achieved: the forces accumulated for the all-out attack had not yet finished their preparations.

In September 1944 small and medium sized Allied units of single and two-engine pursuit planes and fighter-bombers were operating on a large scale over inner Germany for the first time. These activities aggravated the air situation for Germany considerably. From now on Allied air warfare was adapted to achieve short-term results almost exclusively. Utilizing their control of the air, the Allied air forces aimed at facilitating ground operations and at laming German resistance.

All air attacks were clearly concentrated to break down the German communications system, the oil supply, the air armament and the GAF ground services. This strategy showed the Allied desire to smash the entire German resistance as quickly as possible with all means at their disposal. The Allies had fixed as their goal the keeping down of the weakened Germans and to use the results already obtained for final success over the Reich.

The heavy bombing of transportation lines decreased the capacity of the supply system more and more. War material sent to the Western front by hundreds of freight trains, etc., arrived after weeks had passed or did not arrive at all. The German Command no longer governed supply movements. These trying circumstances appeared especially during preparations for the Battle of the Bulge. Military agencies constantly reported that they did not know where the supplies had gone to.

The Anglo-Americans had recognized that the main problem of this war was to "keep the enemy motionless," i.e. to prevent them from recovering, anywhere or at any time. Furthermore, they had realized that the oil supply presented the "nerve-center" of the German war-machine. Indeed, German war capacity was threatened most of all by the neutralization of oil supply plants (Hydrierwerke). The annihilation of these targets, relatively small in number, would bring about the complete paralysis of the air forces, of all motorized ground forces, of the navy, as well as of the public transportation system.

Allied air control proved itself to be the motivating power for the ground advances. If the Allies had not had strong strategic air forces, and if they had not accomplished this type of strategic air war, then such decisive successes by the combined armed forces would not have been achieved! As already mentioned above, the powerful long-range fighter escort over the entire Reich had simultaneously initiated Allied air control and Germany's downfall.

After the "big blow" by German fighters, launched on 1 January 1944 against Allied ground installations, had failed, and the losses inflicted on the Germans had proved so prohibitive, then it was beyond any possibility to conduct any successful air defense with the remnants of the German fighter forces. Some gallant achievements made by individual units and crews could not influence the situation on a larger scale. The jet fighters had come too late.

Desperate measures such as reorganizing the IX Air Corps (bombers) and other bomber units in order to build up fighter units had failed to reinforce the fighter defense. As before and up to the very end of the war, the Air Defense of the Reich suffered from belated and insufficient, improvised efforts.

The combat effectiveness of the AA forces, too, was dwindling more and more, because they were, and had been for years, withdrawn from their proper tasks. Under the pressure of the crucial ground situation in all theaters, they had to support army operations closely. There, the motorized AA units were put out of action or annihilated altogether.

From D-Day on the German collapse could no longer be prevented. It had been possible only to delay the final downfall. Useless and senseless casualties of human beings, of homes and supplies were the results!

Air Defense of the Reich had failed!

German AA Artillery

1.The strength of the AA Artillery in the years 1940–1944 in the zone of interior and in the separate theaters of war:

	Batteries			
	Heavy	Light	S.L.	
1940				
Reichs defense	423	333	143	(German zone of interior)
Western front	368	353	78	(France, Belgium, Holland)
Total	791	686	221	
1941				
Reichs defense	537	395	138	(German zone of interior)
Western front	97	146	71	(France, Belgium, Holland)
Northern front	33	26	0	(Norway, Finland)
Southeastern front	45	45	6	(Rumania, Greece, Hungary)
Eastern front	239	135	25	(Russia)
Southern front	6	5	0	(Italy, Africa)
Total	967	752	240	
1942				
Reichs defense	744	438	174	(German zone of interior)
Western front	122	183	99	(France, Belgium, Holland)
Northern front	44	36	0	(Norway, Finland)
Southeastern front	60	47	9	(Rumania, Greece, Hungary)
Eastern front	148	162	0	(Russia)
Southern front	6	5	0	(Italy, Africa)
Total	1,148	892	282	
1943				
Reichs defense	1,234	693	350	(German zone of interior)
Western front	205	295	33	(France, Belgium, Holland)
Northern front	92	69	1	(Norway, Finland)
Southeastern front	61	39	8	(Rumania, Greece, Hungary)
Eastern front	148	162	0	(Russia)
Southern front	278	80	20	(Africa, Italy)
Total	2,132	1,460	455	
1944				
Reichs defense	1,508	623	375	(German zone of interior)
Western front	412	425	32	(France, Belgium, Holland)
Northern front	126	80	3	(Norway, Finland)
Southeastern front	122	70	3	(Rumania, Greece)
Eastern front	311	328	43	(Russia)
Southern front	176	86	14	(Italy)
Total	2,655	1,612	470	

Explanations:

Heavy – Heavy AA Battery: 4–5 guns (caliber) 8.8, 10.5, 12.8 cm
Light – Light AA Battery: 12–15 guns (caliber) 2, 5, 3.7 cm
S.L. – Searchlight Battery: 16 searchlights (150–200 cm)

2.Personnel Strength of the AA Artillery
(including all units employed at the fronts and in the Reichs defense).

	On 15 Nov 1944	On 15 Feb 1945
German soldiers	573,000	510,200
Auxiliary personnel (Luftwaffe helpers, Foreigners, etc.)	225,400	302,900
Civilian personnel	5,300	8,200
	803,700	821,300

An 8.8cm flak gun in action in 1939. By the time the Allied bomber offensive reached it height, the crews were laregely composed of part-time overage men, teenage boys, women, Russian prisoners of war, and foreign soldiers. (US National Archives)

3.The highest ammunition consumption of the AA Artillery

The monthly highest ammunition consumption these separate types:		From 1939–1944 were for combat on the		
			Western front	Eastern front
2 cm	Nov 1944	11,628,440	9,945,220	1,683,220
3.7 cm	Nov 1944	1,938,470	802,510	235,960
8.8 cm	Oct 1944	3,175,400	2,948,800	226,600
10.5 cm	Sep 1944	255,030	254,360	680
12.8 cm	Oct 1944	102,450	102,430	20

The German Fighter Force

1.The Strength of the German Fighter Force in the Reich Defense

At 6 June 1944	(beginning of the invasion)	Actual strength	1,179
		Operational	656
At 22 June 1944	(after the invasion)	Actual strength	538
		Operational	288

The strength of the German Fighter Force on all fronts (not including the Reich defense).

6 June 1944	Eastern front (Russia)	Actual strength	550
		Operational	282
22 June 1944	Eastern front (Russia)	Actual strength	441
		Operational	298
6 June 1944	Western front (France, Holland, Belgium)	Actual strength	288
		Operational	156
22 June 1944	Western front (France, Holland, Belgium)	Actual strength	704
		Operational	467
6 June 1944	Southern front (Italy, Mediterranean)	Actual strength	171
		Operational	103
22 June 1944	Southern front (Italy Mediterranean)	Actual strength	102
		Operational	71
6 June 1944	Southeastern front (Balkans, Greece)	Actual strength	100
		Operational	44
22 June 1944	Southeastern front (Balkans, Greece)	Actual strength	158
		Operational	82
6 June 1944	Northern front (Norway)	Actual strength	79

		Operational	51
22 June 1944	Northern front (Norway)	Actual strength	78
		Operational	48

Total	6 June 1944	Actual strength	1,188
		Operational	636
Total	22 June 1944	Actual strength	1,473
		Operational	962

2.The Day and Nightfighter Units Employed in the Reich Defense, Status 25 Sept. 1944

Corps Headquarters I Fighter Corps:			Treuanbritten
1 Fighter Division:			Doeberitz
Staff J.G.	300		Finsterwalde
I./J.G.	300		Gahro
II./J.G.	300		Finsterwalde
IV./J.G.	3		Alteno
II./J.G.	4		Welzow
II./J.G.	5	(Recuperation status)	Reinsdorf
I./J.G.	301	(Recuperation status)	Salwedel
I./J.G.	302	(Recuperation status)	Alperatedt
II./J.G.	302	(Recuperation status)	Sachau
Fighter Group	10		Parchim
1./J.G.	400		Brandis
2./J.G.	400		Brandis
2./N.J.G.	10		Werneuchen
3./N.J.G.	10		Finow
II./N.J.G.	5		Stubendorf
III./N.J.G.	5		Luebeck/Blankensee
N.J. Erg. Group			Ludwigelust
Mosquito Commando III./J.G.300			Jueterbog
Training Squadron 1, 3, 5			Koenigsberg/Neumark
Fighter Force Commander Silesia:			Cosel
4. (Erg.) N.J.G.	7		Brieg
Units Tactically Subordinate:			
Staff N.J.G.	102		Ohlan
I./N.J.G.	102		Oele
II./N.J.G.	102		Schoenfeld/Seifersdorf
III./N.J.G.	102		Stubendorf
2. N.J.G.	100		Udetfeld
2. Fighter Division:			Stade
Staff N.J.G.	3		Stade
I./N.J.G.	3		Schleswig

II. /N.J.G.	3	Grove
III. N.J.G.	3	Westerland
IV./N.J.G.	3	Wittmundhaven
I./N.J.G.	7	Kastrup
Assistant Division Leader Denmark		Grove

3. Fighter Division: Duisburg

Staff N.G.	4	Dortmund
I./J.G.	3	Dortmund
III./J.G.	300	Dortmund
III./J.G.	53	Paderborn
II./J.G.	77	Werl
Staff J.G.	11	Guetersloh
II./J.G.	27	Guetersloh
III./J.G.	4	Lippspringe
I./J.G.	75	Steermede
IV./J.G.	54	Planntluenne
II./J.G.	11	Achmer
Staff N.J.G.	1	Lippstadt
I./N.J.G.	1	Muenster/Handorf
II. /N.J.G.	1	Dusseldorf
III./N.J.G.	1	Fritzler
IV./N.J.G.	1	Dortmund
Staff N.J.G.	11	Bonn/Hangelar
Staff N.J.G.	2	Cologne/Butzweilerhof
I. /N.J.G.	2	Kassel/Rothwesten
II./N.J.G.	2	Cologne/Butzweilerhof
III./N.J.G.	2	Guetersloh
Staff N.J.G.	4	Mainz/Finthen
I./N.J.G.	4	Langenliebsch
II./N.J.G.	4	Rhein/Main
II./N.J.G.	4	Mainz/Finthen

7. Fighter Division: Schleisheim

Staff N.J.G.	6	Schleisheim
I./N.J.G.	6	Grossachsenheim
II./N.J.G.	6	Schwasbisch/Hall
IV./N.J.G.	6	Schleisheim
Training Squadron N.J.G.6		Kitzingen

Units Tactically Subordinate:

Staff N.J.G.	101	Ingolstadt
I./N.J.G.	101	Ingolstadt
III./N.J.G.	101	Kitzingen

8. Fighter Division: Vienna

III./N.J.G.	6	Steinamanger
II./N.J.G.	100	Tapics Marton

Units Tactically Subordinate:

II./N.J.G. 101	Paradorf
Fighter Commander, Hungary	Budapest
Hungarian Fighter Group	Vesopren
Hungarian Nightfighter Squadron	Ferihegy

Explanation:
J.G. – Fighter Wing
N.J.G. – Nightfighter Wing

Chapter 2

The Overall Defense of the Reich
1940–1944 (January)
by Generaloberst Hubert Weise

I. Organization
a. Initial

At the beginning of the war, four Luftflotten (Air Fleets) were responsible for the Defense of the Reich. Under these Luftflotten were the Luftgauen. Under the latter were the fighters, the Flak Artillery, air communication troops (Air Warning Service), ground organizations and the civilian passive air defense. The Luftgauen were the headquarters actually responsible for the defense.

The air forces—bombers, dive bombers, reconnaissance planes and nightfighters— were organized in 'Flieger Korps' which were directly subordinated to the Luftflotten, just like the Luftgauen.

The extension of Luftflotten districts to the occupied territory (France, Belgium) the offensive airwar against England and the ever increasing air attacks from England against the Reich (especially at night and against Berlin) led to a reorganization of the air defense in October 1940.

b. Reorganization, October 1940

1. The existing Luftflotten ceased operation within the Reich territory.
2. The Luftgauen III, IV, VII, XI, XIV, and later the Luftgauen in the East (I, VIII, XVII, etc.) were condensed into one command district, under the Commander of the Central District with the powers and the position (rank) of a Flottenchef (Chief of the Airfleet).

Under the command of the Flottenchef came:

a. The already mentioned Luftgauen.
b. The fighter forces within the Reich.

Under the command of the Luftgauen came:

a. The Flak Artillery.

50

   b. The Air Warning Service.

   c. The Ground Organization.

   d. The Civilian Air Defense (Passive).

The fighters which were still under the command of the Luftgauen were transferred from that command and reorganized in Flieger Korps (Air Corps) under the higher command of the Commander of the Central District. The Commander of the Central District, as all other Luftflotten, was directly subordinated to the highest command of the air forces.

II. The Air Defense (Winter 1940/41)

Enemy air activity against the Reich during the Polish and French campaign was negligible. Only after the end of the French campaign did British planes start more extended air activity. This activity increased with the start of the German air offensive against England.

The targets mostly attacked by the enemy were:

   a. The Ruhr District.

   b. Cities close to the coast, such as Emden, Bremen, Wilhelmshaven, Hamburg.

   c. Berlin.

It was not possible to recognize any definite plan in these attacks, e.g. it was impossible to recognize if these attacks were directed against a certain class of targets, like traffic centers or certain industries. An exception from this is the attack on the synthetic fuel plant at Poelitz.

The enemy did not alter the route of approach to the target very much. As a rule the attacks on Berlin came from Holland–Zuider Sea–north of the Ruhr district and Hanover or from the North Sea by detouring the protected area around Hamburg along the Elbe River. Low level attacks were only flown during the winter months when the protective cover of darkness made possible the approach and return. The attacks themselves occurred only when the weather was favorable and visibility was good. The altitude was in general not over 5,000 m. The attack was carried out in such a manner that about 60–80 planes, also many times smaller formations, attacked the target singly, e.g. one after the other. For this reason, an attack on Berlin lasted several hours, many times even half a night, without more than 3–4 planes being over the target at the same time.

The damage and losses among the civilian population were *very* small. The losses of the German defenses were practically zero. Enemy daylight attacks occurred only as exceptions and then in small formations against targets near the coast. The tactics employed by the enemy facilitated the defense.

Nightfighting zones were put on the known approach routes of the enemy. At first these were along the Dutch–Belgian–German border and also along the coastline of the North Sea. The German nightfighting was mainly carried out in the form of "Helle Nachtjagd" or "*bright* nightfighting," i.e. nightfighters and searchlights. At that time the method of *dark* nightfighting was just starting. (Nightfighters and enemy planes were carried and tracked by radar.)

The method of attack by the enemy, who directed his attacks almost exclusively against targets in the Luftgauen III, VI, and XI, made a concentration of flak in these districts possible.

The defensive effect was increased by:

a. Concentration of the searchlight belt.
b. Concentration of the defensive firepower (beginning of the organization of Gross-batteries and double batteries).
c. Prohibition of undirected barrage fire.
d. An intensive training of the defense forces, consisting mainly of reserve units.

The successes of the defense, which were still small by fall, increased during the winter and spring among nightfighters as well as the Flak Artillery. The German losses still were negligible.

III. The Year 1941

Enemy air activity increased at the beginning of 1941, especially with the better weather in spring. This activity increased so much that the air offensive against England had to be more and more limited during the campaign in the Balkans and later against Russia. The attacks of the enemy were mainly directed against the Ruhr district and targets close to the coast, as was the case in the winter of 1940/41. During the summer of 1941, Berlin and eastern, central and southern Germany were completely untouched by air attacks. The last attack on Berlin took place in June.

No noticeable change could be recognized in the tactics of the enemy. The attacks were carried out with insufficient forces, and had only limited success. Daylight raids were very rare and were carried out as hit and run attacks; for example, against Bremen. This was executed in the early hours of the morning with great courage by only one flight (12 planes) as a low level attack The attack did not produce any success and cost the enemy about 50% in losses (shot down planes) by the light and medium flak. The majority of the bombs were duds and did not explode (apparently because of the low altitude). Scattered daylight attacks with only a few planes, and from very high altitudes, gave the impression that the enemy was employing new types of planes.

The German defense increased steadily, as there were scarcely any losses caused by enemy action. The increase in personnel and material could be used for equipping new units, because the tactics of the enemy only demanded the protection of the Luftgauen III, VI, and XI.

This increase was especially noticeable with the nightfighters, where several new nightfighter groups could be organized. The "bright" and "dark" nightfighting zones were increased and extended in depth. Furthermore, the west coast of Schleswig-Holstein and Jutland were included in the nightfighting zones. The Flak Artillery was weakened as, with the beginning of the Russian campaign, all active (fully mobile) units were pulled out of the defense. This loss was not critical, however, as the training of reserve units was quite well advanced and several formations could be quickly organized.

Airwarning service and civilian air defense worked without any trouble. The technical equipment of all defensive organizations was improved, and the nightfighters, the Flak Artillery, and the air warning service were equipped with radars on an ever increasing scale.

The successes of the defenses increased. The year 1941 closed with very small German losses and with a fully successful defense.

Towards the end of 1941, the higher command demanded increased protection of southern Germany and the Ostmark (Austria). The equipment was promised, but the personnel were not available. It was supposed to be formed by employment of the so called "Heimatflak" batteries (civilian workers), alarm batteries (batteries manned only on alerts), and by the use of available military personnel as the primary crews. This measure was only partially successful because, outweighing the advantages of the formation of additional units, there were the following important disadvantages:

1. The alarm batteries, composed of reservists of all arms of the Reich, suffered under a constant change of personnel. They hardly passed a certain elementary level of training.

2. The Heimatflak batteries, organized mainly from the workers of industrial plants, were quite useful if manned by younger personnel (apprentices) and if the weapons (light flak, for instance) were located in the immediate vicinity. By organizing heavy Heimatflak batteries, the question of transport from the plant to the batteries quite frequently created great

difficulties. The Heimatflak batteries needed 3–4 relief crews. After 8–12 hours of work in the factories, the workers were tired out and little inclined for theoretical and practical training. The training of specialists for range-finders and directors met the greatest difficulties. During the night, the Heimatflak batteries were constantly manned. The manning of the farther distant batteries during daylight alerts was not possible. The Flak Artillery in the Reich as a whole was weakened considerably by pulling out the regular military personnel and the formation of new units. This adverse effect was not felt immediately, but its influence did begin in 1942.

IV. The Year 1942

The year 1942 brought quite a few changes in the attack tactics of the British air force:

a. The attacks were more frequent and were carried out in greater strength.
b. It was noticed that the enemy compressed his attacks, as far as time was concerned.
c. The approach routes for the attacks were different.
d. The cities of the Baltic coast and the territories in Westphalia, and along the Rhine–Main, were included in the attacks.
e. During the summer there were several attacks extending far into the Reich.

All these attacks were carried out at night. Only exceptionally were there hit and run daylight attacks, for example against the M.A.N. diesel engine works in Augsburg made by flying across Swiss territory. As before, daylight attacks were expensive to the enemy, as he suffered losses up to 50 percent.

The compression of the attacks into a shorter span of time (2–3 hours) was probably planned by the enemy for the following reasons.

a. To break into the nightfighting zone, with several planes at the same time.
b. To minimize at the target the fire concentration on single planes.

For the first time, so-called terror attacks were experienced, during which a large number of incendiary bombs were used. Especially hard hit were the cities of Muenster, Luebeck and Rostock, where buildings suffered considerable damage.

The losses in human lives were kept within limits. With exception of these terror attacks, no certain tactics could be recognized. In the attack on Rostock for instance, the airplane industry suffered only a little.

V. The German Defense

The strength of the German nightfighter force had been growing steadily with the organization of new units and the lack of losses. The nightfighter division was expanded to a nightfighter corps with several (3–4) subordinated divisions. The few dayfighter groups were attached to these divisions, and special fighter commanders were responsible for their employment.

The nightfigher net was considerably expanded as an answer to the already mentioned efforts of the enemy. The nightfighter belt was expanded as far south as the Rhine front; also Jutland and the Danish islands were included in the nightfighter protection zone. Nightfighters were stationed at the most important targets and those frequently attacked; Bremen, Hamburg, Cologne, the Ruhr and Berlin, for instance.

This night defense was carried out at first as "bright" nightfighting, within the searchlight belt of the Flak Artillery around the target. The defense was carried out so that either the flak or the nightfighters could alternately attack the target which was illuminated by searchlights. The orders for employment of the combined arms came from the Flak Commander; as a rule the division commander. It was up to him to decide which means of defense was to be used and when to employ it. With the flak leader was also the squadron leader of the nightfighters. The transmission of orders (permission to fire, cease fire, firing limitations) as far down as batteries was transmitted by a loudspeaker system. Bright nightfighting, on and over the target, showed surprisingly good results (Hamburg), especially at its beginning.

Within the Flak Artillery, the organization of Grossbatteries proceeded further, and so did the equipping of the batteries with radars and other devices. The efficiency of the searchlight, which was freed from the acoustic listening devices and difficult training for service on the listening devices, increased considerably. The railway flak was increased considerably and proved its value as a highly mobile reserve for the formation of flak concentrations. This was also excellent in respect to the conservation of gasoline which was now necessary.

The program of increasing the equipment of the flak in the South and Southeast of Germany with defensive weapons began. The Russian airforce limited its attacks to a few attacks with a few planes into East Prussia and Berlin. The Russian planes gave the impression that they had difficulties with their navigation and could not even find their target. When a number of planes were shot down by the flak, the Russians gave up their attacks altogether.

The year 1942 closed very favorably for the defense; the nightfighter losses were also very low. The losses of the enemy, as one could see by the English reports, were very high. The damages in the German cities (with exception of

A USAAF B-17 leaves the Focke-Wulf factory in Marienbad burning, 1943.
(US National Archives)

a few small places already mentioned) and the losses among the civilian population were kept within limits. The industrial damages, seen as a whole, were very low.

6. Winter 1942/43

The winter of 1942/43 started the change in the Air Defense of the Reich. A number of measures were started or executed by the Supreme Commander of the Air Forces. In spite of the warnings and pleas by the affected organizations, these measures proved catastrophical for the Air Defense of the Reich. Some of these measures were:

    a.   The organization of air force field divisions (infantry divisions).

    b.   He constant transfer of personnel and equipment without equal replacement.

    c.   Transfer of the last dayfighting units and replacement with completely tired out units (from the front).

    d.   Substitution of stationary flak for the mobile flak artillery.

To amplify these paragraphs:

Under a.   The Flak Artillery of the Reich territory had to give up complete age groups of young soldiers, without any regard whether these soldiers had received specialist training or not, for the formation of airforce field divisions, e.g. infantry divisions. After these soldiers had received training extending over many years on directors and rangefinders, they were used as infantry. Furthermore, the Flak Artillery of the home front had to furnish these divisions with ground artillery; they had to attach flak battalions to these divisions, to be used for ground defense only.

The airforce field divisions were used for their intended mission; however, they did not have adequate leadership. This resulted in high losses so they were dissolved again after a few months and converted into parachute divisions. What the real reason was for the formation of these divisions is beyond my comprehension.

Under b.   The fronts, especially the Eastern and Southern front, demanded an uninterrupted flow of replacements of personnel and equipment because of the high losses. As soon as the regular replacement channels or the equipment production fell down, the forces of the Command–Central District had to take care of these replacements. For this reason, the quality of the troops on this home front grew worse.

Under c. The last complete dayfighter units were transferred to the front and were replaced with completely tired out personnel from the front. They had to be newly organized again, newly equipped and trained for their special tasks (fighting in the North Sea coast area).

Under d. To save material it was ordered that the batteries on the homefront had to be converted as a whole into static batteries. In order to be able to form flak concentrations and to carry out movements quickly, the increase of railroad flak was ordered. This measure also proved a mistake—it was carried out against the pleas of the affected organizations. The savings in steel etc. which were made through the change from outrigger to pivot carriages were small, and these resulting savings were consumed again by the necessary construction of fortifications. A movement of batteries required a matter of several weeks because of the necessary fortifications to be constructed and the difficulties for the transport of the batteries. This was a fact which showed its critical effect, especially in the last phases of the war. All these measures were carried out against continued protests which also called attention to the growing strength of the enemy and the probable early entry in the attacks on all fronts by the American airforce.

VII. The Year 1943
a. Reich Defense

The year 1943 brought a change in the defense of the Reich. *Against all the warnings and protests*, the defense had to give up even greater amounts of Flak Artillery at *three different times* during the winter and spring:

a. As replacements for the losses suffered in the retreat from Stalingrad.
b. As replacements for the losses suffered in the African campaign.
c. For the protection of the industry in northern Italy, upon request by Italy.

Each of these replacements amounted to hundreds of batteries of all calibers.

The replacement of material came later. The replacement in personnel had to be taken from students of the High Schools (15–17 years of age), from the workers in the factories (Heimatflak), and from members of German allied nations, like Italians, Croats, Slovaks, and others. Besides that, women were inducted to a greater extent for the communication service and for the Flak Artillery. The organization of formations composed completely of women was

The Eighth Air Force hits industrial targets in Berlin, 8 March 1944. (US National Archives)

not begun till the middle of the year. In this way the quality of the troops sank rapidly; many of them gave the impression and looked like homeguard (Miliz) outfits.

The few dayfighter formations consisted mostly of tired out combat units which had to be freshened up. The only complete units were the nightfighters. Here, however, direct actions by the Supreme Commander of the Airforce (Goering) showed unfavorable effects. *Against all protests*, constant changes in personnel in higher positions took place. Many divisions and squadrons changed their commanders 3–4 times within a short time. These changes showed their effects among the troops. Uncertain leadership was another consequence.

b. Allied Tactics and German Defense

In contrast to previous years, definite enemy tactics could now be recognized. The separate sectors of the air war were about the following:

1. The air battle in the Ruhr district, which was occasionally interrupted by attacks on the Hanse cities (Hamburg, Bremen, Luebeck) and on southern Germany.
2. Large scale attacks (terror attacks) on large cities such as Cologne, Elberfeld- Barmen, and others compressed, as far as time was concerned.
3. The terror attacks against the Hanse cities during day and night, with dropping of "Window."
4. The day and night attacks against the airplane industry and special industries, such as the ballbearing industry.
5. Attacks against important traffic centers and dams.
6. The terror attacks against Berlin.

The intended attack on the Ruhr district became known and the Commander Central District attempted by a strong concentration of fighter and flak forces to weaken the effect of the attack. It was possible to cause heavy losses to the attacker; during the attack on Cologne more than 50 planes were destroyed for instance, but the destruction in the cities and losses among the population caused by incendiary bombs grew immensely. The highest losses were always in cities which experienced a large scale attack for the first time. In these cities the protective measures were only incompletely carried out, as in Elberfeld-Barmen, for instance.

Towards the middle of summer, American Air Forces appeared in ever increasing numbers, especially in daylight attacks. These attacks were carried out at first without any fighter escort, but after heavy losses, especially on the approaches to the interior of the Reich, attacking planes were escorted by fighters and fighter-bombers in ever growing numbers. The fighter protection of the attacking bombers was so strong that it exceeded in numbers our own employed fighters, especially as they had to divide their activities between two fronts, the west–northwest front and the southern front.

A concentration of all forces was only occasionally possible, because of the large territory and the difference in weather between the separate districts. The attacks from the south, at first against the Danube basin and then against Bavaria, increased. The middle of the year was a specially important and hectic time, with the initial attacks against Hamburg. The use of "Window," for the first time, eliminated in a shocking manner the use of radars for the fighters and the flak. As the night attacks were flown with complete cloud cover, the "dark" nightfighting, as well as the aimed and directed fire of the flak, was completely paralyzed. It took quite some time to find countermeasures and to employ them. Here, also, it had been neglected to warn the troops of this means of combat (which was known) and to prepare countermeasures in time. The enemy, attacking in large formations at night and in bad weather and with the help of the Rotterdamgeraet (radar bombsight), required other defensive tactics than had been applied so far.

The guided "dark" nightfighting and the firing with radar control lost their importance for the time being. In their place stepped the infiltration of our own nightfighter into the enemy bomber formations.

Concentration of strong single and twin engined fighter formations was made over the target, and nightfighting was done in the space illuminated by searchlights and flares. There were considerable difficulties in the coordination of the operations of the separate arms (fighter and flak), as well as in the approach of our attacking planes and the fight over the target. (Firing regulations, limitation of flak ceiling for fire on the approaches, airfields, etc.) Under favorable weather conditions it was quite possible to cause heavy losses to the enemy (first attacks on Berlin, fall 1943, where about 70 planes were shot down), but in bad weather conditions with clouds, snow, fog, and the danger of ice, the multimotored bomber was superior to the nightfighter, especially the single engined fighter. As large scale daylight attacks by concentrations of American bombers were expected, proposals were made to pull the fighters out of nightfighting and hold them for the daylight raids, but these proposals were turned down.

At the end of 1943 the Supreme Commander of the Airforce (Goering) ordered the airforce to take complete charge of the leadership in combat. An A.A.L.O. (Flakeinsatzfuhrer) was attached to each fighter division (fighter wing) who had to regulate the firing activity of the flak within the overall defense. At the beginning of 1944 the airwarning service also came under the command of the fighter divisions. With this, the existing organization was broken up and the Luftgau practically eliminated.

The year 1943 closed unfavorably for the defense. We succeeded in causing considerable losses to the enemy, but the enemy airforces grew in strength and numbers from month to month.

The reinforcement of dayfighters came too late and in insufficient numbers. The losses among the single motored fighters and among the first class twin engined nightfighters were considerable.

The production losses began to be felt, especially within the aircraft industry. The Flak Artillery was in quantity about the same as the year before, but the quality had been considerably weakened by forces sent to the front as replacements. The damage to the attacked cities and the losses among the civilian population were very heavy.

In my opinion, the operations on the front were not coordinated at all by the high command with the requirements for the protection of the home front. The high morale of the troops and the experience of their leaders on the homefront were no longer sufficient.

Chapter 3

Development of Nightfighting
July 1940–15 September 1943
by General der Flieger Josef Kammhuber

General Review

On 17 July 1940, the formation of the first nightfighter division was ordered by the CinC, GAF. On 19 July 1940, I was entrusted with the Command of this division. The staff was organized on 23 July in Brussels, the division then being placed under the 2. Luftflotte (commanded by Kesselring). On 1 August the HQ was moved to Zeist near Utrecht, Holland, where it remained till 1943. On 1 April 1941, the 1st Nightfighter Division was placed under the command of the Luftwaffebefehlshaber Mitte, Generaloberst Keise, this command having been newly formed in the meanwhile.

On 1 August 1941, the 1st Nightfighter Division was remodelled into the XII Fliegerkorps, of which I was appointed commanding general. Simultaneously, I assumed the task of the "General der Nachtjagd" (General of Nightfighters), with capacity of supervision and inspection throughout the Luftwaffe.

On 15 September 1943, the XII Fliegerkorps was split up into I and II Jagdkorps and an independent (7th) Fliegerdivision. I merely retained the task of General der Nachtjager up until 15 November 1943. On this date I relinquished my duties in nightfighting and assumed command of the Luftflotte 5.

Beginning of Nightfighting

At the time of my taking over the Nightfighter, there were in existence:

1 Nightfighter Geschwaderstab Command in Dusseldorf with 1 Nightfighter Gruppe (2 Staffel Me-110, 1 Staffel Do-17Z)

furthermore

1 Flak Searchlight Regiment.

In the area of Munster L/W a nightfighter zone had been formed, where "illuminated" nightfighting (i.e. nightfighting in collaboration with searchlights) was operating. These nightfighter forces were under the command of Luftgau VI, Munster.

At the formation of the first nightfighter division, these forces came under my command and formed the core of the proposed new division. Up till 1 August 1940, less than 10 aircraft in all had been shot down by German nightfighters (according to results actually confirmed).

My Task

My duties were: To carry through the entire equipment of the 1st Nightfighter Division and of any additional unit to be formed later with regard to material and personnel. Furthermore to create the basis for technical and tactical development, as well as the organization and training, which was essential for arming and carrying through effective and radical attacks on enemy night bomber raids.

Execution of My Task

In the course of August 1940, my conception of the fundamentals of nightfighter practice became clear and the organization, as described further below, could thus be envisaged. It will be understood that the experience gained from operations was immediately applied, resulting in continuous amplifications and improvements of nightfighter organization and tactics. This development was facilitated since there existed in the command of the 1st Nightfighter Division and later the XII Fliegerkorps one central authority, which by personal union with the General der Nachtjagd was anchored with Ob.d.L. Thus, any experience, newly gained, could at once be turned to practical use and the long and infertile official approach was avoided. After the dissolution of the XII Fliegerkorps, however, as from 15 September 1943 the situation changed to the considerable detriment of nightfighting.

As from 1 September 1940, nightfighting began to function according to the principles laid down in the following chapters.

Long Range Nightfighting

Its purpose is to hit the enemy where he is most vulnerable, i.e. on the ground, in his dispersals, when lined up for the take-off, at the take-off, when coming in for landing and when taxiing. Vigorous and correctly launched long range nightfighter operations are, in my view, the *most effective tactics of any kind of nightfighting*, especially if they are combined with continuous attacks on the ground organization by bomber units. If one wants to get rid of a swarm of wasps, it is better to destroy the hive together with the wasps instead of trying to follow the individual wasps in order to kill them. It has, therefore, right from the beginning, been my intention to lay the strongest stress on long range nightfighting. To carry through this intention, however, I had, at the beginning of my activities, only one flight equipped with Do-17Z at my disposal, later one squadron with four flights of Do-17Z and Ju-88 and later still Ju-88C-6, the latter being stationed at Gilze-Rijn in Holland.

Statements by enemy prisoners of war testified to our successes: numerous enemy casualties, considerable disturbance of enemy night operations at an increasing rate, unrest and irritation among enemy crews, which in their turn augmented the losses. In spite of these successes, confirmed by the enemy, all applications to raise the number of nightfighter units or to further develop this weapon, combining utmost efficiency with lowest expenditure, were turned down. The Fuhrer himself did not believe in the efficiency and the successes of long range nightfighting. When, in August 1941, lack of force began to make itself felt in other theaters, he ordered long range nightfighting to be stopped entirely and the long range nightfighter squadrons to be transferred to Sicily and Africa. Thus, the enemy bomber forces were able to expand in comfort, to develop their bases, including those of the USAAF, entirely without disturbance, and to apply any tactics according to their own choice. Neither was the enemy ground organization attacked by bomber units since that time, not counting a few exceptions. It can be assumed that these mistakes caused by neglect have materially contributed to the destruction of the German homeland and to be loss of the war.

Close Range Nightfighting

Here a distinction must be made between "illuminated" nightfighting (with searchlights) and "dark" nightfighting (without searchlights).

Illuminated Nightfighting

This kind (with searchlights) was in the initial stages the only form of nightfighting with any prospects of success at all, since there were not then in existence any radar sets, neither on the ground nor aboard the aircraft. The first problem, therefore, was to find the best solution for the collaboration between searchlight units and nightfighters. Decisive factors for the success of illuminated nightfighting were:

Favorable conditions for the searchlights to pick up the targets and a sufficient period of time to hold on to them. In order to fulfil the first demand, it became necessary to choose a site in front of the object to be protected, where favorable conditions in respect of atmosphere and general suitability of the terrain were encountered—thus protecting the "Horchgeraete" (sound apparatus), which operated on an accoustic basis, from the roar of the flak, and the searchlights from the smoke of concentrated fire. The second demand necessitated an arrangement of the searchlights in such a way that they "joined up" in an area of sufficient width and depth. Since the minimum "Haltezeit" (holding on time) necessary to shoot down an aircraft was approximately three minutes—in most cases, however, even more—a depth of 30 km became necessary in the case of an enemy aircraft passing through the searchlight zone from straight ahead.

The width of the searchlight zone automatically resulted from the geographical situation of the objects to be protected, which called for a continuous uninterrupted belt from the Skagerrak to the Swiss frontier. Owing to the shortage of material and personnel, the completion of this belt could only take place gradually, step by step. Thus, in the beginning, the nightfighter forces (i.e. flying units and searchlights) had to change their positions repeatedly in order to be "thrown in" at particularly hard hit points. This catching up with the bomb craters, however, was exceedingly inopportune and inefficient, quite apart from the disadvantages which had to be taken from the point of view of readiness for action and training, the latter having had to be carried out in whatever positions occupied.

Only in proportion with the gradual increase of the searchlight units, as well as the nightfighter squadrons, an increased calm prevailed, positions remained occupied by the same units; the belt extended into a continuous area stretching from the region of Schleswig over Kiel–Hamburg–Bremen–Ruhrgebiet–Arnhem–Venlo to the Liege area and further to the south. A second belt for the protection of Berlin covered the Gustrow–Standal area and extended in the direction of Gardelegen.

General Kammhuber postwar, as *Inspekteur* of the *Luftwaffe*, with one of his wing commanders, the 352-victory ace Colonel Erich Hartmann. (US National Archives)

The waiting space of the nightfighters was placed behind the searchlight belt to prevent the disturbance of the (accoustical) detection apparatus. The waiting space was marked by lights to be switched on at the request of the nightfighter and by "leichte Funkfeuere" (radio beacons). The take-off took place after the receipt of "Fluko" warnings, which again were based upon the reports of the "Flugwachen," which at first were obtained in a purely accoustical way. The nightfighter flew into his waiting space (one per searchlight battalion), gained altitude (approx. 12–18000 ft), and waited till searchlight action indicated to him the approach of many aircraft passing through his sector. By the formation of a searchlight "spider" it was revealed to him whether a target was picked up and passed on. He would then approach the "spider" and begin the aerial combat. This procedure was still very primitive and led to the miscarriage of many nightfighter operations, for the nightfighter was very often deluded in approaching a "spider" that did not pass on an enemy aircraft or that had lost it again while other aircraft actually caught by spiders passed through the nightfighter section unattacked.

The first decisive improvement was effected by the appearance of the "Wurzburg A" radar set. This device had already been developed before the war and ordered by the Ob.d.L. (Chief NVW) as a radio location set. At its appearance in October 1940, it was at once obtained by the flak to replace the "Flakschiessgeraet," the development of which had not been completed in time. Now to these demands, that of nightfighters was added, for which up until then detection sets had been envisaged. Since deliveries were very scanty in the beginning (approx. 20 sets per month) the sets had to be distributed by the Ob.d.L. personally, with the natural result that none of the interested parties could actually be satisfied.

On 16 October 1940, the first set of the Wurzburg A type was installed for operation in nightfighting in the neighborhood of Zytphon, Holland. The first trial failed as nobody was able to operate the set and there were no clear conceptions whatever about its tactical application and purpose.

Therefore, the technical and tactical possibilities for use at the front had to be tested next along with the training of the necessary personnel.

Plotting tables invented by the operating personnel were constructed, but owing to their varying accuracy, they did not always meet the requirements. In the beginning of November, the second test was run, this time successfully.

The most important task (as will be appreciated from the foregoing) was to check upon the position of our own nightfighter and to lead him from the ground by mean of R/T, i.e. to bring him into combat with such enemy aircraft as were actually picked up by the searchlights and were flying in his proximity in a position suitable for an attack. As long as the scarcity of these sets prevailed, one "Wurzburg A" set was put into operation for leading our own nightfighters within the sector of one searchlight battalion. Since the position of the nightfighter was now known and could be transmitted to the searchlights by telephone, the waiting zone could be placed into the center of the searchlight zone without confusing the own accoustic aircraft detecting service. Hereby the time of approach was cut in half at the nightfighter could reach all sides very quickly.

As more sets became available, a second "Wurzburg" set was placed at the far edge of each searchlight battalion, in order to pick up enemy approach at a greater distance and to be able to send up own fighters earlier, to have them close at hand as soon as the searchlights picked up the enemy aircraft.

As still more sets became available, a third "Wurzburg" set was placed at the rear edge of each searchlight battalion, in order to have the same advantage on return flights.

The "Wurzburg" sets which were employed for enemy detection were of course simultaneously used to direct the searchlights. For this purpose they were

A "Würzburg" radar captured by the US Army at Bad Godesburg, 7 April 1945. Range 170 kilometers; frequency 560 MHz; range precision 100 meters; angle precision 0.2 degrees. (US Army Military History Institute, via Steven Zaloga)

coupled with a neighboring searchlight, which thus became a "Leitschweinwerfer." For the directing of several "Wurzburg" sets at the same time, multi-plotting tables were used.

Further improvements were achieved with the introduction of "Wurzburg C" and "D" sets, and also by the use of 200 cm searchlights as lead s.l. instead of the 150 cm s.l. used so far.

In the meantime, during the winter of 1940/41, the number of aerial victories had been increased month by month (up to 31 December, 40–42 enemy aircraft had been shot down by nightfighters). Practically all aerial victories had been achieved by illuminated nightfighting, except for the successes of long range nightfighting. The latter, as well as the others in positions near the coast, equipped with "Freya" AN sets, clearly proved that aircraft could be brought down without searchlights. This fact, being gradually realized in wider circles, encouraged nightfighter crews to shoot down planes in the dark also. Thus, a number of such aerial victories would be achieved during the following months, including nightfighter sectors equipped with searchlights; this, however, only in clear and moonlit nights. Thus the confidence in dark nightfighting was strengthened to such an extent that further steps could be taken to improve this method systematically on a broad basis.

The following had to be improved or established:

Considerably greater range of the ground detecting devices ("Wurzburg"), with equally good results as with the "Wurzburg D" sets. Considerably improved and more accurately working plotting tables.

Faultlessly working scanners, which meant at first the same range as altitude, later on, further range than altitude. Close range detection to 200 m. and identity.

In winter 1940/41, the technical and tactical requirements for these sets were made by the nightfighter division and issued to the industry in cooperation with the Ob.d.L. (Chief NVW).

The "Wurzburg Giant" ground detecting set, although not meeting the requirements to full satisfaction yet yielding reasonable results, had been developed as a large scale warning device. It had a range of some 80 km and the same accuracy as the "Wurzburg D" sets. The "Seaburg Tisch" was developed as a plotting table which permitted a satisfactory radius of action of 36 km, with a 1:50,000 scale. As a scanner, the "Lichtenstein" set was developed, which, however, at late as in winter of 1941/42, under the name of "Lichtenstein B/C," yielded satisfactory results. After an interview with the Fuhrer I had on

22 July 1941, these sets were being produced in mass production and were put to number one in industrial importance. However, not before autumn 1941 did the sets reach the front line in larger quantities.

As the majority of the nightfighter crews went on achieving their results by illuminated nightfighting, I built the positions for dark nightfighting within the searchlight zones, in order to avoid a setback by all means. Thus, a kind of combined nightfighting came into being—illuminated and dark nightfighting side by side, at one's discretion.

As both "Wurzburg Giants" had to be switched on one plotting table ("Seeburg Tisch"), whose tolerance range was only 2 km, both had to be installed within the tolerance range.

To promote dark nightfighting and to intercept enemy aircraft as early as possible, I moved the positions of the sets to the foremost edge of the searchlight zones. Thus an area of 36 km was available for dark nightfighting exclusively in front of the equally large sector covered by searchlights. The interception therefore took place in the dark zone first. If this interception failed for some reason, illuminated nightfighting could be applied as soon as the searchlight zone was reached. Thus, the old method could be used with the advantage of the nightfighter being in action already. All which was now necessary was to switch on the searchlights and to pick up the target with them to achieve success. Thus, sometimes 1–3 minutes of holding the enemy aircraft in the searchlight beacon were sufficient to shoot it down. For this reason, the depth of searchlight zones could be reduced from 30 to 20 km without hesitation, and therefore the width of the total sector increased. Each regiment thus spreading over a large area represented a "Grossraum" (width some 90 km, depth some 20 km), each of the three battalions being equipped with one position of sets. The overlapping of neighboring positions was about 50%. In winter 1941/42 the "Grossraums" were thus completed, their positions as mentioned above. As the completion progressed and all other improvements mentioned above were being put into action, the numbers of aircraft shot down increased.

Aerial victories by illuminated and dark nightfighting were about equal by spring 1942. Then, in spring 1942, the Fuhrer gave orders to have all but one searchlight regiment moved out of nightfighting and to be used by the flak, protecting special objects within the Reich. All my protest remained without success. Thus, nightfighting was compelled to rely on dark nightfighting only. The last searchlight regiment remained in action for experimental purposes in the area of Venlo to complete the experience of illuminated nightfighting, should it be resumed in the future.

Dark Nightfighting

In summer 1940, right from the start of nightfighting, it became evident that illuminated nightfighting alone could not be fully successful as the efficiency of searchlights depends largely on weather conditions. With 10/10 overcast it is ruled out; with more than 6/10 it becomes extremely difficult. At 10/10 overcast the enemy aircraft can fly above the clouds and carry through its raids; therefore my chief attention, right from the beginning, was concentrated on the development of dark nightfighting.

A-N Method   No preparation had been made the dark nightfighting, neither from the ground nor from the air. Before the war, German planners had not expected the possibility of bombing attacks during the night. Therefore only a few "Freya" sets existed, built for the Navy. Some of these sets had been borrowed by the Luftwaffe, which used them for aircraft detection purposes near the coast.

In September 1940, the first trial to carry out dark nightfighting failed, as the altitude could not be measured and the sources of errors were too numerous. Only the AN method made an interception possible, which in the course of winter 1940/41 led to success and strengthened the confidence in the possibility of dark nightfighting. The results, however, depended largely on the ability of the fighter control officer, who had to possess both technical knowledge and a good sense for flying. A number of experts were trained who achieved very good results. It was, however, impossible to increase the number of experts beyond a certain degree; therefore, easier methods for dark nightfighting had to be adopted.

The disadvantage of the lacking altitude measurements with the "Freya" set was eliminated later on by adding a "Wurzburg" set ("ACD," later "Giant"); the method, however, was simplified.

As the final solution, all "Himmelbett" (Four-Poster Bed) positions were equipped with "Freya" AN sets, which made it possible to lead with AN from every position. In reality, however, owing to the shortage of experts, the practical use was confined to the positions near the coast and in the open flanks (utilization of range).

"Himmelbett" (Four-Poster Bed) Method   As mentioned above, the development of the first "Himmelbett" positions arose as a combination—dark nightfighting, supplemented by the possibility of illuminated nightfighting within the same position. Then, in spring 1942, the searchlights were withdrawn. I left the positions of the sets intact, although their range would have allowed them to be spread further apart. This was done to retain the greatest density of interception possible. Simultaneously, in front and behind this zone, the entire fore sector up to the coast, and gradually also the entire hinterland around the main area to be protected, were equipped with "Himmelbett" positions, with the aim:

Nowhere to leave a gap, so as to attack the enemy continually along the penetration and return flight. The concentration of set positions within the usual "Grossraum" was retained; new positions were combined with new "Nachtjagdgrossraums" (nightfighter areas) under the command of a "Nachtjagdfuhrer" each. In the end each nightfighter division usually had 4–6 of those nightfighter areas at its disposal.

A "Himmelbett" position consisted of the following sets:

1 "Freya" set equipped with AN.
2 "Wurzburg Giants."
1 "Seeburg" plotting table.
1 Ground air transmitter.
1–2 Light radio beacons.
1 beacon.

Furthermore, positions near the coast were equipped with ("Wassermann" or "Mammuth") "Grossuchanlage."

Directing of nightfighters by means of the "Himmelbett" method caused no difficulty to the fighter control officer; thus, very soon the basis could be widened, and there were always well-trained fighter controllers in sufficient numbers available. As a rule, owing to the lack of personnel, only one fighter was led at a time. The method permitted, however, the control of several fighters. The remaining fighters hung on to the light radio beacon, flying at different heights, and were called up one after another. This method was repeatedly used on return flights when the situation was clear. The nightfighters of the neighboring sectors were then directed as desirable reinforcements to the zone which was crossed by enemy aircraft. As regards to its accuracy, the "Himmelbett" method was based upon the fact that the nightfighter had a scanner aboard.

At the time of its introduction into nightfighting (winter 1941/42) very few planes were equipped with "Lichtenstein B/C," which meant that most of the interceptions had to be made without scanners. Not until the course of 1942 were round about 60% of all planes fitted with it. By 1943, no newly built nightfighter was delivered without "Lichtenstein B/C" (C1 for Ju-88). Obviously, as long as in the beginning nightfighting was carried out without "Lichtenstein," many interceptions failed, particularly during dark nights with bad visibility. As the "Lichtenstein" sets reached the front in larger quantities, the number of successes increased rapidly. The "Himmelbett" method reached its highest peak in spring 1943, with ever increasing numbers of victories, until at the point of 23 July 1943, there came a sudden stop by the RAF's use of "Window."

Round about this time—apart from the stop caused by "Window"—the "Himmelbett" method had by no means reached the end of its development, but was right in the midst of it. Only 3/5 of all positions planned were completed. The automatic transmission of the readings from the "Wurzburg Giant" (and their sets) to "Seeburg" tables was just being developed. The same applied to the ground control of the fighter by the "Y" system and to the automatic transmission of orders from ground to aircraft (Uhu 2). Furthermore, what is most important, the "Lichtenstein" SN 2 was being started, whose bigger range (4–6 km to 200 m) inaugurated a new form of dark nightfighting, the so-called "Verfolgungsnachtjagd" ("Zaehme Sau"), where the interception took place by means of the "Himmelbett," while the nightfighter was supposed to pursue the target picked up by the "Lichtenstein" SN 2 and fly himself into the bomber stream. All these technical developments died down as soon as I relinquished nightfighting. Also the most important anti-jamming of the sets was not given the necessary attention. The "Wilde Sau" was stressed instead, and when this method proved to be less effective, it was too late to return to the old system again, as by then the badly damaged industry would not have been able to fulfil the requirements any more, if such orders would have been given.

Single Engine Nightfighting

As the manufacture of twin engine nightfighters (Me-110, Ju-88, Do-217, He-219) caused a considerable expense of labor, the order to try single engine aircraft for nightfighting was given by the Ob.d.L. personally and to convert dayfighter pilots to single engine nightfighting. Both experiments were carried out in the Cologne area, each by a staffel, owing to the fact that only rather inefficient dayfighter pilots had volunteered while the real experts declined to switch over to nightfighting.

Not until the bomber pilot Colonel Herrmann, who had become jobless, surrounded himself with other bomber pilots of the same status and began to convert on Bf-109 to nightfighting, did the situation change. These personnel had real fighting spirit apart from the necessary experience in night and instrument flying.

Major Hans-Joachim ("Hajo") Herrmann, fighter ace with over 300 missions. He was instrumental in the development of "Wilde Sau" tactics, but was personally and politically disliked by Galland. (US National Archives)

When these men, after the introduction of "Window" in July 1943, were put into action in freelance fighting above the target of the raid ("Wilde Sau"), they achieved successes (for the first time over Cologne at the end of July 1943). The "Wilde Sau" was a welcome method of overcoming the stop, which had arisen on 23 July. Unfortunately, the Ob.d.L. overestimated the possibilities of this system in the course of time; therefore, as already mentioned, further development of the technical part of nightfighting was neglected, with the well-known result.

Combined Nightfighting

To utilize all possibilities of defense to obtain the utmost result, in spring 1941 combined nightfighting was started, i.e. especially over the particularly important objects, Berlin f.i., nightfighting was introduced, in addition to flak. This necessitated a specially equipped control station for the fighter controller, combined with the flak under a joint command, which was always in the hands of the flak. Nightfighting was usually done by illuminated nightfighting, i.e. the nightfighter shot down a target which had been picked up by the flak searchlights. For this purpose, the operations by the flak in the respective sector, in which the target appeared, was suspended during the time the nightfighter stayed in this sector. (The zone was usually divided in 6 sectors of 60° each, counted from the center of the towns.) The suspensions were regulated by a flak transmitter. This method was in fact complicated and required a big technical control apparatus, but it avoided casualties and achieved considerable success. If the local flak commander and fighter controller worked well hand in hand, when experienced nightfighters were operating in the air, every possibility and finesse, which this method allowed, could be applied, as f.i. in Hamburg, Bremen, Kiel, Ruhrgebiet, Koln and Frankfurt-Darmstadt. With the introduction of "Window," this method lost its power.

Nightfighter Aircraft
Me-110, Do-17Z, Do-217, Ju-88C-6, Ju-188, He-219 and Me-262

The development, and, above all, the output of nightfighter aircraft did not keep pace with the technical and operative requirements, although the He-219 and, towards the end, the Me-262 would have represented superior nightfighter aircraft. This theory was proved by the number of Mosquitoes shot down by Me-262s over Berlin during the last months of the war.

The number of units and serviceable aircraft were not halfway sufficient to raise nightfighting to a level which would have been necessary to oppose the raiders and inflict such losses upon them as to achieve an operative success. It is quite likely that the reason for this was the underestimation of home defense right from the start. When this mistake was realized, the industry had been weakened to such an extent already that it could not fulfil the requirements any more. The necessity and importance of home defense with all its consequences was repeatedly pointed out, both by the flak (General Weise) and myself. Owing to the general opinion of the Fuhrer, as mentioned above, our advice was disregarded.

Scanners

Experiments with infra-red ("Spanner") were conducted as early as winter 1940/41, but they failed. It was due to the electrical detection sets that the first successes were obtained after a first experiment with "Lichtenstein A" and "B" in winter 1940/41 (Oblt. Becker in Leeuwarden) had also failed.

The importance of "Lichtenstein B/C" esp. "C1" and of "Lichtenstein SN 2" has been mentioned already. Simultaneously with the latter, other sets came into use to approach the enemy warning and identity sets and the H2S ("Naxos," "Neptun," "Flensburg," "Rosendahl"). They were mainly used in action after I had left; during my time their development and trials were conducted.

Jamming

The jamming by "Window," which affected nightfighting acutely, had started suddenly on 23 July 1943. This blow could only be counteracted by all conceivable means and the greatest energy on the part of the German high frequency industry. Immediate evading and conversion on a wavelength on the ground as well as in the air was the only possibility to master the jamming and come into action again.

My requests along these lines were not given sufficient consideration by the Luftwaffe (Ob.d.L.), as the main stress of action was by now laid upon the

Dornier Do 217J (top) and 217N night-fighters. (US National Archives)

"Wilde Sau," whose initial successes had been overrated. The industry did not have enough energy to switch over and master the situation. Thus the technical side of nightfighting fell short of the enemy, whose advantages could not be overtaken in the end.

Situation in the Air

In order to have a reliable picture of the air situation at all times, I developed right from the beginning of nightfighting all radar positions simultaneously as (accoustic) "Flugwachkommandos" and coupled them with neighboring "Flugwachen." Observations by eye and ear in all positions were supplemented by readings of the sets. The positions of sets were switched on the "Raumfuhrer," and these, coupled with the fighter divisions, and the aero-strategical situation, were always dual controlled (eye and ear and instrument results on one side and "Fluko" reports on the other side). As there existed only one control center for the entire nightfighting organization—the XII Fliegerkorps—the air situation was always uniform and clear, even after the introduction of "Window" jamming; for now only the accoustic section was in action, while the electrical part was switched off.

This uniformity, however, changed when the XII Fliegerkorps was divided up into three different control centers working separately. Since thus the "Flugmeldedienst" was separated too, instead of being kept together, the picture of the aerial situation was blurred considerably. It would probably have been blinded altogether, had the enemy not made it possible to plot his position by switching on his identity sets or warning devices—or, what was more effective still, his H2S sets. Towards the end, this alone made it possible for the nightfighters to intercept, and, in connection with own reconnaissance aircraft over the presumed targets, to meet the enemy bomber stream.

PART TWO

A BATTLE OF INCREASING NUMBERS AND TECHNOLOGY

This section starts with another 1946 Von Rohden piece introducing the technologies that were key in the defense of the Reich: radio, radar, "Y" Service, fighter control and meteorology. The technologies—and the history of how they are used—are discussed by "Beppo" Schmid, who was one of the major Luftwaffe commanders opposing the bomber offensive at its height in 1943–45. The two Schmid chapters look at a broad range of technologies and relate these to German efforts and to the different phases of the bomber offensive.

The German authors concentrate most of their descriptions in the earlier phases of the war, even though the bomber offensive did not enter its decisive phase until after D-Day. Some 72 percent of total bomb tonnage was dropped between July 1944 and the end of the war.

D.C.I.

Chapter 4

Technical and Communications Equipment used in the Reich's Defense

by Generalmajor Hans-Detlef Herhuth von Rohden

I. The Radar Service

An overlapping net of radar positions was constructed for the requirements of nightfighting; these were densest in northwestern Germany, Holland, Belgium, and northern France. In 1943 the Skagerrak and Denmark were covered. However, in the Reich itself there remained a big gap for a long time, which could only be closed up in the spring and summer of 1944. This was the area of Muenster–Bielefeld–Hamm–Marburg–Fulda–Suhl–Erfurt–Kassel–Holzminden.

The daylight fighters only benefited by this tremendous organization after the day and nightfighters were incorporated into the nightfighter division. Prior to this time, a line of radar stations was their sole service—running along the coast to give warning before the Aircraft Warning Service could operate effectively.

Radar positions were furthermore lacking in the Alps, Luxemburg, and Alsace. The performance of the equipment in mountainous regions was very poor. Most of the general line of Berlin–Vienna expansion work began taking place only after 1944, after the net had been expanded from a 40 to a 60 kilometer radius from the most important objectives, but without ever attaining full coverage of the area.

The German radar industry had to compete against tremendous difficulties following its belated beginning. The chief bottleneck was the lack of special personnel: every new apparatus built by the industry required specially trained personnel for servicing. In addition to this there was an endless chain of personnel being transferred from the Luftwaffe to the parachute troops and Luftwaffe field divisions. The signal communications troops were also hit particularly hard. The widespread employment of women filled this gap only partially.

The standard set of the radar service—the "Freya" set—was, technically, quickly obsolete. Modern constant search sets (panoramic) could first be turned over to the industry in the middle of 1944. Production was converted from this time on. Eliminating the interfering effects of the "Window" from the "Freya"

79

—which the RAF used for the first time on the night raid of 24/25 July 1943, in their big attack on Hamburg, and henceforth in every large day or night attack—did not completely succeed in practice. However, it was possible to follow the flight path despite the "Window" and transmission interference.

The electrical recognition between friend and foe (IFF) was never satisfactorily attained. When the radar service and a proportion of German planes (first the nightfighter planes) were at last equipped with suitable sets, then the flak lacked the accessories for operating its electrical sighting equipment.

II. The Radio Monitoring ("Y") Service

During the course of the war radio intelligence continuously increased in importance:

a. Establishing the strength of the enemy, enemy organization, and enemy armament.
b. Observing the enemy's tactical Air Force operations.
c. Observing the activities of the enemy's operational Air Force (Air Force and US bomber formations in the British motherland and southern Italian bases).

The last duty was of special value for the Reich's defense. The effects of the radio monitoring service were generally very good. All of the facts were forwarded to the operations commander after a quick evaluation, starting with the preparations of the Allied air forces, weather forecast in the approach and target areas, start and termination of the assemblies, switching on of navigational aids from plane to plane, following the courses of the approach and return flights and observations and direction finding through voice transmissions of plane to plane and plane to ground, and of bearings of almost all high frequency sets ("Rotterdam," nightfighter warning apparatus). Important decisions for operating were often based on radio intelligence. An evaluation of large scale air offensives in the making, and forming of clear aerial situation map, would have been impossible without these.

The German fighter commanders often dared to timidly delve into the secrets of the enemy missions in advance of the operations. The results of the radio monitoring service could only be made practicably helpful to the Reich's defense in the fall of 1943, because until this time the results were forwarded through channels by a complicated organization. For example, the "Radio Monitoring Division – West" in Holland was subordinate to Luftflotte 3 and the results were first forwarded to Paris, and to Berlin by way of Paris. This resulted in a delay of almost 24 hours: they came too late to be of importance to the Reich's defense. For a long time an insignificant monthly activity and recognition report of the division was of more importance than an immediate evaluation for continuous operation. The demands of the 1st Fighter Corps and of the Luftflotte Reich about this remained fruitless.

When the invasion of the Western Powers finally ended with the loss of France not only almost all of the radar and bearing apparatuses were lost but a large number of special personnel of the outer Reich's defense as well. There was a tremendous monitoring and bearing gap in the Eifel–Swiss border sector. At first no sets were available to fill this gap in September–October 1944. Not only were the necessary towers lost in Paris but unnecessarily also in the east (Lvov). The remaining organizations of the radio monitoring service in the west worked mainly for cooperation purposes. The effects of the loss of the outer zones personnel and equipment was so great on the Reich's defenses that even the radio monitoring service could no longer successfully stand by the radar service.

III. Technical Means of Command in the German Defense

Under the above heading we must understand the technical means and methods with which the day and nightfighters were led to their targets from the ground.

The battle of England had brought a surprise to the German High Command, namely, that the English motherland had already a well built out radar and fighter escort service for operating in her air defense. The English used an aerial voice communications set for this purpose. These especially marked direction finding signals which were transmitted by the sets were received by 2 to 3 towers on the ground. The point of intersection of the individual towers gave the location; by following the location coordinates an established time rhythm of the flight of their own formations was followed.

At that time Germany was only beginning with experiments. The following method was generally used. The command post gave their own formations a sort of an enemy air situation report by way of radio. Further actions were left up to the formation leaders. This so-called report procedure, however, did not in any way meet the requirements, and this was particularly the case when overcast sky, visibility, or misorientation of their own location was unknown. This system was in no way a match for the large scale flights of the USAAF. The air situation which became so entangled by fighter escorts and preliminary fighting could no longer be completely transmitted by radio to the employed formations. In spite of all of these weaknesses, this system had to be retained as a supplementary and evasive solution until the end of the war. A unified frequency was used for this during the day—the Reich's fighter wavelength. This was used especially for the alarm units of the fighter pilot schools, supplementary fighter groups, industry defense flights, and for the second wave of active formations of the Reich's defense during large scale daylight attacks. During the night the fighters were kept informed of the aerial situation by radio, voice communication, and broadcast.

In 1940 a net of fighter towers was erected in the German Bay which served the primary purpose of flight security on missions over the sea; later on it was also used for the fighter command. Similar to the English system, the fighter command lacked, above all, automatic direction finding signal transmitters so that recognition and D/F signals had to be given by the pilots.

In addition to the continued expansion of fighter D/F nets in the fall of 1941, the "Benito" procedure came into use along the western coast of the occupied countries. With this method the aircraft did not have to give any kind of signals. Direction and distance were measured from a grand position. The expansion program of the ground organizations and aerial equipment for aircraft was started once again in the German Bay. Holland–Ruhr, Berlin–central Germany, and the area of Luftflotte 3 in southern Germany followed. The higher priority of the nightfighters stood in the way of a more rapid application of this system for the dayfighters.

The interference weakness of the system and the lack of D/F towers and range finders for the ground organizations resulted in the "Egon" system. This system worked in cooperation with the recognition set in the aircraft and the "Freya" set on the ground.

In 1942 a rivalry existed between the adherents of both systems. Nightfighting again settled the matter; the "Benito" system—which was more suitable, because it was more exact—was introduced as a standard system for day and nightfighting in the fall of 1942 after Goering's decision. The "Egon" system, which was more advantageous to the unit leaders, was used as an alternative system in the event of effective enemy interference, and the ultra short wave flight safety service was ordered to expand generously on the basis of the D/F system.

The High Command of the Luftwaffe first took an interest in these basic questions of aerial defense at the end of 1942. The clear path which was attained as a result was maintained by the fighter command service until the end of the war.

Neither the "Benito" nor the "Egon" system was ever effectively jammed.

After 1944, all of the fighter planes were equipped with a 5-channel voice communications set. This made it possible to change over from one system to another while in the air. Moreover, the Reich's fighter wavelength and also the near and far distant flight service could get in contact with the pilots as they chose.

A large number of special technical difficulties frequently arose when the command had to be turned over from one fighter division to the neighboring division during operations covering large areas.

On the whole, the fighter command organization was sufficient from 1941 on.

The war year 1945 had to bring about the change of further developments of the navigational system of the Reich's defense for fighter missions in bad weather, for the actual large scale missions of 40–50 fighter formations of every division, and for the mass operations of the jet fighters. Preparations for this had started.

Although it had been said before that the fighter control system was greatly injured by these interference measures, this did not apply to the connections from the Headquarters and fighter control stations to the pilots in the air, and vice versa. The night operations were especially hit in this respect. The ether was filled with code and voice, long and short waves, with tone or OW, radar search, commands, talking music and bell tones. Those who had to listen too the war of the wavelengths during the night believed they were at a fair at a late hour or were listening to a transmission of an excited parliamentary debate. In spite of this, the enemy never succeeded in cutting off all of the command methods at the same time.

The Meteorological Service in the German Defense

The weather reports about conditions over the British Isles and Western Europe were of the utmost importance for the command of the Reich's defense. Important conclusions could be drawn therefrom.

These weather reports came from the weather reconnaissance aircraft, which had always been successful and reliable during the war. They were substantiated by individual observations of reconnaissance and combat planes which brought back important reports. U-Boats and naval vessels also gave weather reports; however, due to coding and radio mistakes, these did not always suffice. In addition to this, the automatic weather radio sets (weather buoys) which were set up by the weather service of the Navy in the later years of the war gave useful atmospheric pressure and temperature reports.

The reports of agents from the unoccupied territories were of little meteorological value. These observations of the laymen often gave the wrong atmospheric pressure values. As a result of the extensive relay methods other errors were added. Especially, synoptic reports were lacking. The agents reports from the northwestern and western sections of Europe were small in number since the German espionage service had little success in this field; the fear also existed that the agents' service would be discovered too quickly on account of the fixed-time transmission of the weather reports. Reports were also received from England regarding the London area; their value, however, was also questionable.

On the other hand, the reports of the German monitoring and decoding service were of the greatest value. Usable reports of the weather situation over England were received from the tactical monitoring receivers which intercepted gam reports or parts of gam reports. At the same time, weather forecasts, e.g. from Ronaldsway and Liverpool, were intercepted and proved to be of great value.

Specific weather conditions in certain areas could also be arrived at through the subject matter and contents of the radio traffic of RAF training and practice flights. Radio commands of the transfer of training and practice flights to other areas indicated favorable or unfavorable weather conditions. Some reports of landing aircraft were also picked up. The radio traffic of the returning bomber units, and the individual weather reports which were sent from the ground stations to the planes in the air, could be made use of.

Later, the German monitoring service also supplied valuable information on atmospheric pressure conditions in the Azores, in England, Ireland, and Greenland; this information originated from the Flight Safety Communications of the ferrying route from America to England. Through the close cooperation between the meteorologists and the decoders, individual conclusive QFF-values (atmospheric pressures at sea level, which were of special meaning to the analysis of the European weather situation) were decoded, despite many difficulties. During the last months of the war these QFF-values were the only reports that were available from western and northwestern Europe.

The best source was beyond a doubt the Copenhagen Weather Code, which decoded weather reports, but whose decoding had only been a success in the first years of the war. The immense difficulties of decoding were great due to the continual changing of the code.

Chapter 5

German Nightfighting
From 15 June 1943 to May 1945

by Generalleutnant Josef "Beppo" Schmid
Beaconsfield, England, 1 October 1945

Operations Rooms

Up to autumn 1943 the ops rooms had become an excrescence of the control of one single fighter ("Himmelbett" method). They were built in oversized dimensions almost as an end to themselves and required many personnel for their functioning. The object for all the staffs was not to find out the enemy or our own air situation. With the help of all modern means of instrument mechanics, of electrical engineering, of optics, and of cartography, personnel tried to fix the position of the enemy and one own single flying aircraft on large-scale maps by various light reflexions. This kind of ops room failed completely since the time when the RAF flew to Germany in a narrow bomber stream and the own operations could no longer be carried out with the "Himmelbett" method. It was neither possible to show up the enemy bomber stream in a sensible way nor to carry out a free combat. These "Richard Wagner Theatres," as I called them, were mere "Himmelbett" automatics.

Until the end of 1943 such giant ops rooms for fighter divisions had been built at the following places: Doeberitz near Berlin, Stade, Deelen, Metz, and Schleissheim near Munich. Apart from the ops rooms in Deelen and Stade, one giant ops room each had been built there in concrete to give the necessary protection against 2,000 kg bombs. In my view the work (for the responsible fighter commanders and their staffs) was very hard, if not perhaps impossible, in these gigantic ops rooms, with the constant artificial light and bad air and among so many noisy people. The atmosphere in these giant ops rooms certainly did not contribute to successful control and clear decisions during the operations. Apart from these great ops rooms of the fighter divisions, there existed others which were a little smaller, such as that at Koenigsberg-Beumark.

When I took over the I Fighter Corps it was one of my first and foremost tasks to simplify the work of the ops rooms, reducing the personnel and saving material, and to adjust them above all to the requirements of a modern and flexible fighter control. Unfortunately, owing to lack of time and material, one had to stick to the existing buildings of the giant ops rooms. It was not intended

A Luftwaffe operations room in combat during the Defense of the Reich, showing the staggered tiers of officers with telephones who ran the battle under the eye of the commanding officer (standing at the rear). (US National Archives)

to work out a uniform scheme for the equipment and setting-up of the ops rooms. Although this had been demanded by Luftflotte Reich and the CinC Sigs. Communications, I could defend myself successfully against them.

The demands which I raised for changes of the ops rooms were, on the whole, the following:

1. Removal of the divisional commanders and their personal staffs out of the great commotion of the ops room.
2. Simplified method of representing the enemy forces—representation of the bomber stream (beginning, end, and width of the stream)— representation of Mosquitoes and enemy weather reconnaissance aircraft— representation of different components for the formation of the enemy situation (results from D/Fs, "Y" Service, set reports, and Air Rep. Serv.), statement of times, flying heights and flying speeds.
3. Clear representation of the positions of the own aircraft in general—no representation of single aeroplanes—use of the plotting procedure and observation of the own identity devices (FuG 25).
4. Simplification of the large-scale maps by leaving out all dates for organization, purposes ("Himmelbett" areas, sector limits, and so forth),

but marking of big towns, rivers, lakes, high mountains, beacons, radio beacons, and other points of orientation.

5. Renouncing the over-minute methods of representation with light projectors and other electrical sets subject to frequent disturbances.
6. More frequent use of the frosted glass screens and marking the positions from behind in mirror writing.
7. Concentration of all incoming news about the own and enemy situation in two places, which must be separated from the ops room proper by glass screens because of the noise.
8. Reduce organization of the body of commanders, including signals commanders and meteorologists.
9. Drastic reduction of personnel by no longer marking every single flying friendly or enemy aircraft.
10. Extensive use of the Air Reporting Service (Eye-Ear).
11. Close cooperation of the AA and fighter commanders.

These demands were in fact welcomed by all fighter divisions. By spring 1944 all ops rooms were converted. The fighter divisions had solved the problems in different ways according to their mentality. This was good, because now the best solution of a first-class ops rooms could be chosen by the different commanders in case a new room was to be installed. It must be pointed out that in the ops room of each division, reductions were made of about 75 officers, 14 officials, 3,290 NCOs and men, and 2,360 female employees. The corps ops rooms in Zeist, Brunswick, and Treuenbrietzen could always be kept small and simple. There the bulky apparatus for the formation of the air situation (the Gen. Kdo. generally took over the air situation of the fighter divisions) and the equipment of the commander of the "Y" Service were omitted by introducing briefing desks for the fighter control officers. A masterly equipped and concrete ops room had just been finished in Freuenbritzen when in January 1945 the Russians approached Berlin.

The technical equipment of all sorts concerning the sigs service in all ops rooms and their reliability can be called excellent; they had been built by the construction staffs of the CinC Air Sigs Corps. Finally, it must be mentioned that, naturally, the equipment and functioning of the ops rooms had to be adjusted to the various methods of operation and were subject to changes caused by new HF sets. With the further development of the roundabout radar sets, these would have been necessary also in the ops rooms. If the war had been carried on longer, it might perhaps have been necessary to move the ops rooms to sites higher above sea level (e.g., Brocken in the Herz Mountains).

Signals Communications
(a) Wire Network

It was dense and on the whole excellent. The reliability kept up with the great demands and the strain put on it. The disturbances and interruptions caused by enemy bombing were quickly overcome and were therefore scarcely felt by the command, even up to the end of the war. There was no assurance that the telephone lines were not being listened in to, especially in the occupied countries. In Holland, e.g. in the Army telephone exchanges, Dutch subjects were being employed under very weak German military supervision. I suspected that there all long-distance calls about operations were listened-in to. Only thus can it be explained that on the very morning after night operations the British radio station for soldiers could broadcast details about the German nightfighter activities. A change could not be brought about with any of the superior officers, above all not with the Military Commander in Holland.

The coding of the long-distance calls could only be demanded to a certain extent. Otherwise the operational calls would have become too long, the strain on the telephone lines unbearable, and the contents of the calls too confusing, owing to the unavoidable coding errors. How much strain could be put on the command net is shown by the following example:

On 19.4.1944 the Gen. Kdo. I Fighter Corps had the following direct telephone connections from the ops room at Treuenbrietzen:

To 1st Fighter Div.	4 lines
2nd Fighter Div.	8 lines
3rd Fighter Div.	7 lines
4th Fighter Div.	5 lines
7th Fighter Div.	7 lines
8th Fighter Div.	5 lines
JaFue East Prussia	2 lines
Silesia	2 lines
C in C	1 line
O.K.L.	9 lines
Luftflotte Reich	4 lines
Zentrale "Y" Service	3 lines
Wehrkreiskommando Berlin	1 line
R.L.M.	2 lines
Chief of Gen. Staff	4 lines
Min. of Propaganda	2 lines

Rundfunkhaus Berlin	2 lines
Leipzig	2 lines
II Fighter Corps	6 lines
Fighter Corps	6 lines
Fighter Sector Darmstadt	2 lines
Area Commander Muenchen-Gladbach	5 lines
Ops Room Zeist	5 lines
Brunswick	4 lines
Luftgau Berlin	8 lines
10 Air Force Exchanges	38 lines
Flugwachkommandos Berlin, Leipzig, Magdeburg, Bremen, Hanover, and Hamburg: 1 each	6 lines
Flugwachkommandos Brussels, Muenster, and Amsterdam: 2 each	6 lines

Total: 148 direct telephone connections

The fighter divisions had sufficient telephone connections to their flying units, to the JaFues, to the section commanders, and to the radar sites. They were also

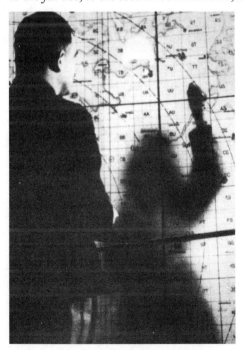

several times crossconnected with one another. The total wire net had weak points which had geographic reasons (mountains). They were in the Eifel, Taunus, and Vogelsberg, and impaired the telephone connections from the Frankfurt area to the 3rd Fighter Division. Other areas with a poor wire net were the Erzgebirge and Riesengebirge, which had a detrimental effect upon the connections with the 8th Fighter Division. Finally, telephone connections did not exist across the lower part of the Elbe, which impaired the con-

A German operations room: plotting the course of an incoming raid. (US National Archives)

Batteries of slide projectors, each showing the location of a friendly or enemy formation, were a feature of the largest German fighter ops rooms. The images were projected against a map on the wall. (US National Archives)

nections with the 2nd Fighter Division, the Fighter Sector Grove, and with the radar stations in Schleswig-Holstein.

The command net of the units (division to staff of the geschwader to gruppe, as well as and amongst themselves) was partly mediocre. The Luftgaue refused to put sufficient useful lines at our disposal. They themselves, however, and the AA units subordinated to them, were amply equipped with telephone lines for economic and private calls. Furthermore, the Air Reporting and Meteorological Services led their own lives and had therefore their special networks. CinC Signals Communications was not judicious enough to interfere here with a strong hand in order to raise the striking power of the Defense of the Reich.

(b) Decimeter Communications (Directed R/T)

In the beginning, the wireless telephone communications (RV) were mostly being used in the Eastern theatre of the war. They were introduced in Germany by spring 1944, and completed then in a safe way for communications in times of frequent interruptions of the network caused by bombing. The supposedly great danger of listening-in reduced the possibility of the RV being used considerably.

(c) W/L Connections

All telephone connections of the working and command sets in the Defense of the Reich were overlapped by wireless connections. Gen. Kdo. I Fighter Corps had ordered that all instructions and orders for operations, which were given out by telephone, were always repeated in coded W/T messages. Nevertheless the W/L connections were no perfect substitute in case of collapse of the telephone system. The W/T personnel of the GAF never reached the achievements of the Navy.

Formation of the Air Situation
(1) Own Air Situation

Until summer 1943 it was hardly of any importance. It was merely indicated in the ops rooms which "Himmelbetten" were being occupied at one particular time. Then the little lamps, which had been provided for that purpose, were glowing on the great map screen. This method could however no longer suffice after nightfighting round the target area and pursuit nightfighting had been introduced. I therefore ordered that the greatest stress had to be laid on an accurate registering of the own air situation. This was necessary for the following reasons:

(a) To have a general survey and to be able to find out how many aeroplanes could be used for the different methods of nightfighting.
(b) As a means to find out which units could be sent on operations against the various enemy raids.   .
(c) For all cases in which plans had to be changed during the nightfight owing to a changed enemy air situation.
(d) For the control of units and crews.
(e) For the continuous instruction of the AA and the Air Warning Services. Thus false warnings and AA fire on friendly aircraft were to be avoided.

Apart from the regular reports to the QMG according to schedule, the units had to report the number of serviceable aircraft to the Gen. Kdo. by telephone through the tactical and operational channels one hour before sunset. These reports served as material for the planning of the commanders. They were given decoded according to types of aircraft as follows:

Number of a/c serviceable for "Himmelbett."
Number of a/c, stating the serviceable scanners.
"Lichtenstein BC" or SN 2 or special and experimental sets.
Number of top crews for bad weather operations.
Number of serviceable reconnaissance a/c.
Number of illuminators.

Plotting the courses of own a/c had to be ascertained by various means:

(a) Take-off reports of the units to the fighter divisions.
(b) Plotting the courses by the units and the fighter divisions by personnel specially trained for this purpose.

(c) Reporting the positions of single flying a/c, later (from summer 1944 onward) during the pursuit nightfighting of the units from the air by W/T or R/T (reporting the arrival over target or the radio beacon).

(d) Reports of the Air Reporting Service Eye/Ear; in most cases they were wrong as the engine noises of friendly a/c and those of enemy planes were difficult to distinguish.

(e) Reports of the radar stations after IFF had been introduced. The problem of identification had been solved in late summer 1943. Fitting the nightfighter a/c with FuG 25, and above all equipping the radar stations with the additional "Gemse Erstling" set, were not finished before spring 1944. It was found that the own crews did not like to switch on the identification set on board as they suspected the enemy plotting them.

It was a long time—up to about April 1944—before the fighter divisions learned how to register the own air situation to some extent. The problem was never solved completely.

(2) Enemy Air Situation

It was simply called air situation. For a long time there was an absolute confusion in this field. This was mainly connected with the development of the factors for the formation of the air situation. Since the beginning of the war, every department that was in need of it, procured for itself its own picture of the situation in the air (big filter centers of the Air Reporting Service, nightfighter and AA offices, local air warning stations, police stations, political leaders, and a number of other offices, even if they procured their material from ordinary wireless reports).

As late as 1.2.1944, the fighter divisions (for the Air Force) were generally made responsible for determining the enemy air situation for all those who needed it. Up till autumn 1943, the picking-up of enemy a/c for reasons of nightfighting was almost exclusively built up on the reports of the radar stations in view of nightfighting on the "Himmel-bett" method. Until then, other means of finding out about the

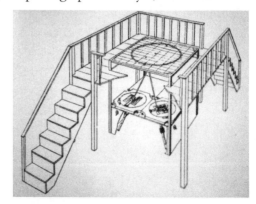

A German plotting table. The positions of friendly and enemy formations were projected upward in the lower level. (US National Archives)

enemy were scarcely being used. Therefore, the I Fighter Corps had to reorganize the formation of the enemy air situation, almost completely. Until the end of the war, this organization fought a continuous battle both against the increased enemy radar warfare and against stubborn superior officers. To the latter belonged, first of all, the CinC Air Signals, who regarded the Air Reporting Service and the "I" Service as independent "branches of the service" with an end in themselves.

At first, I was of the opinion that it would be a great relief to nightfighting, and that it would mean at the same time a reduction in work and personnel, if a faultless and correct picture of the air situation could be taken over from some organization which was not under my command. For I was afraid of taking over the bulky apparatus of the Air Reporting Service of the Reich and with it the additional responsibility of the Air Warning Service and the warning system. As a responsible man for the creation of the air situation could not be found outside Fighter Command, I decided, at the turn of 1943/44, to take over this task myself within Fighter Command, and demanded therefore the subordination of all feeding services for the formation of the air situation.

The fighter divisions supplied most of the material. There, all the information about the strength and the activities of the enemy a/c flowed together within the respective areas. The COs of the fighter divisions were made responsible that the enemy air situation was reported by telephone to those concerned. Fighter Corps gave a summarizing survey of the enemy air situation on the basis of the reports of the fighter divisions and other information. They made this survey known in the form of a corps "reportage" to all concerned on the ground by telephone, and, via the fighter divisions, to the units in the air by R/T and W/T. The first links in the chain of this procedure, which were of great importance, were the radar stations. The main factors necessary for the formation of the air situation are:

Radar Service.
Air Reporting Service Eye/Ear.
"Y" Service.
Air Reconnaissance.
AA Spotting Service.
Experience of all experts in the formation of the air situation, in particular of the COs of the fighter divisions and commanders of radar stations.

Up to 1.2.1944, when all the above-mentioned services were subordinated to the Fighter Corps (with the exception of the "Y" Service), the flowing together in time of the information from all sources for the formation of the air situation had been difficult and painful.

(a) Radar Service

It is of importance to state that since 1941 the entire radar ground organization had exclusively been built up and organized for the purposes of directing nightfighting ("Himmelbett" method) and not also for the general Air Reporting Service. The network of the "Himmelbett" positions in a 30 km radius was far-spread, and up to the end of 1943 their construction was finished for the time being.

The construction is perhaps one of the greatest merits of the organizational achievements of General Kammhuber. The network was particularly dense in northwest Germany, Holland, Belgium, and northeast France. In these territories the radar stations frequently overlapped. Furthermore, they were still further overlapped by a special switch line (formerly an illuminated switch line) along the general strip Flensburg–Stade–Bremen–Rheine–Enschede–Nymwegen–Hasselt–Charleroi–Hirson–Rethe–Somme–Py–St Dizier–Joinville. In the rest of France, positions had been built in the area of Paris and in the Rhone valley. In Rumania there were 12 positions in the oil fields and around Bucharest. Denmark and the islands in the western Baltic Sea as well as the southern end of Norway were covered. In the south, Sicily and the northern part of Tunisia were equipped with sets.

In the Reich, on the other hand, there yawned a great gap round the area of Bielefeld–Muenster–Hamm–Siegen–Marburg–Fulda–Suhl–Erfurt–Kassel–Holzminden. Only in spring and summer 1944 was this territory ready for radar activities in an emergency way. In the west, the radar stations were missing in Luxemburg and in Alsace-Lorraine as well as in the Alps. The eastern limit of the radar ground organization ran along the line Pressburg–Lundenburg–Bruenn–Trebitsch–Bayreuth–Plauen–Karlsbad–Aussig–Kottbus—Frankfurt a.d.O.–Schneidemuehl–Elbing–Allenstein–Johannisburg–Lyck–Eydkuhnen–Memel. In spring 1944 the equipment with sets was finished in the territory Bruenn–Pressburg–Wiener–Neustadt–Agram–Fuenfkirchen–Budapest–Olmuetz. On the island of Bornholm a new radar station was built. Lastly, there were 45 truckborne radar stations. They operated mainly in Russia, and only towards the end of the war they were being used in the area east of Vienna and in the west of the Reich. The radar ship *Togo* was to be used in the Skagerrak, but it never arrived there; it was most of the time in the eastern Baltic.

Until autumn 1943 the radar stations had about 160 soldiers and female personnel each. In October 1943 I decided to loosen the network of radar stations and to reduce their personnel. This was possible because the "Himmelbett" method no longer formed the main part of nightfighting. My first proposal of November 1943 was a general extension of the radius of radar stations to 60 km; use of this saved up personnel and equipment for filling the existing radar gaps in the Reich, in Austria, and in Hungary; as well as reduction of the personnel in the stations to about 120. The proposal was not totally accepted by CinC Air Signals Communications. To begin with, only a small proportion of radar stations were to be transferred from northwest Germany to Austria. It was only towards the end of the year 1943, when the total war was becoming imminent again, that my proposals were carried out to the letter, but the personnel of the radar stations were reduced to 100 persons. Only the stations along the coast kept their former strength, and were staffed with male personnel only. Apart from some controllers and specialists, who were men, all the remaining posts had to be filled by women. Unfortunately, in the course of the year 1944, experienced radar specialists, too, were removed to be used in frontline fighting. Fully qualified male or female replacements never turned up. Finally, it must be mentioned that the female personnel from the Reich Labor Service generally proved to be particularly good.

(b) Air Reporting Service (A.R.S.)

Here I must go a bit further back. Before the war (being then a member of the Gen. Staff of the GAF 1. Abteilung), I witnessed the formation of the ARS. At first it was then (1935?) decided it was the duty of the CinC Sigs Communications to organize the ARS because there were telephone connections necessary. Therefore the CinC Sigs Comm organized the ARS. The necessary orders, however, were given by the Gen. Staff of the GAF, 1. Abt. But, on the other hand, it was the duty of the police to carry them out. It was only in wartime that the entire ARS of the Reich was to be under the command of the CinC of the GAF.

A distinction was made between the ARS of the Forces and the ARS of the Reich. The former was meant for the purposes of air defense (fighters and AA) and for the warning and alarms in the area of operation of the Army. It was organized into air rep. companies (mot., i.e. mechanized) and air rep. battalions (mot.), and consisted exclusively of members of the Air Sigs Corps. During the first part of the war these air rep. battalions and companies were under the command of the "Kolufts" with the "Armeen," and later on they were subordinated to those Fliegerkorps or Fliegerdivisions, respectively, which cooperated with the Army. The foremost parts (air rep. posts) of the ARS of the forces were practically joined together with the front line of the Army. The rear parts had direct connections to the communication network of the ARS of the Reich in the home defense area near the limit of the operational area of the Army.

In the first part of the war, the units of the ARS were well mechanized and sufficiently equipped with sigs sets (telephone, W/T, R/T sets). They had, however, only acoustic sets and no radar equipment. The ARS of the Reich was under the command of the Luftgau. It was organized into Flugwachkommandos, great and small ARS filter centers and AR posts. It was a mere eye/ear service, without any sets. Its personnel consisted only of old reserves of the AS Corps, older remustered organs of the police, civilians unfit for military service from communal offices, and chiefly female personnel. Its use and organization were directed according to targets. The Flugwachkommando was in the target. The Flugwachkommandos were connected amongst themselves and with the local Luftgaukommandos by telephone. Those authorities and other establishments interested in the reports of the Flugwachkommando were connected with them by telephone (aerodromes, AA units in the home defense, warning services, railways, hospitals, political offices, etc.). The AR filter centers and the AR posts were grouped in a ring around the targets. Shortly before the war the distance from one ring to another had to be increased according to the greater speeds of the a/c. Thus the entire Reich, and, during the war also the occupied territories (these only very thinly), were covered with an irregular spider-weblike network of AR stations.

Perhaps it would have been better, in the interest of a reduction in personnel, and of a clear organization and, above all, of a faster transmission of reports, to arrange the AR stations in the entire air defense area (Reich and occupied territories) according to the boundaries or the fronts in one line. The efficiency of the entire ARS of the Reich was mediocre as most of its personnel were too old and badly trained and without any radio-location sets almost throughout the war. As late as 1938 the CinC Sigs Comm had intended and demanded to equip the ARS with radar sets first of all. However, when the first sets appeared, they were given to the AA as firing devices, and in 1941 and 1942 most of them went into nightfighting. In reality there existed now 3 AR organizations which worked side by side: the radar ground organization for nightfighting, the Reich ARS of the Luftgau for the AA and air warning centers, and the ARS in the territory of naval fortresses subordinated and belonging to the Navy. For a long time, the Reich ARS had remained the own creation of the sigs troop and formed, so to speak, a branch of its own within the GAF.

Only in January 1944 were the demands of the I Fighter Corps for unification and subordination of the ARS complied with, after it had obviously failed under the very eyes of the CinC of the GAF. On 24 January 1944 the weather was dull.

There was an 8–10/10 cloud layer 1,000–1,200 meters. The USAAF attacked the town of Dueren in western Germany in daytime. The enemy approach was recognized in time and followed up by the radar stations of the I Fighter Corps. The withdrawal was registered by them, although the tinfoil swept away to the east by the wind had been measured as far as the Rhine. In any case, it was beyond any doubt with the Gen. Kdo. I Fighter Corps that no enemy a/c had crossed the Rhine to the east.

On this day the CinC of the GAF took a personal interest in the air situation and had, amongst other things, his reports also from the ARS. They registered the enemy approach from Dueren further inland via Frankfurt and Schweinfurt to Dresden and Pilsen. Goering ordered all available dayfighters to take off for the protection of Schweinfurt, of the oil refineries in central Germany, and even of the Skoda factory in Pilsen. In reality, there were only German fighters east of the Rhine, and partly above the clouds. They were regarded as enemy planes by the ARS. One Flugwachkommando in central Germany pretended to have even seen 4-eng. enemy bombers, which can be proved by written reports. The AA in the same territory reported alleged strong jamming by "Window." There was, however, no bombing reported east of the Rhine. The whole drama resembled a big hoax. It became the subject of a great conference with the CinC in which the CinC Sigs Comm fought for the independence of the ARS for the last time. On 1.2.1944, however, the amalgamation of the ARS of the Reich with the radar organization of the I Fighter Corps was ordered by the CinC of the GAF.

The main work for the formation of the air situation was now done by the radar controllers. They were now also supplied with all the reports from the eye/ear service of their areas. The radar controllers, who were either fighter control officers or efficient persons from the ARS (the first deputies were always of opposite origin), had the responsible task of giving a clear picture of the air situation by telephone reports to the superior fighter division and by using the results gained from the sets and all the observations made by the ARS stations in their areas.

A vast organization was necessary to create a communication system between the ARS stations and the radar stations. This proceeded at a slow pace only, and lasted until spring 1945. By the reorganization, a reduction of wire personnel was possible. It was, however, much too late and did therefore not contribute towards a successful Air Defense of the Reich.

(c) "Y" Service

In order not to be misunderstood, I repeat that the general achievements of the "Y" Service were excellent on all fronts in peace as well as in wartime. However great these achievements may have showed themselves, the total organization was just as bad. This fact had a particularly tragic effect on the command of the Defense of the Reich. The "Y" Service may have recognized an enemy night raid at the right time and at the right spot. The reports on it, however, reached the responsible unit commander in the Defense of the Reich only the following day. Therefore all the good work of the D/F stations was of no use, if the higher command organized its operations in the wrong way. On the whole, the "Y" Service had three different tasks:

1. Find out the enemy strength.
2. Find out the enemy dispositions.
3. Find out the movement of enemy aircraft.

Observing the operations of the TAFs of the enemy, these results were especially used by those branches which operated for army cooperation; observing the operations of the strategic AFs of the enemy (RAF and USAAF bomber units on the British Isles and the south Italian bases), the results of the "Y" and D/F Services were vital for the commanders in the Defense of the Reich.

The three clear tasks of the "Y" Service had to be taken into consideration in view of its use and organization. A possible solution offered itself in the following way:

1 "Y" controller with the Intelligence Dept. of the CinC GAF.
1 "Y" controller with Luftflottenkommando 3, later Luftwaffenkommando West.
1 "Y" controller with Gen. Kdo. I Fighter Corps.

Several "Y" controllers were on the Eastern front, according to the command organization of the Air Force there.

Every "Y" controller had to be given an adequate number of "Y" and D/F troops and be put under the command of the units for which he worked. Only if the unit commander and the "Y" controller both experienced the actual fighting together, could the "Y" be used and work successfully for the command.

In reality, there was a complete confusion in the use of the "Y" Service. My repeated and urgent demands and proposals to use the "Y" Service in the way mentioned above were mostly disregarded or accepted too late by the CinC Sigs Comm. Up to autumn 1943 there was practically no collaboration at all between the XII Fliegerkorps and the "Y" Service. This happened at a time when, in Zeist in Holland, the "Y" Service unit was stationed in the immediate neighborhood of the ops room of the Gen. Kdo. This "Y" Service unit, whose base was between Heligoland Bight and the middle of the Channel, was under the command of Luftflottenkommando 3 in Paris.

An efficient officer of Y Battalion West, Oberleutnant Rueckheim, was called to the Gen. Kdo. to be present in the ops room of the Corps during several night operations: this turned out to be a full success. Until November 1943 he organized a useful and fast reporting D/F organization, which procured the reports on H2S concentrations for the Gen. Kdo. I Fighter Corps. Until April 1944 these reports were the only reliable data for the plotting of enemy courses and thus the cause of a successful control of nightfighting. The only tragicomic fact was that Y Battalion West had orders to pass their D/F results not directly on to the Gen. Kdo. I Fighter Corps, but to forward them via Paris. When this "impossible" instruction could not be observed, radar sets and personnel of the Y Battalion in Zeits were removed to Paris.

The successful work of the Y units could only be carried on because the I Fighter Corps replaced the removed sets and personnel from out of its area. The tomfoolery reached its zenith when I obtained Rueckheim's promotion by selection to Hauptmann and his appointment to CO of an Abteilung from the CinC GAF. Rueckheim's transfer to the East was announced at the same time by his superiors. The Luftflottenkommando 3 and the CinC Sigs Comm did not want the successes of the reserve officer Hauptmann Rueckheim to pass. Even a personal interview, which I had with the higher Sigs Commander of Luftflotte 3, could not alter this. All I could achieve with the CinC was that Rueckheim was not transferred. Until the collapse of the German front in France, Y Battalion West remained under the command of Luftflottenkommando 5. The Gen. Kdo. I Fighter Corps attained neither a subordination of Y Battalion West to the Gen. Kdo. nor a uniform organization of the "Y" Service suited for the tasks of the Defense of the Reich.

However, with the Befehlshaber Mitte (later Luftflottenkommando Reich) there grew up a new and absolutely inexperienced "Y" Service instead, which was solely at the disposal of this unit and whose reports the Gen. Kdo. I Fighter Corps were received at second hand only. In theory the state of affairs was therefore that the Gen. Kdo. I Fighter Corps was dependent on the passing-on of the D/F reports from Paris and Berlin. This happened at times of the most intense night bombing activities, when delayed and wrongly interpreted D/F reports at second hand to the commander of nightfighting might have devastating effects upon his decisions.

When, finally, the invasion of the enemy forces resulted in the loss of France, not only practically all radar and D/F sets and a great number of expert personnel were lost in the advanced area of the Defense of the Reich. In addition to that, a gigantic "Y" Service and D/F gap was opened in the sector between the Eifel and the Swiss frontier. At first, in September and October 1944, no sets were to be had to fill this gap. The necessary D/F equipment had fallen into the hands of the enemy, not only in the Air Sigs Depot in Paris but also, unnecessarily, in the East (Lomberg). As late as autumn 1944 the Gen. Kdo. I Fighter Corps was supplied with a "Y" controller (not Hauptmann Rueckheim, but a colonel from the ARS), but without any troops. These still remained under the direct command of the CinC Sigs Comm. On the Western front, the "Y" Service did chiefly AC work. In view of the Defense of the Reich, the result of the loss of the advanced area, together with the expert personnel and the equipment, was that even the "Y" Service could no longer successfully wage the radar war.

(d) Air Reconnaissance

Up to autumn 1943, night air reconnaissance did not exist at all. It was first introduced by Gen. Kdo. I Fighter Corps in October 1943. To start with, first a kette, then a staffel was formed with each fighter division; night air reconnaissance and day shadowing aircraft were combined in these units. Experienced nightfighter crews were used for this purpose.

The night air recce staffeln were equipped with Ju-88s for reasons of range. Already in autumn 1943 the aeroplanes were equipped with a scanner (SN 2) and with experimental sets. From April 1944 onward, they were generally fitted with the "Naxos" set. After the day shadowing units had fallen away, the night recce staffeln with the fighter divisions were scrapped and the crews were incorporated in the staffs of the nightfighter geschwader.

Night reconnaissance flying had been started for the purposes of target area nightfighting ("Wilde Sau"). It was to make it easier for the commands of nightfighting to follow up the route of the bombers by means of the enemy track markets (flares and ground markers). Furthermore, the night recce units were to notify the commanders in time of the target of the enemy raid and to recognize above all spoof attacks and spoof markings.

During the six winter months 1943/44, the night recce units repeatedly solved their first tasks in an outstanding way. From April 1944 onward their use began to decline when only pursuit nightfighting was practiced, after all nightfighter aircraft had been equipped with SN 2, and when the enemy and our own use of illuminating devices had reached such an extent that with their help conclusions could no longer be drawn, neither on the courses nor on the targets.

When, in summer 1944, the enemy started to jam our radar sets from the ground and to carry out diversion flights on a large scale with the RAF 100th Group, a new task grew up for the air recce units. They were to find out the enemy bomber stream or streams in the air by plotting the enemy airborne detecting sets (bordzielgeraete). They solved these tasks only incompletely; in most cases they did not solve them at all. It is true that the "Naxos" set was able to plot the single H2S equipment, but not the concentration of H2S of the bomber stream This could only be plotted by chance.

(e) AA Spotting Service

In the course of the years of the war, the stationary AA units in the Defense of the Reich had gathered great experience in judging the local air situation. They were therefore instructed to communicate to the fighter control stations all impressions on night raids (illuminating devices, spoof attacks, Mosquitoes and s.o.) as a contribution towards the formation of the air situation.

(f) Experiences of the men in charge
of forming the air situation (Erfahrung der Luftlagebildner)

Great experience, special talent, and a constant study of the enemy are necessary for a correct appreciation of the enemy air situation. There were many diligent and gifted officers who never learned this activity. Owing to the quick march of events during a night raid and the multiplicity of the incoming reports true and false, nervous men were just as unsuitable for this kind of work as phlegmatic people. Numerous radar controllers, especially young officers who had been active since the beginning of nightfighting, did excellent work. To the detriment of nightfighter command, in 1944 a great number of these young officers were removed to be used on the front line. They were lost for the work of gaining the air situation. Of all the sector commanders, Major Ruppel in Darmstadt was by far the best man. General Grabmann, the Commander of the 3rd Fighter Division in the advanced area, could be regarded as an artist in this field. Oberstleutnant Bode and Oberstleutnant Schaller-Kaüde headed the team of the General Staff officers. With the Gen. Kdo., the Chief of Staff Oberst i.G. Wittmer (Heinrich) had a lucky hand. The Personnel Department of the GAF paid no heed to the proper distribution and appointment of the air situation specialists.

Goering maintained repeatedly that in most cases he had known the target of the enemy before the raids had been carried out, or that he had recognized it in time. Unfortunately, he failed to forward his knowledge to me, too, beforehand. Perhaps then many a night battle would have been more successful for the troops and many houses would have been saved. For the Germans, the most important part of the command of nightfighting belonged to the most interesting and exciting activities of the handling of troops during the past war.

Radar Technology and Radar Warfare

May I state in advance that I know little about technology and therefore I have not enough knowledge about technical particulars to be able to judge every move in the chess game of modern radar warfare. But I was able to follow up the high frequency development of the enemy and at home before and in the course of the war. As commanding general of the I Fighter Corps, I saw radar in such intensive action during the tragedy of nightfighting that I may try to pass a preliminary judgement. The development of radar on both sides during the war may be compared with the artillery of a ship and the amourplating in the battle of navies or tanks and antitank guns in gthe battle of armies. The stronger element will win; I therefore speak of radar warfare.

(a) Radar technology before the war

Both countries, Germany and Great Britain, prepared radar for purposes of war. In both countries it was known that aircraft could be detected by cathode ray tube. Each country believed it to be the sole owner of this new implement of war—or, at least, to have a great margin of progress ahead of the other. How the stage of development compared in reality, I do not know.

(b) Beginning of the War

For the beginning of the war, especially for the so-called Blitzkrieg, radar did not mean anything. During the Battle of Britain and during the then following bombing raids on the British Isles, it came into effect for

Left: A "Freya" early-warning radar (with a "Würzburg" dish in the background. Range 120 kilometers; frequency 125 MHz, range precision about 125 meters, angle precision 0.5 degrees. (US National Archives)

the first time. Great Britain was on the defensive. To master the crisis it had to mobilize all its national technical and scientific forces. It was overcome by colossal progress in the field of radar. At the same time, in Germany, who believed herself in successful offensive, little or nothing was done. When the big advantage of Great Britain was realized in Germany, it was started there to make up for the time lost. The leadership in the field of radar research and development was rather poor. In the sphere of personnel, the political and racial policy showed its disadvantages. It had caused the loss of a great number of good men. The principle of standard in the German radar industry showed in all fields only a considerably small basis, quite in contrast to GB and especially the USA, where the wide activities of amateurs had created a fertile soil for the high frequency technics. Lastly, it is important to state that in radar warfare Germany had always to catch up, had therefore to parry or follow up the hits. In connection with nightfighting and radar warfare I distinguish 3 phases.

(c) First Phase

The landmark for the beginning of the effective bombing war against Germany was the British night raid on Koln on 30.5.1942, which was carried out with 1,000 aircraft, according to the statement made by Churchill in Parliament. The British methods of night raids at that time still consisted of a considerably staggered incoming and outgoing flight of the bombers and of a considerably long duration of the attack (1–1½ hours). The losses in all British night raids in 1942 and in the first half of 1943 were great. German radar and nightfighting tactics had parried the British bombing warfare for the first time. The establishment of the radar bases with "Freya" and "Wurzburg" sets and the equipment with the "Lichtenstein" scanner ensured successful nightfighting in connection with the "Himmelbett" method. This was not changed by the British jamming attempts in 1942.

It was an astonishing fact that at the time Germany did not try to take up pursuit nightfighting with the "Lichtenstein" scanner. The German defensive success found its acknowledgement in the fact that in the middle of 1943 the British Bomber Command changed its tactics of attack and introduced new scanners and jamming devices.

(d) Second Phase

It was initiated with a blow in August 1943 by the two effective big raids on Hamburg. The British had made their surprise countermove in the field of high frequency. They surprised with very effective "Window", even more though with the target-finding H2S, and a well practiced method of attack. This became a catastrophe with its PFF, illuminators and the short duration of the raids. The massed bomber stream and "Windowing" made the "Himmelbett" method only partly effective. Nearly all frequency islets of the detection sets were jammed. The "Lichtenstein" scanners could only be used by the best crews any more, and only then in part, for the target approach. The enemy jamming from the ground took effect on the German long range detection sets and made the forming of the air situation very difficult. The "Window" made it difficult to control the nightfighting units in the air. On the whole, German nightfighters had come into a very disagreeable position.

As the first countermove, illuminated nightfighting was taken up. This could, however, be only an emergency measure, as the H2S enabled target finding in dark nights and even in bad weather through the clouds. Furthermore moonlit nights were avoided by the enemy.

At this stage of the high frequency warfare, I took command of the I Fighter Corps. At first we had to keep on fighting with emergency measures (object and single seater nightfighting). The first signs of the German countermeasures against the British innovations of the summer became visible: for the planes, the aircraft set SN 2. Technically it was completed in early fall, however, without minimum range.

Now a strongly impeding factor arose. In contrast to many other opinions this must be pointed out. In summer and fall 1943 the British night raids on German towns had affected the small shops of the radar industry very much, especially in Berlin. For this reason, the equipment of the flying units with SN 2 was postponed for another half a year. Furthermore, there was always a great shortage of tubes, as f.i. the bottleneck of LV 1, of which alone about 20 were needed for the SN 2. How slow the equipment with SN 2 was, is shown by a note in my diary on 20.10.1943, that mentions that 19 aircraft in the sphere of the I Fighter Corps were equipped with SN 2. Still in March 1944 the nightfighter Geschwader 2 and 6 flew with few, the nightfighter Geschwader 4 still without, SN 2. In spite of the fact that the "de-Windowing" of the ground sets and the minimum range in the SN 2 scanner did not become effective before spring 1944, already in December 1943 the effectiveness of the German countermeasures became visible. A small British carelessness, however, was very useful to the German command. The British nightbomber units kept their H2S sets switched on from takeoff to landing. Therefore the German detecting service was able to follow closely the path of the British bomber stream from the rally point to the target and back to the landing. From November 1943 until May 1944 it was therefore no problem to form the air situation even with jammed ground sets. During the night of the raid on Nurnberg on 30-31 March

1944, the British bomber stream, and H2S tactics felt the German parry strongly. The German nightfighters achieved with de-jammed ground sets and the SN 2 with minimum range the biggest defensive success of the war. At this point nightfighting had reached its peak. Soon afterwards, by the time of the invasion, the last phase of the radar war was entered upon.

(e) Third Phase

Already in June 1944, "Window" (with a new kind of long tinfoil) and jamming of SN 2 on the invasion front were reported by the flying units. The more careful handling of the H2S sets and the very smooth deceiving and jamming maneuvers of 100 Bomber Group and the tactics of separate bomber streams with the admirable feats of the British 5 and 6 Groups aggravated the forming of the air situation and the flight path tremendously. The spoof and diversion attacks of the Mosquito units, the disturbing effects by the British long range nightfighters and the disregard of the Swedish and Swiss neutrality by British bomber units brought additional difficulties.

The German nightfighter command was confronted with new problems. The German technics, however, afforded more favourable conditions to master the third phase than it had been the case during the high frequency warfare of the second phase.

I shall relate about the end first. The bomber command had won the game. The German players lay on the ground. They could not use their balls anymore.

The acute shortage of fuel and the loss of the advanced area, France and Belgium, showed their effects on all elements of command and operations. Research and development offered the SN 3 and the FuG 218 as new scanners as well as the new all-around-view radar ground set. The progress in the field of optical and heat measuring for scanners was big. The possibility of a sudden change in scanning methods had arisen. But all technical progress was of no use any more—they had come too late.

The fuel shortage dictated the further happenings. Since September 1944 this diminished the readiness for operations of the nightfighter units in regards to personnel and material. Sensitive scanners cannot be checked without trial flights. The high frequency sets suffered very much by accumulation of moisture during cool nights or in damp weather when the aircraft were parked on the airdromes in a wide dispersal. Without petrol it was not possible to keep the crews in training on the scanners and new methods of pursuit nightfighting in difficult situations. Without petrol it was not possible to run the dynamos of the radar sections to generate the current for the sets. Since September 1944, the supply of public electricity fell off in an alarming way.

The crews of the radar stations with their new reserve personnel could neither, without current, be kept in practice on the "de-Windowed" sets in difficult situations, nor could they be trained on the "Jagdschloss" set, which was difficult to handle. The latter was a very useful new set, which, however, still had plenty of teething troubles (dead zones, stationary blips, difficult detection switching, window sensitiveness, it used a big amount of current etc.). Crews well trained and experienced with the "Jagdschloss" could have fully mastered the following up of the flight path also in the third phase of radar warfare, in spite of enemy jamming. The "Jagdschloss" personnel, however, could neither be trained, nor bring many of these 100 all-around-view radar sets into use. This number was at the disposal of the home defense towards the end of the war.

The breakdown of the "Y" Service in connection with the loss of the advanced area and the gap in direction-finding on the Western front, as well as the disadvantageous consequences for forming the air situation, has been dealt with already. The quality of the nightfighter units had also much deteriorated since the invasion, because of the other uses of these crews (railway and street staffing at night and attacks on airdromes).

If it is taken into consideration that the basis of confidence in the high command had disappeared completely, that the policy of personnel in the distribution of posts was not very fortunate, it is easily understood that, in spite of the technical means, Germany could not cope with the third phase of the high frequency warfare.

I am convinced that, without the unfavourable indirect influences on German nightfighting, in case of continuation of the war, the British methods of the third phase could have been overcome. I am, however, also fully convinced that the British Bomber Command would have introduced a fourth phase of high frequency warfare with further advanced developments in radar and new tactical methods. In the age of the radar warfare, after all, not successful defensive but the offensive wins. Whether German radar would have been in a position to carry out a successful offensive with an appropriate number of modern bomber aircraft, I cannot know.

Methods of Operation
(a) Preparatory measures

In the staff of the "Generalkommando" of the I Fighter Corps a briefing took place every noon in which the ops staff participated in presence of the commanding general. There, the events of the night before were reported and the necessary consequences taken from the experiences gained on operations. The most important part of the briefing was the weather forecast for the following night. Experiences gained on operations and weather forecasts were the basis for the advance orders for the coming operation. They were given still in the early afternoon and generally contained:

1. Experiences, reprimands, acknowledgments, etc.
2. Judgment of the Generalkommando about the weather situation.
3. Judgment of the enemy and its supposed intentions.
4. Intended own operations based on supposed enemy intentions and weather forecast; concentrations of the various fighter divisions ("Himmelbett" or pursuit nightfighting). Operations of crack crews.
5. Transfer of units according to supposed weather situation.
6. Measures in the field of signals, especially call signs and frequencies for ground–aircraft communications.
7. Special references.

Very often, the summarized advance order was given orally by the commanding general by means of "Reportagegesprich" (a single call to many listeners), to all the division commanders.

(b) Methods of operation

It is the art of the fighter command to lead the biggest possible number of own aircraft against the enemy, considering the best conditions for the battle (weather, visibility, fuel, etc.). This is only possible with an energetic and centralized command, considering the technical possibilities. Also, with the further development of technical progress in this field (all-around-view radar sets), a centralized command station would have been needed for successful fighting. The reasons for such centralized command are:

1. Unified judgment of the enemy. Only one command station can judge the correct, i.e. the valid, air situation. To this end all elements of the air situation must be relayed to the central command station on good and overlapping signals system. The central command station has to inform the lower and middle command continually about the air situation and has to give general short judgements on the enemy from the first sign of the impending operation on and during the penetration flight. The calmer and more objective the air situation is formed and transmitted, the easier it is to intercept the majority of the enemy. In the age of the bomber stream I reject a de-centralized command of nightfighting. A number of varying air situations would be gained simultaneously and only by sheer luck all own forces would contact the enemy.

2. Own forces. The total force of German nightfighters was always small
   in comparison with the enemy bomber forces and with the size of the
   area of defense. The concentration of small forces on long stretches,
   considering enemy, weather, flying time, and aircraft equipment, calls for
   a centralized and energetic command.

It is not necessary that the supreme command station of nightfighting be
strong in personnel or have a giant ops room. Also a small staff in the smallest
room can work successfully on a map of 1:1,000,000 scale. Needed are,
however, calm and objective command as well as a sufficiently large and faultless
communication network. The Generalkommando has to take care that, from
dusk to dawn, his own ops room, those of the fighter divisions and of the units
are constantly superintended by a responsible officer to lead the operation.

Only by preparedness of the staff and ops room (connected telephone lines)
could enemy surprise action be prevented. Precipitate action by a surprised
command which had not followed up the development of the air situation never
brought any success. It was thus vital that all important officers lived in the
immediate neighborhood of the ops room, because every minute wasted was
disadvantageous for the units. At the first sign of enemy action over their
airdrome, the ops rooms had to be fully manned.

Stress was laid on getting the unit into readiness as early as possible and on
not changing the degree of alarm. For this reason I had to abolish many kinds
of alarms. Only a short, a long, or a sitting in the aircraft stage of readiness were
used. During the first type, the crews had to be in or near the a/c within the
hangars or the parking space. During the second type, crews could stay in the
dispersal rooms or near the aircraft, with their equipment at hand. According
to airdrome and taxi conditions as well as the stage of unit training, the
Generalkommando counted, after the order for action was given, to the time
of takeoff by the first aircraft with crews already sitting in the planes 15–30
minutes and with the second stage about one hour. It was also very important,
when conditions were difficult due to bad weather, that the crews were given
their rest in time.

According to the development of the enemy situation, the air situation
reports of the fighter divisions to the Corps, reports of the rec. aircraft as well
as of the "Y" Service, the command activity of the Generalkommando set in.
It consisted only of short ops orders transmitted by telephone. As to carrying
them out, the fighter divisions were to be given the largest liberties possible. But,
above all, the fighter divisions had to control the units by R/T. The order of the
Generalkommando given during a night of operations usually ran about as follows:

1. Brief assessment of the enemy during the entire penetration flight, enemy speeds, altitudes, diverting attempts by Mosquitoes, spoof attacks, nuisance raids, changes of course, supposed target, etc.

2. Directing the "Reportage" and command communication lines appointing the fighter division, which had to carry through the reporting, change of reporting during the penetration flight.

3. Demand for radio and light beacons from the Ob.d.L., keeping wireless stations in readiness.

4. Fixing the stage of alarm for the units.

5. Ordering air reconnaissance, and fixing their tasks.

6. In bad weather conditions, informing all fighter div. about airdrome on which the units can land. The crews are to be informed before take off.

7. Communicating with the various fighter divisions about the presumed intention of operation, in case there remained enough time for it.

8. Ops orders: Appointing the "Himmelbett" sectors, which had to be set in action; f.i. ' "Himmelbett" in action in the area of the estuary of the Schelde and North Jutland." '

   Releasing the take-off for pursuit nightfighting, f.i. to switch in the 3rd Fighter Div. at radio beacon "Ludwig," units of the 2nd and 1st F.D. first to radio beacon "Berta" and "Otto," presumable switching in at Osnabruch and at Steinhuder lake.

   Object nightfighters rally: 1st F.D. at radio beacon "Ludwig," 2nd to 7th F.D. at "Philip" and "Fritz." Number of aircraft in action and times of take-off were automatically reported to the Corps. During the penetration flight dispositions had to be made according to the development of the situation of the operations of the pursuit and object nightfighters.

9. Flak fire ceiling had to be applied for by the Generalkommando at the Luftflotte Reich.

10. Each F.D. was informed by the Generalkommando about the operations of the neighboring divisions. The order to take over other units in the air was given in time.

11. When several separate enemy bombers streams were in the air, the various formations of units were ordered to intercept them. The different bomber streams were given different colours, as f.i.red, blue, and green.

12. When the enemy jamming was strong, change of frequencies for reporting was ordered and if necessary the reporting was carried out by the Corps by means of regular wireless stations.

13. The flying time of the units was checked to draw the attention of the divisions to times of impending landings.

14. After the enemy target could be guessed beyond doubt, orders to attack the enemy on the return flight by "Himmelbett" and pursuit nightfighting were given.

15. Rally areas for single engine nightfighters over light beacons or flak flares were fixed.

16. If the weather was suited, searchlight signs and illumination by magnesia for "Leichentuch" was ordered, when the object of the target was recognized.

17. After the enemy raid was over, the stage of alarm for the landed units was ordered according to weather conditions and enemy situation in case of a possible second raid.

The main task of leading had to be done by the fighter divisions. This was mainly to form the air situation. In this respect it was important to bring about a constant exchange of ideas between the fighter divisions and the radar stations and to give the latter continually correct directions for searching. Considering the reports of the "Y" Service, air reporting service, the flak, and the air rec., the division commander had to and could commit himself for a short period of time.

For the control of our own units successfully, a well prepared organization was the most important need. This included: appointing the "Himmelbett" crews (who and where), appointing the pursuit—and object—nightfighters, activity of rec. aircraft, distribution of call signs and frequencies and "Epsilon linien," agreement on taking over of units in the air with neighboring divisions, distribution of personnel to the ops room functions. etc. When the fighter divisions and units had taken care of the preparations carefully, the activities of control could run smoothly.

For the units, it was of primary importance that they were given a clear picture of the air situation before the take-off and that, during operation, the reports were transmitted by the fighter divisions to the airmen over as many channels as possible. For the nightfighter units, it was important that the control officer of the gruppe transmitted the air situation from the ops airdrome to his flying crews on the "gruppen" control frequency. Lastly, it may be pointed out that, especially during the last half year of the war, a centralized command had become necessary. Owing to the fuel shortage and the many enemy jamming measures, operations which might turn out to be failures had to be avoided. Such failures happened more frequently when, on suggestion of the "inspectour" of nightfighting in fall 1944, more freedom of action was granted to the nightfighter geschwader 1 (NJG 1) in order to protect the Ruhr basin.

Means of Control

When controlling the units in the, air the main task was to inform them about their own and the enemy locations. For this purpose a great number of possibilities for ground to aircraft communication were created. The enemy tried to jam all these means and in most cases succeeded in doing so.

In this field, the war at night was most interesting. The air was filled with key-tapped long and short waves, which were jammed by whistles, continual dash and frequency sweep. In our own and the enemy R/T a mix of reporting orders, talk, music, and bell tones could be heard. Whoever had to watch the wave ranges could believe to hear the noises of a fair during its late evening hours or the transmission of excited debates in Parliament. In spite of all, the enemy never succeeded to jam all means of control simultaneously or cut them off altogether. He had, however, ensured that the use of the means of control became extremely difficult. Only very good and experienced nightfighter crews had enough experience and flexibility to play the manifold and complicated instrument of the wireless sets. Since the middle of 1944 it was not possible any more to keep such crews in practice or even more train new ones. This way the enemy had succeeded in general to indirectly paralyse the simple means of control anyhow.

The enemy situation was transmitted to the crews in the air by means of reporting, i.e. by continually informing them of the enemy location and action. This most valuable basis for the nightfighters was transmitted on numerous

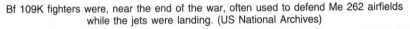

Bf 109K fighters were, near the end of the war, often used to defend Me 262 airfields while the jets were landing. (US National Archives)

frequencies. Two VHF transmitters transmitted the reports of the Corps on two frequencies. If those waves could not be heard or were jammed, the reports were then made available on the frequencies of the divisions. In case reception of these were impossible too, the R/T transmission of the radar stations could be heard. All reports were given over R/T and were key-tapped in addition. At any rate, it was practically impossible to prevent well experienced crews from receiving some kind of report.

Last but not least there still was the "gruppen" command frequency, on which it was possible to transmit the enemy action from the ops airdrome to the units. The easiest method of control of the units in the air was by means of the "Epsilon" control method. It was carried out by the fighter divisions or the subdivision controllers. The "Y" control was hardly jammed at all until up to the end of the war. Unfortunately it could not be introduced generally because there were only a small number of frequencies available. Therefore they were reserved for the command of reconnaissance and the unit commanders. The "Egon" control was not used in nightfighting, because the two way R/T was not possible.

In order to facilitate the transmission of reports and orders, already in 1943 the experiment to use regular wireless transmitters additionally was made. The "Soldatensender Annemarie" (Reichs wireless transmitter Stuttgart) was the first one to be available for this purpose. In cases where the enemy jammed the usual reporting channels too much, then enemy situation, target or orders were successfully transmitted by the Generalkommando, who made short coded announcements over the Stuttgart wireless station. After this station had been used for about 4 weeks, the enemy suddenly introduced a continuous dash. Also the use of women's voices proved to be futile as the enemy had the very same at his disposal and could even transmit misleading orders. The wireless stations remained of a certain importance for the nightfighters in so far as, by means of different kinds of music, the approximate path of the bomber stream could be transmitted, e.g. waltzes meant the Munich area, jazz the Berlin sector, church songs the area of Munster, Rhenish music the Cologne area, etc. Enemy jamming of this emergency measure for the nightfighters was never noticed.

The searchlights of the radar stations, pointing trowards the bomber stream or showing its direction, was only of limited importance on account of its dependence on weather conditions or the possibility given for confusion which came about by flak searchlights. Weather permitting, the searchlights allowed for good orientation in regards to towns.

Flak flares which were shot in the arc on parachutes proved to be very successful. They could be placed above the usual overcast with various identifications and would light for a considerabe time. They were visible from far away and made good orientation possible, a fact which was most important for single engine nightfighters. When, with the increase of enemy jamming of our frequency ranges, the flak flares were supposed to be used as markers for the bomber stream, their industrial manufacture was stopped.

The use of light beacons as navigation aids depended on weather conditions. The big identification radio beams could not be dispensed with for all nightfighting preferably attacked near these beacons, but they could at least be used as long range directly points. In the neighbourhood of the big beacons, the crews were supposed to use the small beacons of the radar stations as emergency directing points. By this method our nightfighters could, on their way towards the bomber stream or while rallying, evade the enemy nightfighters. The IFF sets (FUG 25) made it possible for our ground stations to identify own nightfighters. The latter was of vital importance for checking the operations and for the controller in cases where the air situation had changed to a considerable extent. The crews had repeatedly to be forced to switch on the IFF, as they believed the FUG 25 could be taken bearings on by British nightfighters. How far this presumption proved to be correct was never known.

German research and development offered a number of very useful control sets, but these could not be realized any more owing to the lack of industrial capacity. Of these, the "Bernhardine" set seemed to be most suitable. This allowed for transmission of a number of letters by wireless. Thereby air situation, orders and commands could be teletyped into the air at a distance of about 300 km. This means of control was especially suitable because it was visible and did not prey on the hearing and thinking capacities of the crews, and it took up only little space in the aircraft. On the other hand, the respective ground stations were of gigantic volume. Furthermore, it took about half a year to build a "Bernhard" ground station and it was very sensitive against enemy action. At the end, the introduction of the "Bernhard" method failed for this reason. Whether the method could have been jammed by the enemy is not known, but probable. The "Kuckuk" was a similar set: it allowed transmission of commands on the principle of the watch hand. In 1944 its mass production was not possible any more.

S.-E. Nightfighters and Illuminators
1. S.-E. Nightfighters

S.-E. nightfighting was born in an hour of distress after the heavy attacks on the Ruhr valley and on Hamburg in the summer of 1943. It was believed that the insufficiency of T.-E. nightfighter units in the "Himmelbett" could be made up for by S.-E. nightfighting. A large number of distinguished old-experienced pilots and a large quantity of aircraft were put in action, only to achieve expensive success in a fight that did not pay. It might have been considerably cheaper to use other methods and employ a larger number of T.-E. aircraft in time. Thus it had been a road strewn with heavy losses both in personnel and material that finally led to the conviction that S.-E. nightfighting might perhaps mean a useful complement of T.-E. nightfighting for target protection by illuminated procedure (helles Verfahren), but did not mean the solution of the nightfighting crisis.

No doubt it had been quite a great merit of the then Major Herrmann to have, by means of exceptional powers, put up the first S.-E. nightfighter units within the short space of 6 weeks. However, he had conducted his operations without any regard for losses in personnel or material. Weather conditions or endurance of aircraft were not taken into consideration at all. "If the fuel has run out and there is no possibility of landing, bail out," was the watchword. The great mass of S.-E. N.F. crews soon had more parachute jumps on their records than kills.

The operational organization for S.E. nightfighting was established independently from T.-E. nightfighting. Thus under Luftflotte Reich and the Luftgaue a separate so-called "Wilde Sau" Command was formed side by side with the XII Fliegerkorps (later I Fighter Corps). Again it swallowed a lot of telephone and telegraph wire, W/T transmitters, signals troops, and staff personnel, and led a life of its own apart from others to such a degree that the T.-E. commands and, before all, the T.-E. units never knew when, where, and how many S.-E. nightfighters were being engaged.

The long-nose Ta 152 was considered the ultimate in German single-engine day fighters. (US National Archives)

Focke-Wulf FW 190A fighters. The short-nose 190 was used by day and night in the Defense of the Reich. (US National Archives)

The organization of orientation, illumination, and navigation aids for S.-E. nightfighting was extensive and good. It also helped the T.-E. nightfighters a good deal. The fact remains without doubt that S.-E. nightfighters were putting up a splendid fight and also achieved good success in nights offering good visibility and favourable conditions for searchlight operation in the target area. But they had also become the terror of the T.-E. nightfighters, for they would open fire from the greatest distances upon all targets illuminated by searchlights. In doing so, many a T.-E. N.F. aircraft with twin rudder (Me-110) illuminated by searchlights was hit and also brought down. The S.-E. claimed all the aircraft they saw coming down, hereby contesting successes achieved by old-experienced T.-E. nightfighter crews. It was a striking fact that in such nights when only T.-E. nightfighters were fighting, our own claims for aircraft shot down nearly always agreed with the losses admitted by the enemy, whilst in the case of mixed operations our own reported victories were considerably higher than what the enemy admitted as losses.

By September 1943 the commander of S.-E. nightfighting had been promoted divisional commander and his nightfighters had been stamped national heroes by their outstanding exploits and the corresponding additional propaganda. All this changed when, in autumn, the bad weather period began. The losses of S.-E. nightfighters rose considerably, their operation being enforced even under the most critical weather conditions. There were losses of 20–25 a/c of a total of some 60 S.-E. fighters engaged, and no success. In winter 1943/44 these forceful attempts were continued, and then silence fell upon S.-E. nightfighting. In spring 1944, after the scrapping of the staff of the 30th Fighter Division, the S.-E. N.F. units, bled almost white, were placed under I Fighter Corps.

The courage and bravery of the S.-E. nightfighters must be fully acknowledged. Their leadership had, however, been rather inconsiderate, so that success and losses were in no bearable relation to each other. These losses meant that the aircraft of at least two full-strength dayfighter geschwaders would be lacking for dayfighter operation, and that at a most crucial time. In my opinion the operation of S.-E. N.F. units is only justified in the following cases:

(a) Operation in illuminated nightfighting (helle Nachtjagd) over targets in fair weather with good altitude visibility and suitable illuminating conditions.
(b) Use for illuminated nightfighting over targets in such cases when, as a result of an uncertain air situation, enemy surprise, and slow rate of climbing, T.-E. nightfighter aircraft would arrive late.
(c) Use against enemy aircraft of speeds and service ceilings superior to those of T.-E. aircraft.

After all, S.-E. N.F. aircraft constituted an expedient in all those cases, too, since their operation by means of a properly working scanner was never successful.

2. Illuminators

Concurrently with the introduction of S.-E. nightfighting, a kampfgruppe equipped with Ju-88s (1/7) was put in action for illuminating purposes. It was to arrive in time over the target attacked by the enemy in order to illuminate the sky over target by all sorts of flares. This gruppe was stationed at Muenster Westph. and would launch on those nights when S.-E.nightfighters were put in action. It was under the 30th Fighter Division.

On its operations the unit flew in the approx. direction of the enemy bomber stream and then with it, as far as this was made possible by the picture of the air situation. They had to be very lucky to arrive in time over the target attacked. Frequently the illuminator gruppe would be over the enemy's alternate or his dummy targets and arrive late over the real object of attack. The activity itself was very tedious for the crews, the more so as they were flying without any armament and could therefore not defend themselves in case of attack by enemy long-range nightfighters, besides not being able to bring down enemy bombers. A clear appreciation of the value of illuminating by parachute flares was never given by the N.F. crews. It seems that the blinding effect and the advantage resulting from illumination were as great for the enemy bomber as the casual help in target-finding afforded to our own nightfighters. After the enemy had made ample use of illuminating effects of all kinds already in winter 1943/44,

I converted the Illuminator Gruppe 1/7 into an N.F. gruppe in February 1944. A demand for illuminating the sky over the target by means of flares was never again uttered by GAF units.

Cooperation with Flak Artillery

The first Chief of the Gen. Staff of the GAF, Gen. Lt. Wever, held the opinion that in the Air Defense of the home country one single command should in each case operate and direct all the air defense weapons. This found its expression by way of organization in the fact that the Luftgau (as the responsible organs of Reich Defense) had under them at the same time fighter, barrage and smoke screen units.

This solution of the problem was weakened (verwaessert, lit. diluted or adulterated) by the offensive wars of the years 1939–1941 and by the fact that enemy air action against the Reich in particular was almost completely absent. When nightfighting came into being, it did not come under the Luftgau as part of the Air Defense of the home country, but was, by way of command, organized with the Corps and thus stood apart from the Luftgau, to whom only Flak Artillery was subordinated. In the meantime it had become usual since the beginning of the war for all the commanding staffs in the home Luftgaus to be

A railroad-mounted 8.8cm flak gun. "Flak trains" were a part of German air defenses and could be moved quickly to reinforce threatened targets. (US National Archives)

filled with Flak generals. The Air Defense of the home country was then predominantly flak-minded. When at last more and more dayfighter units were added to the Air Defense of the Reich besides the nightfighters, the Higher Commands of the GAF were on the one hand reluctant to place flying units under Flak commanders and on the other hand hesitated to fill the Luftgau commands with suitable personalities.

Thus there really never was a uniform direction of the Reich Defense. There were the Flak Artillery under the Luftgau organized into flak divisions and the day and the nightfighter units under the I Fighter Corps organized into fighter divisions. The two organizations existing side by side had only one thing in common, viz. the enemy. Otherwise they claimed different operational staffs, sigs. communication systems of their own, enemy location organizations of their own and different supply channels.

Over the fighter corps and the Luftgau there was Luftwaffenbefehlshaber Mitte, later redesignated Luftflottenkommando Reich. The staff of this command, too, was mainly filled with Flak Artillery men. They thought themselves capable of directing the night operation of combined arms and therefore never submitted proposals for a change in the organization of command. It was exactly as if in the war on land, an army had operated with infantry and artillery corps, thereby no infantry general being allowed to put a gun, and no artillery general to put an M.G. into action.

In my opinion the organization of the Reich Defense is one of the greatest mistakes made by the High Command of the GAF. A double equipment of staffs, personnel, Signals and Air Reporting Services was used to defend the Reich insufficiently by means of a faulty organization of command in the heaviest bombing war of all times.

When I took over the I Fighter Corps a liaison of command with the home Luftgau or the flak divisions did not exist at all. FlakArtillery in the Reich conducted the fight at night quite independently from the nightfighters. They were firing under all weather conditions—when, where, as long and as high as they pleased. The Fighter Corps had no influence on the fighting activity of the Flak Artillery.

It is true, there existed most bulky and complicated instructions of the Befehlshaber Mitte which were to ensure the cooperation of the nightfighters with the Flak Artillery. These instructions, however, were based on the supposition that fighter and flak divisions should agree during the battle. In all other cases, the decision of the Luftwaffenbefehlshaber Mitte should be brought about. It was, however, practically out of the question to obtain, during the fast unrolling night operation decisions, which could have come in time to the knowledge of the firing flak batteries and to the nightfighter units in the air. Regarding this, I remember a large number of instances: To quote them here would lead too far.

At any rate, the faulty organization of command and not the fighting units must be blamed for the fact that frequently fighters and Flak Artillery impeded each other or could not come into full effect during the battle. Moreover, a number of our own fighters were shot down unnecessarily by Flak Artillery. During the time between 15.9.1943 and 20.4.1944 Flak Artillery shot down an ascertained number of 15 of our own nightfighters besides damaging a considerably larger number. This happened especially when the enemy had long withdrawn and when our own aircraft were flying back to their stations or even already landing.

By autumn 1943 I had realized that a change in organization of command within the Reich Defense, e.g. into defense corps or defense divisions with subordinated fighter and flak units, was, for personal reasons or for reasons of signals organization, to be attained only slowly or, in view of the then already advanced stage of the war, maybe never. To ensure cooperation without friction between nightfighters and Flak Artillery, I submitted the following propositions to the High Command of the GAF:

(a) Unification of the ARS by merging the Reich ARS with the radar ground organization of the I Fighter Corps for improvement of reporting on the air situation.

(b) Stationing of fighter and flak controlling staffs at one common ops room in each area; by this it was intended that fighter and flak controllers should witness the course of the battle in common. Putting the staffs together locally would have been possible without any difficulties.

(c) Right for fighter division COs to give the home flak divisions orders for fire control. The disciplinary subordination and tactical operation of Flak Artillery under Luftgau was to remain untouched.

I illustrated my proposition by practical examples of day and night operations in the form of a planspiel (tactical demonstration on map) at Zeist in Holland on 10 December 1943. In the planspiel took part: all the COs of units, representatives of OKL Fuehrungsstab, of Luftwaffenbefehlshaber Mitte and of the Luftgau. It passed without result in as much as nothing was changed in the existing organization. At the beginning of 1944 I made the same proposition to Gen. Oberst Stumpff, who, on 1 January 1944, had taken over Luftflotte Reich, but this time, too, without success.

Already in the late autumn, Flak Artillery officers of field rank had joined the Gen. Kdo. I Fighter Corps and the staffs of the fighter divisions as so-called flakeinsatzleiter (flak ops controllers). Their task consisted in passing, during the battle, requests of fighter control regarding fire control, limiting of fire as to height, change of air situation and clearing of doubts, etc., to the flak divisions. They had no powers of command and were subordinated to the Luftgaukommandos, i.e. were qualified and proposed for promotion by the latter. For these reasons the flakeinsatzleiter showed the greatest reserve in their activity as liaison officers to the Flak commands. They improved, it is true, the connections between fighters and Flak commanders, but, being according to their instructions mere puppets, could not ensure a successful cooperation. In autumn 1944 a General der Flak Artillery joined the Gen. Kdo. I Fighter Corps, although without any authority of command over the Flak authorities (flakbehoerden) in the Reich territory. Thus conditions remained to the end of the war. Fighters and Flak Artillery defended absolutely separately from one another the Reich territory against the enemy's day and night bomber attacks.

Appreciation of the Enemy

Judgments on certain measures taken by the enemy are stated in all chapters of this report in connection with other considerations. It shall now be tried shortly to recapitulate and sum up the essential points of appreciation of the enemy. It is an indubitable fact that the British Bomber Command developed the procedure of attack of nightbomber formations to a very high standards and that the enemy formations achieved considerable exploits in the night bombing war. The war having been decided in favor of the enemy, it may not be taken for arrogance if different measures taken by him are criticized here.

1. Aircraft

The performance of British 4-engined bombers as concerned range and loading capacity was remarkable. One might, however, wonder why their service ceilings and speeds were not improved more. A bomber stream approaching at 7,000 m (23,000 feet) and at an average of 250 mph would have paralyzed the bulk of German T.-E. nightfighters. Perhaps protection of the 4-engined bomber by armoured plate against attacks from below might have saved a large number of losses through fire from the oblique armament of the nightfighters. The quality and effect, of the British bombs were greater than those dropped by the Americans. The Mosquito was, I think, the most successful achievement in the whole field of aircraft construction. Its multiple use contributed in a very large measure to render the defense against British night attacks more difficult.

2. Effects of Attack

Up to the attack on Cologne in May 1942, the British attacks on the Reich territory were to be valued merely as pinpricks. Even after that they could not be regarded as a factor deciding the issue of the war. Not until the beginning of the bomber stream technique in conjunction with the introduction of the H2S did the British nightbomber war actually prey upon the nerves of the German war machinery. It is true, German talent of organization, dispersal and tucking-away of industries, and the strong morale of the German people (largely under official pressure), slowed down the rate of expansion of bombing effects considerably.

I strongly decline to follow the judgment of those who maintain that the British night attacks did not have a decisive influence on the downfall of Germany. It may be right to say that the mass of British bombs did not hit the German war economy directly. But the systematic planning and the continuity of those attacks increased their indirect effects, in particular in connection with the USAAF day attacks, to a quite unbearable extent. The success in target finding by night and in bad weather had increased in an astonishing measure by autumn 1944. It serves no useful purpose to discuss the question whether the weight of British night attacks alone, without the USAAF day attacks, would have sufficed to paralyze the German war economy in a decisive way. However, in view of the increased accuracy of aiming of the British bomber formations, I am inclined to answer the question in favor of the RAF in as much as the achieving of the final goal would only have been a question of time.

The nightbomber attacks of the British Mosquito units did not cause any decisive material damage, although it was surprising to see what large quantities of bombs these "graceful" planes brought to the targets. On the other hand, the nuisance value of the Mosquitoes was considerable. They had caused us to increase the extent of air raid warning by day and by night and had therefore a strong effect on production and on the people's nerves. Also their influence upon the Higher Commands must not be underrated. For more than a year almost daily several staffeln of dayfighters launched against reconnaissance Mosquitoes for an almost hopeless mission, only because the Highest Command of the GAF wanted to see enemy photographic reconnaissance of the effects of bombing attacks prevented.

3. Methods of Attack

It may well be assumed that Great Britain had drawn certain conclusions from the German bombing attacks in the years 1940–41 for the development of her own night bombing tactics. This was quite simple in as much as the German night bombing attacks at that time had been carried out almost without any methodical planning. They showed how little economical night bombing war is without a highly developed and cultivated method of attack. But Bomber Command appears to have gone a way of very careful and systematic development until, in 1943, they were able to achieve a telling effect with an efficient method of night attack. What the Mosquito represents in the achievements of British aircraft industries, the British method of night attack may be said to be in the field of air tactics. The reasons for the efficiency (durchschlagskraft, lit. percussion) of this method were:

(a) The surprisingly high standard of training of the bomber crews.
(b) The discipline of air crews as regards both flying and W/L operation.
(c) The tactics of massed approach by night in one or several bomber streams.
(d) The highly developed orientation and navigation aids.
(e) The H2S and therewith the independence from weather conditions, and reliability in target-finding.
(f) The short times over target (lit.: times of attack).
(g) The realization of the importance of incendiary effects.
(h) The generous and comprehensive measures taken in the field of jamming German W/L traffic and H.F. sets of all kinds.

The following details seem to be worth mentioning. Most unpleasant for the German Fighter Command were Mosquito screening or camouflage (Mosquito Verschleierung), Mosquito spoof attacks, and before all bomber streams (of different Groups) succeeding one another at intervals of 2–3 hours, in some cases attacking the same target by different routes. The operation of bomber streams of different groups on different targets meant splitting up and lessening of effects, i.e. 4 targets attacked once each by 4 bomber groups at a time had a greater effect than if those targets had been attacked 4 times each by one bomber group at a time. For Nightfighter Command the former was more favorable.

The direct success of British long-range nightfighting was very modest. The nuisance effect must, however, be assessed high in as much as the German nightfighter crews were strongly worried and in their majority prevented from working calmly at their scanners and their W/L sets (Flugsicherungsgeraete). Shooting down German nightfighters had to be done by surprise, otherwise the German nightfighters could not be outmaneuverd by the Mosquito.

British bombs, dropped occasionally in small numbers on German nightfighter stations, were hardly worrying us, but were almost always presaging the ensuing night attack of the bombers. It was surprising that the British command did not disturb more frequently the vulnerable nightfighter bases in Holland and in northwest Germany by day or by twilight attacks with larger formations—from the British methods of attack the German fighter command derived a number of advantages for forming a picture of the air situation:

(a) *Jay Beams*. By their turning on the intended night operation was announced. In many cases the number and the direction of the beams permitted to decide whether the target was in northern or in southern Germany.

(b) *Warning Messages* to British shipping.

(c) *Fighter Warning Sets* (Jaegerwarngeraet) such as "Fishpond." By taking bearings on them, the positions of enemy aircraft were obtained. As not all the aircraft had turned on their sets, the bearings resulted in an incomplete picture of the enemy operation.

(d) *H2S*. Bearings taken indicated the position of the bomber formations, and from November 1943 to May 1944 served as the most reliable basis for plotting the enemy's courses.

(e) *Weather Recce Aircraft*. They flew ahead of the bomber stream. The weather reports they transmitted were listened in to. Their contents permitted reliable interferences as to depth of penetration and target, besides indicating the location of the aircraft.

(f) *USA Air Warnings*. The Americans in France occasionally transmitted open warnings by W/L of expected British nightflying over France to their airfields and AA units, e.g. Reims 20.00 400 British bombers crossing. After the loss of our advanced bases in France, from autumn 1944 onward, these messages were important for the German Fighter Command.

(g) *Oboe and Gee H. Methods* (Bumerang and Diskusverfahren). The traffic was listened in to and therefore Oboe targets could mostly be found out at least 30–40 minutes before the first bomb was dropped. On that occasion it was ascertained that the cooperation between Oboe-directed Mosquitoes as target markers and the bombers did not work satisfactorily on several attacks on the Ruhr valley in summer 1944. The bombers had to wait for the delayed Mosquitoes and could be attacked by the nightfighters while still in the waiting area before target.

From a number of other small points of British nightflying tactics the German Fighter Command also drew periodically limited advantages. It must, however, be stressed that either the British bomber crews practiced excellent

W/L discipline or that on the British side W/L traffic was carried on within wave bands which were not, or could not, be listened in to by their opponents. The enemy ground jamming measures were generally less effective than jamming from the air. It was a striking fact that British bomber groups only seldom attacked the target from different heights. Such a procedure would have been unfavorable for defense by nightfighters. Last of all, the German Command wondered why Bomber Command, considering the weakness of German dayfighters from the late summer of 1944 onward, did not generally shift their Mosquito and bomber attacks to the daytime in order to heighten their effects.

4. Personnel

The British aircrews were on a high level as regards toughness in operations. Contrary to the Americans, the crews of 4-engined bombers left their aircraft only in cases of extreme emergency. Frequently crews were observed to still fire by night with all their aircraft armament from burning or crashing aircraft.

Nightfighting Procedures

In all services and arms, the tactics during the war were rapidly changing, especially in a technical area. This also applies in particular to nightfighting. In reviewing these tactics, I leave out the first unsuccessful experiments in Illuminated Nightfighting (Helle Nach-jagd), because I did not witness it and am therefore not able to judge from personal experience.

1. "Himmelbett" Procedure

The description of the different functions of the procedure is uninteresting. It is in the main based on both enemy and friendly aircraft being plotted by radar. In doing so it is left to the skill of the fighter controller on the ground and to the fighter in the air to solve an interception problem (friend/foe) within a circle of 20 (later 40) miles possibly even in case of enemy W/L jamming. If the "Himmelbett" procedure functions without trouble, it forms the ideal solution of the problems of nightfighting, provided that the area to be defended and if possible also the advanced area of approach are covered without any gaps by fighter control centers (radar stations) (Jaegerleitstaende, Funkmess-Stellungen). The main disadvantages are:

(a) It is very vulnerable against jamming by the enemy and against effect of arms against radar stations.
(b) The usefulness of radar stations depends on the quality of the terrain.

(c) The whole system depends on the enemy using certain tactics of approach.

(d) The whole system fails in the case of the enemy approaching at a height lower than 3,000 feet.

Enemy jamming rendered the R/T and W/L traffic difficult, to such an extent that only the best crews could bring about a communication at all. The dropping of great masses of tinfoil practically paralyzed the measuring activity of the sets in the area crossed by the enemy. In very hilly country, and more so in the mountains, work with radar sets was almost impossible. The bomber stream, in contrast with the more loosened form of approach, offered only a few "Himmelbetten" an opportunity for putting fighters in action. It was difficult to pick out and control one single aircraft out of the bomber stream. Summing up, it may be stated that by introducing the bomber stream and the beginning of extensive enemy jamming measures (including "Window"), the "Himmelbett" procedure lost considerably in importance and could then only be successfully employed in the case of the enemy flying back in loose formation or in the case of mine-laying units approaching in a broad front. In all other cases, only the very best fighter controllers and the old-experienced crews (both air and ground crews being in good mutual practice) could achieve kills in the "Himmelbett."

Current practice by day including "Windowing," operation in the same "Himmelbett" again and again and close collaboration by day and by night, also in the personal exchange of experience between the crews and the fighter controller, are indispensable presuppositions for successful "Himmelbett" fighting. The air situation by day, gradual deterioration (lit. dilution) of personnel, the fuel situation and, in part, an insufficient number of nightfighter aircraft could not but forcibly relegate, after 1944, the importance of the "Himmelbett" to the background.

Thus a discussion becomes superfluous about whether it was right to neglect the "Himmelbett." Crews engaged in other "Himmelbetten" than their own almost always returned without success. It is true that, probably, the controller as well made mistakes. The fighter controllers, as the essential factors for ground-controlled "Himmelbett" nightfighting, were at the same time COs of the radar companies and were therefore stationary. It would, no doubt, have been better to couple the fighter controllers with "Himmelbett"-specialized nightfighter gruppen and to make them parts of those gruppen. Then both might have been transferred to other areas as the situation required, which would have been equally advantageous for "Himmelbett" fighting and for the purposes of switching in fighters into the bomber stream for pursuit nightfighting. Trials regarding this change were made by me successfully in summer 1944. They had, however, met with almost insurmountable difficulties because neighboring commands tried to hinder in their activities fighter controllers of the I Fighter Corps that had entered their area.

2. Target Area Nightfighting (Objektnachtjagd)

It can be the most effective kind of nightfighting because it upsets the enemy bomber's aimed bombing. On the other hand, T.A. nightfighting is one of the most primitive methods of nightfighting. The changes of success depend on many factors:

(a) Good conditions of visibility and of illuminating over target.

(b) Skill of the Higher Command, which must succeed in bringing as many nightfighters as possible over the target attacked. This can be managed only rarely as it is most difficult and often mere chance to have one's own units start just in time to lead them over large distances to the right object of attack which cannot be anticipated.

(c) Reliable means of control. In T.A. nightfighting, the enemy can most easily interfere by spoof markers, spoof attacks, fake orders, etc.

(d) Correct reporting on the air situation.

(e) Cooperation without friction with the Flak Artillery.

The main disadvantages of T.A. nightfighting are:

(a) The bomber stream and short times over target implied offer the night-fighters only a short opportunity for shooting down over target. Nightfighter units mostly arrive late for action over the target area if they lose time owing to detours caused by enemy feints or by winds or owing to a late start.

(b) Cooperation between the nightfighters and the Flak Artillery is made extremely difficult. One of the two arms is generally hampered in its fighting activity. Only few nightfighter crews pass right over the target in case of flak activity, but prefer to fight over the periphery.

(c) Friendly and enemy aircraft crowd over the target for a short time. Opportunity for killing is too short and the possibility of mutual firing of friendly aircraft is great, particularly in the case of mixed operation of S.E. and T.E. nightfighter units.

(d) Difficulty of the proper local distribution of the nightfighters. In case of equal distribution of the nightfighter forces over the whole Reich

Messerschmitt Bf 109E-3 fighters: a frame from a wartime newsreel. The original Bf 109E design was intended to be, in large part, a defensive fighter, operating against French, Polish, Czech or RAF day bombers attacking Germany (hence the early introduction of 20 mm cannon), but the system for effective defense of the homeland had to be improvised. (US National Archives)

territory, only parts of them will contact the enemy, especially in case of attacks on targets near the frontiers. If the forces are near the frontier and arranged in close order, they are completely lost for defense purposes in case of unfavorable start conditions owing to bad weather, on the occasion of enemy attacks on targets in the center of the Reich. The total number of nightfighters was too small to permit stationing an adequate number of nightfighters in certain definite areas and engaging them mainly in the protection of the targets of their respective areas.

Seen as a whole, T.A. nightfighting is obviously a makeshift. It will always be necessary as an additional procedure in special situations, such as uncertain air situation, limitation of operations by bad weather, and in case of the breakdown of other systems (e.g. in the case of a Mosquito chase).

3. Pursuit Nightfighting

This is the most elegant method of nightfighting, and has the greatest chances of success. The following conditions must be given:

(a) Aircraft with scanner and with long endurance.
(b) Well disciplined crews disposing of W/L operators, very skilled in the use of the scanner and the traffic control sets and procedures.
(c) Higher and middle commands of quick reaction.
(d) Smart and quickwitted fighter controllers.

(e) Clearly ascertained air situation. Its transmission by many different ways and the marking of the bomber stream by optical means of all kinds are most urgent.

(f) Use of bomber stream tactics by the enemy. In case the enemy aircraft fly in very loose formation, pursuit nightfighting offers little chance of success.

In pursuit nightfighting, Fighter Command must aim at leading its own forces to meet the enemy as far out as possible, in order to enable them to fly with the bomber stream as long as possible. In this case the chances of spotting and shooting down enemy aircraft are the greatest. Thus it happened, e.g., that a nightfighter crew flying in the stream from Venlo to Magdeburg brought down, with certainty, 7 aircraft.

Furthermore, it is important that the nightfighter units should, if possible, not be switched into the bomber stream at right angles, because in this case it may happen that the nightfighters fly right across the rather narrow bomber stream without noticing it. Leading the nightfighters into the bomber stream on a reciprocal course is the safest way of switching them in. Frequently in this case,

A two-man Bf 110 crew poses for a wartime propaganda photograph prior to a mission. Most German night-fighter crews had three or four men: the presence of RAF night-fighters meant that a rear gunner had to keep a constant lookout while the pilot and radar operator carried out their attacks. (US National Archives)

and if the height at which the enemy is approaching is known, the nightfighter crews are warned by the propwash of enemy aircraft of the fact that they are already flying in the stream.

It is of the greatest importance that these aircraft that have become aware with certainty of their flying in the bomber stream should make the fact known to the other nightfighters by special W/L or light signals. The best way of marking the bomber stream is by aircraft shot down ablaze.

Aircraft flying in the bomber stream will find it expedient to zigzag in order to increase their chances of picking up enemy aircraft with their scanners. Experiments made with long-range scanner "Naxos" to locate the bomber stream have been negative. Recce aircraft equipped with that set mostly homed on aircraft flying alone and found the bomber stream only by chance. Good crews having a correct picture of the air situation and their own exact position can switch into the stream by themselves. Otherwise there are the following possibilities of switching in: by means of radio beacons, on "Y" lines by fighter divisions, by fighter controllers at radar stations or by gruppen command wave from base.

The most successful and at the same time most difficult operation of pursuit nightfighters was the close operation of a whole gruppe (geschlossener Gruppeneinsatz). The gruppe assembled over base, set course under the command of their CO and were switched in by the latter. This method of operation had the advantage that the CO was able to check (or control) his crews, to lead them by air to air traffic or by means of optical signals, and switch them in safely on a "Y" line. The chances that a nightfighter gruppe flying in relatively close formation under an able CO arrived safely in the bomber stream and contacted enemy aircraft were general. However, this required continuous preliminary training by day in the air and in the schoolroom as an essential condition of success. Only few nightfighter gruppen disposed of good and energetic COs of that kind, who could employ the method of gruppen operation in pursuit nightfighting successfully.

Generally, the nightfighters went on pursuit nightfighting alone. This led, however, to the splitting-up of nightfighting in view of the enemy tactics of flying in several bomber streams and in view of the enemy ways of jamming and of camouflage (or screening; German: Verschleierung) by Mosquitoes, and had therefore only little chance of success. The tactics of pursuit nightfighting never came into full application as the nightfighter units, owing to enemy jamming, no longer mastered or could no longer master the manifold uses of means of control, especially of scanners. Last of all, it must be taken into consideration that the all-around-view radar sets (Panoramageraete) were an excellent means for switching in units and, if further perfected, would have played an eminent part in pursuit nightfighting.

As a counterpart to the 100th RAF Bomber Group. the organization of listening-in and jamming staffeln had been envisaged by me in autumn 1944. This intention was, however, never realized because I no longer succeeded in hunting up the necessary aircraft equipment and also because there was a lack of understanding on the part of fighter authorities for the urgent necessity of my design.

Taking into consideration the standard of enemy tactics and our own technical facilities in the last year of the war, it was probably right not to prefer one method of nightfighting, but to employ all the different methods and combine them according to the situation. In doing this, the main rule of conduct was: pursuit nightfighting against closely bundled bomber streams, "Himmelbett" nightfighting against loose formations or single aircraft, and target area nightfighting in case of surprise attacks and against Mosquitoes.

Chapter 6

German Dayfighting
in the Defense of the Reich

15 September 1943 to the End of the War

by Generalleutnant Josef "Beppo" Schmid

Preliminary Remarks

The control of dayfighting and nightfighting in the Defense of the Reich lay in one hand. Both arms have a great deal in common as regards the different factors of command. For this reason it shall be tried to enumerate the essential characteristics of dayfighting in the Reich Defense. In this connection it may be pointed out in particular that data concerning the distribution of units and dates of battles may be incomplete or in some cases even incorrect, as I am in many cases quoting them from memory. As far as reference from the War Journal of the Gen. Kdo. I Fighter Corps is concerned, this will be indicated. Such small blemishes should, however, not blur the general outlines of a picture delineating the characteristics of the principles of command in dayfighting in Reich Defense.

Formation of Air Situation
1. Own Air Situation

Our own air situation was formed by the same means by day as well as by night. In contrast to nightfighting the daily reports by the Ia channels (Ia corresponding to the American G-3, S-3, etc.) comprised:

Number of fighters ready for operations
  (Me-109 and Fw-190)
Number of Zerstoerer ready for operations ⎫ specified
Number of planes ready for "Y" operation ⎬ by units
Number of shadowing a/c ready for operations ⎪
Names and ranks of combat formation leaders ⎭

In contrast to nightfighting, it was in most cases no longer possible by day to get a clear picture of our air situation once the units had gone into action; for, after having engaged the enemy, the fighter could no longer indicate his position. Nor did the all-around-view radar set, introduced later, give a clear picture at first of friend and foe during the engagement. It could only be ascertained that friendly units were mixed up with those of the enemy.

131

2. Enemy Air Situation

The formation of enemy air situation was very much simpler by day, even in the final phase of the war. From the R/T, traffic between fighters and bombers and process of assembly, both over the English and the Italian bases, could regularly be listened in to. As the assembly would last a long time (up to several hours) there was sufficient time left for forewarnings and for preparation of our own operation. Also, the assembly areas of the three enemy bomber divisions were ascertained. From the enemy's behavior during assembly, the weather difficulties and a possible early abandoning of the operation became also known. The courses of the enemy weather and target reconnaissance aircraft flying into the Reich territory in the first hours in the morning permitted almost unmistakable conclusions as to the probable target for the day.

As long as the US forces in England were weak (as in 1943, when there was only one bomber division), and were as yet flying without deep penetration escort as well as without high fighter cover, diversion maneuvers, especially in the North Sea, had a very unfortunate effect on the German Command. This was compounded by the weakness of the fighter forces at our disposal, and—as long as the German fighters were flying without extra tanks—our very short operational endurance (1 hr 10 mins.).

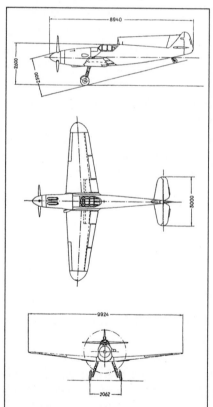

Beginning from about spring 1944, the enemy, much to our surprise, hardly ever used these tactics of diversionary approaches any more. The approach of the bomber aircraft from the time of leaving the assembly area was as a rule ascertained, no matter whether it took place in one combat division or several, and on one single or on different courses. The plotting of the approaching aircraft over Belgium, Holland, and the Reich territory never caused any difficulties in good weather. Likewise, the distinction between

General arrangement of the Messerschmitt Bf 109 G-2. (From manual in US National Archives RG 165)

fighters and bombers was nearly always effected correctly. On the other hand, the plotting of the bomber course through the areas of France, Italy, and Dalmatia, sparsely provided with air reporting facilities, was subject to frequent interruptions at a time when the US bombers were not as yet flying with "Mickey" sets.

The badly disciplined R/T traffic of the US bomber units facilitated the plotting of the courses and the early finding out of the target in cases of bad weather. Thus, messages such as "Crossing the enemy coast" or "30 minutes to target" or "No clouds over target" could be picked up again and again. As long as the enemy bombers were flying above the clouds during the day and were not using "Mickey," the work of the radar sets was frequently hampered, but never completely arrested. Later, bearings taken on the "Mickey" sets in bomber aircraft and on the R/T traffic of fighter aircraft would always result in an exact picture of the air situation, even in case of bad weather conditions. From the summer of 1944 onward, the plotting of aircraft approaching from the south became increasingly difficult owing to the events of the war in Italy and the uncertain situation in Dalmatia and Croatia.

Radar War

Radar war originated in the day operations of the Battle of Britain, but entered its most important stage owing to the night bomber war and the war at sea. Jamming and "Windowing" by day affected German fighter control only slightly. One may hold the opinion that the introduction of "Mickey" and of longrange fighters and, resulting from these, the almost complete independence of bomber warfare from weather conditions, might have formed the starting point of an enforced radar war. This might have been the case particularly if there had been a bad-weather aircraft available for defensive purposes on the German side, and if the all-around-view radar sets (Panoramageraete) had been perfected or their operation and their manifold uses been generally understood and practiced by the specialized ground personnel. If such had been the case, dayfighter control on a large scale might have taken on similar forms to those of nightfighting.

Operational Methods
1. Preparatory Measures

The operational principles and methods of nightfighting apply essentially also to dayfighting. First of all, a careful survey must be made of the weather outlook. On it depends the decision as to the shifting of fighters over a large area already on the eve of an operation. In view of the ever insufficient forces, this was of particular importance. Moreover, it was necessary for Fighter Command daily to check the standards of operational readiness. In view of the proneness to trouble of the aircraft and in view of the rather heavy losses, a methodical, frictionless, and speedy supply of aircraft, implements, and personnel was of particularly great importance.

2. Procedure in Operations

A centralized control was of still greater importance for dayfighting than for nightfighting, because the relation of strength between friend and foe was always by far more unfavorable by day, and because, by day, it was more important to bring, if possible, all the forces available into effective simultaneous action in the same area, under due consideration of weather conditions and of the enemy air situation. In the issuing of orders by the Gen. Kdo., an essential presupposition for dayfighter command was to begin the preliminary discussion of the situation and of the operational intentions already at day-break. On it depended the shifting of units, if such was to be made. Shifting of units would only serve a useful purpose if it was effected early in the morning, and, as experience taught, only in the summer months. In any other case the units transferred were mostly not yet ready for action again when the enemy activity began.

In the preliminary discussion which, depending on the development of the weather outlook, was resumed repeatedly until the enemy activity began, the operational intentions of the Gen. Kdo. for different eventualities of approach had to be clearly defined for each case. For these different cases, it was of paramount importance, nay even a presupposition of a successful fight, that each fighter or Zerstoerer crew should know as long as possible before the actual start:

(a) Organization of the combat formation (light fighters, heavy fighters, Zerstoerer).

(b) Manner and form of assembly of the gruppen and of the combat formation (units meeting one another by the shortest routes or rendezvousing over agreed landmarks), in other words, how and where do the units form, starting from different airdromes and taking into consideration the times of start and the shortest routes, and at what heights (usually 1,000–2,000 m) will they join the combat formation.

(c) Assembly area of the combat formation or later of the geschwader at operational height (6,000–7,000 m). For this, certain landmarks were used (lakes, river bends, well-marked towns, AA directing shots, etc.).

(d) Exact weather situation in the expected fighting areas and safe landing strips.

(e) Names of the COs of the gruppe and of the combat formation as well as those of their deputies.

Regarding the issuing of orders by Gen. Kdo., the following details may be added:

(1) Information as to the possible target of the enemy attack as inferred from the course of the enemy weather reconnaissance aircraft.

(2) Appointing that fighter division which, during the raid, will report over the ReichsJaegerwelle (Reich fighter frequency) (reportage of enemy activity for the units in the air). Change during battle.

(3) Laying down the degree of readiness for the personnel. There were only two degrees of readiness: Instant readiness (Alarmbereitschaft)—pilots ready to start, sitting in aircraft near the place of start. 10-minutes readiness—pilots in flying equipment near the aircraft, ready for start in the hangars or at the dispersal points.

(4) Operational orders on R/T or broadcast reportage would run according to the preliminary orders and discussions, e.g.

"To assemble at operational height:"

1st Ftr. Div. over Muritz-See; free to start, after leading enemy bomber elements are over Heligoland.

2nd Ftr. Div. over Steinhuder Meer, free to start.

3rd Ftr. Div. over Lake Duelmen, free to start.

7th Ftr. Div. over Donauwoerth, free to start.

"Tasks of Fighter Divisions:"

3rd Ftr. Div. principally to engage and tie up enemy high cover fighters, coming from the direction of the Zuyder Zee, in the area of Oldenburg.

2nd Ftr. Div. flanking enemy fighter cover to attack enemy bombers' leading elements in the Hannover area.

1st Ftr. Div. beats up enemy bombers before reaching the presumed target Berlin. For this it must be aimed at leading the fighter and Zerstoerer units of the division from the east (out of the sun) into the flank of the enemy bomber stream NW of Berlin.

7th Ftr. Div. terminates assembly at 3,000 m and leads units up to operational height in the direction of Dessau. It is intended to lead the division in the Berlin or the central German areas to the enemy. Flak directional fire at Dessau.

2nd and 3rd Ftr. Div. aim by all means at a second operation of maximum strength and report number of aircraft engaged as well as the resp. airfields.

Nightfighters of 1st Ftr. Div., northern part and of the 2nd Ftr. Div., Jutland, are to be operated against enemy aircraft trying to escape into Sweden.

It was most important that the Gen. Kdo. should effect a most exact and foreseeing work of dead reckoning (Koppelungsarbeit), taking into consideration: high altitude winds, speed of enemy aircraft, performance of own aircraft and our own standard of training, weather and high altitude visibility. Only then was it possible to avoid the danger of our own units, in the case of premature start, running out of fuel even before contacting the enemy—considering the extremely short operational endurance (1 hr. 50 mins.)—or of being, in the case of late start, attacked by enemy fighters whilst still in the process of assembly.

Careful work of command and control at the HQs of the fighter divisions was as important for dayfighting as it was for nightfighting. For a large part, success depended on their ability and the quality of the fighter controllers in the ops rooms. At all dayfighter stations, the enemy air situation had to be plotted carefully according to the divisional telephone reportage. Only then was it possible for fighters, flying their second mission for fighting the returning bombers, to contact the enemy.

Means of Control

In contrast to nightfighting, the means of control for fighter control by day were by necessity much simpler. Reasons for this were:

(a) Lack of space in the S. E. German fighter planes available did not permit to carry several or bulkier and more modern wireless sets in the airplane.

(b) The absence of small, modern wireless sets and, resulting from it, the lack of a simple procedure making possible a simultaneous exchange of communications air ground with all crews.

(c) The difficult tuning in of German radio sets, involving bad R/T connections, in contrast to the quartz controlled enemy radio sets affording very clear R/T connections.

(d) The absence of suitable D/F and navigation sets in one seaters, or belated and neglected mass production of such sets.

(e) Insufficient war production capacity of the German electrical industry as a consequence of the enemy's bombing war, or lack of planning and foresight of the competent planning departments of the High Command of the GAF.

(f) Low standards of training of dayfighter personnel replacements owing to short periods of training.

USAAF bombers encounter flak. After the defeat of their day-fighter force in early 1944, the Germans relied increasingly on flak for daylight defense as the bomber offensive reached its height. However, German night-fighters remained highly lethal until the last month of the war. (US National Archives)

(g) Signals specialists of the ground personnel of dayfighter units of little efficiency.

(h) Failure to develop early methods of fighter control and to put the corresponding demands on the authorities responsible for technical development.

(i) Too narrow basis of experienced young fighter officers within Fighter Command, for conceiving ideas for technical means of fighter control, thus helping the development of such means.

Consequently there remained as the safest means of control:

(1) Well qualified COs of units (COs of geschwader and gruppen as well as of combat formations).

(2) Careful preparation of operations at the units on the basis of the preliminary orders of the fighter control centers (Jaegerfuehrungsstellen).

(3) "Y" control and Egon control with all their drawbacks. In dayfighting, too, "Y" control was preferred to Egon control. The latter had been

employed successfully in the main with 8th Ftr. Div. only. "Y" control nearly always created difficulties when passing dayfighter units from one divisional area to another, such difficulties mostly occurring through faulty tuning in. This kind of control, moreover, required understanding and careful training of unit commanders and crews. Where these conditions were given, "Y" control was a quite safe means of control, limited though it was on account of the few frequencies available. Even in the last phase of the war enemy jammings of "Y" lines were rarely effective.

(4) Flak indicator bursts for assembly above the clouds and in case of bad visibility.

(5) Flak rockets as landing help in case of overcast. It would show the possibility for landing and the position of aerodromes, even through the clouds, but only to a limited height.

The mounting of a model of the "Bernhardine" sets in the S.E. fighter had been successfully achieved by summer 1944. This set might have meant a great advance in fighter control by technical means. Serial production of "Bernhardine" was said to be too costly and was no longer possible in 1944 for reasons of war production capacity.

Unfortunately the all-around-view radar set (Panoramageraet) arrived too late to be generally employed as the excellent means of control for dayfighting it might have constituted.

Radio beacons were not used for dayfighter control.

Cooperation with Flak

It was missing by day as well as by night. By day, too, fighters and flak should in all circumstances be put in action and controlled by one and the same control center. It was no rare occurrence that, in spite of being warned previously by Flak liaison officers (Flakeinsatzleiter), our own fighter and Zerstoerer units were fired at and our own aircraft brought down by flak. The commanders of home flak units always believed they had a better picture of the air situation in their small sector of defense that did the fighter control centers.

Appreciation of the Enemy

In the years 1940 and 1941 it seemed that the theory of Douhet was only valid any longer to a limited extent and then only during the night. The Luftwaffe and the RAF both had shifted their bomber operations to the night. Both nations were of the opinion that it was not possible any more to use the usual type of bomber aircraft during the day, because the losses inflicted by even an inferior enemy fighter force would make operations during the day uneconomical. The bomber escort of T.E. fighters had proved unsatisfactory to the Luftwaffe. The S.E. fighters of both air forces had not such ranges as to enable them to escort bombers on great and greatest distances, or even to achieve and keep up aerial predominance over the entire enemy territory.

So much the greater must therefore appear the achievements of USAAF, when in 1943 they initiated the strategic aerial warfare against Germany. They proved, by achieving, already in 1944 the air supremacy, that large scale operations of bombers during the day time are possible, and hereby bringing about the present day precedence of the Air Force over other branches of the armed forces. As a matter of fact, it has hereby been proved, for the time being, that air power may mean world power. In summer 1945 the latter fact was enlarged and hardened by the appearance of the atomic bomb.

In summer 1943, the USAAF carried through its first daybomber attacks without fighter escort, but suffered considerable losses. In contrast to the German High Command during the Battle of Britain, the USAAF High Command did not lose their nerves. Not only did they continue the attacks, but also made them economical by creating and putting into use a strategic fighter force. Therefore, it must be stated that not the American fleet of bombers was the new, effective and decisive means, but in the end only the strong fleet of long range fighters created the presuppositions for the use of bombers and was the key for the secret of unobstructed operation of daybombers.

It is not apparent from the course of events whether it was the acknowledged aim of the USAAF Command right from the start to create the conditions for a war of attrition by bombing against Germany by means of long range fighter units. It rather seems that the Americans came to this conviction in the course of the operations in 1943, and then implemented their conclusions hurriedly but with all their might. Should this conception not be correct, then it would be hard to understand why, in 1943, the USAAF flew their costly bomber raids without fighter escort, and did not wait with the initiation of large scale bomber operations until the time when sufficiently strong long range fighter forces were available. In detail, the following achievements of the USAAF daybomber warfare against Germany were especially remarkable:

(1) Planning of operations as regards choice of targets, reconnaissance of bombing effects,continuity and keeping in tune with the British nightbomber operations.
(2) Mastering of the methods of carrying out missions with very large units

of mixed forces and excellent cooperation between bombers and fighters.

(3) Technical performance of the long range fighters.

(4) Flying achievements of the long range fighters as regards bad weather flying and orientation.

(5) Formation of flying of the bomber units.

(6) Discipline of mixed units while carrying out attacks (tactics of attack), assembly, penetration flights, the attack itself, return flight.

(7) Independence from weather conditions while carrying out the operation.

(8) Bombing accuracy by means of the H2 radar sets also in bad weather (bombing through the undercast).

During the American daybomber raids, the following facts were especially remarkable:

(a) The comparatively late initiation of bomber raids on the German synthetic gasoline industry.

(b) The infrequency of raids on the GAF ground organization.

(c) Unsatisfactory cooperation between the bomber commands and the TAF.

(d) Little use of deceptive maneuvers.

(e) Continuation of flying at high altitudes during penetration and bombing after air supremacy had been achieved, especially in 1945.

(f) The absence of large scale radio jamming and deceptive radio activity.

Dayfighter Procedures
(a) Fundamentals

Right from the start, the dayfighter component of the Reich Defense suffered from neglect by the Supreme Command of the Armed Forces and of the GAF. They realized not at all, or very much too late, its importance for safeguarding the German armament potential.

In the beginning of 1943, it was thought impossible that the enemy could at all carry out effective day raids. Should the enemy try them, it was the conviction that he could be warded off by small German forces and with big enemy losses, and that the attacks could thus be prevented. When things turned out differently, one surprise followed the other. For dayfighting, these surprises turned out to be technical and tactical catastrophes. In both fields, dayfighting was very poorly prepared for large area defense within the German territory, and in both fields it was very slow to counteract any new move of the enemy, and was, therefore, always lagging considerably behind.

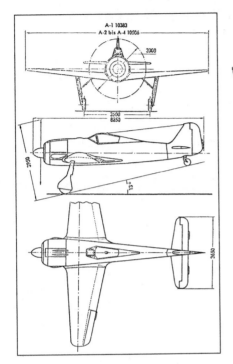
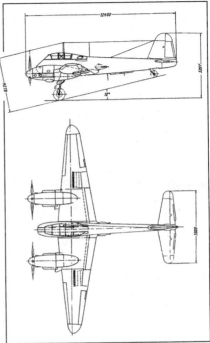

General arrangement of the Focke-Wulf FW 190A-2–4 (left) and Messerschmitt Me 410.
(From manual in US National Archives RG 165)

It may be expressly pointed out that CinC Fighter Command had realized at a very early date the dangers of the USAAF bomber raids, the resulting situation for Germany in general, and for the fighter forces in particular. His organizational, tactical and, above all, technical demands were either not complied with at all or much too late, and then only in part. Thus, the methods of operations were developed and continually changed under unfavorable presuppositions all through the period of the American daybomber warfare, from spring 1943 up to the end of the war.

In fall 1943, at the very latest, therefore, just about the time when I took over the 1st Ftr. Corps, the German Luftwaffe High Command had made the capital mistake in the Air Defense of the Reich. Assuming that the enemy bomber units would be the primary opponent, tactics of attack, equipment of aircraft, training, armament, and ammunitions were designed for the exclusive use of fighting the bombers.

Not until summer 1944 did I myself become fully convinced that, first of all, it would have been the main task of dayfighters engaged in the Defense of the Reich to regain the air supremacy over their own territory by shattering the enemy fighter forces, before taking up the battle against the enemy bombers. For this purpose, few fighter battles would have had to be won in order then to take up the battle against the enemy bombers. This fact was not realized at all or very late, and then only in part, by the Supreme Command of the GAF.

The accepted compromise, to fight enemy fighters and bombers simultaneously, could not be successful, considering the relative strengths. In my view, it was, in fall 1944, too late to switch the entire dayfighter armament to the battle mainly against fighters. I was neither able to stress my convictions after the operations sufficiently, not did I have enough influence on the distribution of the units, whose airports of operations were very often ordered as far down as the gruppe by the CinC GAF himself.

How little the problems of the dayfighter defense of the Reich were understood, is shown by Hitler's worries during spring 1945 about bigger and heavier armament for fighters to take up the battle against enemy bombers. The contrary was the fact: armament and ammunition were the best existing qualities of the fighters. Suitable types and the number of aircraft were lacking which could have taken up battle with enemy fighters. The facts mentioned above are important presuppositions for an understanding of the changes and developments of dayfighter tactics.

The dayfighter operations of the Reich Defense were in detail determined by the following main elements:

1. Single orders given by the Ob.d.L. and O.K.W., who often demanded the protection of certain objects. With respect to the unknown intentions of the enemy, weather and small own forces, the demand for protection of single targets by fighters has to be rejected. The enemy must be hit wherever he can be met under the best fighting conditions.

2. Frequent changes in relative strengths forced to change the methods of attack continually. Resulting from the misjudgment of the importance of the Reich Defense, the total strength had always been left too weak. Furthermore, fighter units which had got used to the difficult fighting conditions in the Reich Defense were frequently removed to centers of action for cooperation with the Army ground forces, from which job they mostly returned weakened. This happened fall 1943 and spring 1944, after operations in the East, after the battle against the invasion troops in July 1944, and finally in December 1944, on the occasion of the Ardennes offensive.

3. Although the battle of the Reich Defense called for higher flying qualities of the fighters, in the beginning of 1943 and up to the summer of 1944

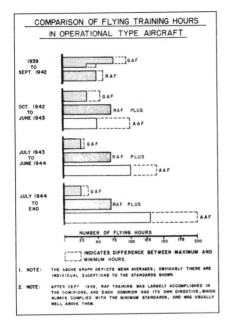

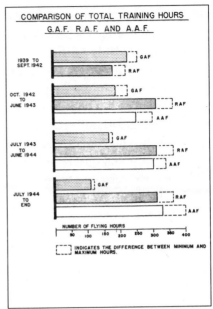

the units consisted of new formations and various, mostly bad or tired out S.E. or T.E. fighter gruppen, whose sister gruppen of the same geschwaders operated in ground support work. Therefore, the Supreme Command had, for a long time, not put the best part of the fighter forces at the disposal of the Reich Defense. Up to summer 1944, the dayfighter units lacked the strong service and tactical cohesion of a geschwader, a demand made by the 1st. Ftr. Corps in fall 1943.

4. The fighter models Me-109 and Fw-190, with the exception of the latest series Me-109K4, K10, Fw 190 and D12, as well as the Ta 152, which arrived much too late, were inferior to the enemy fighters and unsuited for high altitude fighting. These facts could not be overcome by the emergency measures of GM I and G supercharger. In the Reich Defense, the T.E. fighter types Me-110 and Me-410 equipped with 5 cm cannon proved to be errors in tactical operation. The Me-163 rocket aircraft proved to be tactically unsuitable. The Me-262 as a fighter came one year too late. In S.E. fighters, the protection against icing and the protection against dimming of the cockpit windows were insufficient. From summer 1944 onward, the reliability of the engines decreased rapidly, on account of their short time of running on the test beds at the factory and inexpert test flying.

5. The use of 20 cm rockets as aircraft armament against bombers was only effective as long as the enemy bombers were flying without fighter escort.

All other attempts at destroying close-flying bomber formations with bombs or big caliber armament usually failed.

6. The standard of fighter training at the dayfighter units was rather poor; that of the reserves was insufficient. The physical and mental qualities of the replacements in personnel were generally unsatisfactory up to summer 1944. RTU training at the schools was practically nonexistent. The biggest bottleneck existed in the field of tactical and technical training of the unit commanders (geschwader, gruppen, and staffel COs). The number and quality of highly qualified technical specialists within the ground personnel were insufficient.

7. The problem of operation of dayfighter units in bad weather conditions remained unsolved up to the end of the war. A part solution failed on account of the much too short time of training resulting from the shortage of fuel. Thus the operation of units depended generally on the following conditions:

— take off at a cloud base of 100 m or higher landing at no less than 500 m cloud base in flat country

— ascent through overcast up to a thickness of 500 m.

The achievements of single aircraft (a few experienced pilots to each gruppe) are hereby not touched. In my view, it would have been rather doubtful whether, even with the best of training, it would have been possible with the available types of aircraft and technical means of control to bring close flying units into operation in bad weather conditions (e.g. at 200 m cloud base and 4,500 in cloud tops).

8. The shortage of suitable commanders for middle commands (fighter division COs) and assistants (General Staff officers who had been fighter pilots) was very big. Owing to the prejudice against fighter pilots before and especially during the war, it had been neglected to train a suitable reserve of young commanders at schools and academies. It, therefore, was a poor sign that I, not being a fighter pilot, had to take over the command of the 1st Ftr. Corps.

(b) Division of Time

In order to give a clear picture of the development of the methods of dayfighting, I divide the events into three periods.

1st Period, 1943   The US bomber units were flying without or with only little fighter escort of limited range (extreme range of escort in the west: Aurig–Rheine–Dortmund–Cologne–Sedan).

2nd Period, Spring 1944   The enemy bombers were flying with close fighter escort (range of escort in the west up to the approximate line: Bremen–Hannover–Kassel–Frankfurt/Main; in the south into the area of Vienna and that of Munich).

3rd Period, from summer 1944 to the end of the war   The enemy was flying with close fighter escort and ever increasing fighter high cover almost over the whole Reich territory.

(c) 1st Period

Orders for the CinC GAF:

Interception of bombers during the period of their flight over Germany. If several bomber streams are in the air, it must be aimed at concentrating all S.E. and T.E. fighter units as well as industry and night ighters available on one and the same bomber stream, and at destroying it completely. The continuous attack was to induce the bomber crews to spend all their ammunition. The Luftflottenkommando 3 was ordered to put, upon request, fighter forces at the disposal of the 1st Ftr. Corps, to fight enemy aircraft approaching from the West.

Organization and Distribution of Units:

3rd Ftr. Div.:	J.G. 1—Holland
	J.G. 3—northwestern Germany
	Z.G.26 (2 gruppen)—northwestern Germany
	N.J.G.1—Holland
	N.J.G.2— Holland
	Erprobungskommando 25—Achmer
2nd Ftr. Div.:	J.G. 11—Heligoland Bay/Holstein
	N.J.G.3—northwestern Germany/Jutland
	Industry fighters in the Hannover and Bremen areas
1st Ftr. Div.:	III/54—Parchim
	N.J.G.5—Berlin Area
	Industry fighters in central Germany
7 Ftr. Div.:	III/53—Frankfurt Basin
	II/27—Frankfurt Basin
	Z.G. 76—Ist Gruppe ready for ops in Bavaria
	—IInd Gruppe forming in Bavaria
	Industry fighters—Augsburg–Regensburg, Bavaria

Jafue Ostmark:

N.J.G.6—Bavaria
J.G.27—Vienna area
I/Z.G.1—Wels
Unit Commanders Training School
Industry fighters—Wiener Neustadt

Total number of S.E. fighters ready for ops: on an average 400 a/c
T.E. fighters ready for ops: on average 50 a/c
Nightfighters for dayfighting: 100 a/c
Industry fighters: about 30–40 a/c

Aircraft Equipment and Armament:

2/3 of S. E. fighters (light): Me-109. Armament: 3 MG 151 and 2 MG 131
(2 gruppen with Me-109 with 1 mortar and one MG each)

1/3 of S.E. fighters (heavy): FW-190. Armament: 4 MG 151 and 2 MG 131

Z.G.26:   I/26 Me-110. Armament: 1 MG 15 1, 1 MG 131 and 2 mortars
II/26 Me-410 (1 staffel). Armament: 1 MG 151, 1 MG 131 and 2 mortars
Me-110 (2 staffeln). Armament: 1 MG 15 1, 1 MG 131 and 2 mortars

S.E. Fighters: 10% fitted for "Y" operation (FuG 16)

Manner of Operation:

Largest combat formation: Gruppe.

Control: Bulk on Reich fighter frequency, 2–3 gruppen by "Y" control, J.G.27 by "Egon" control. The gruppen were directed to the enemy one after another for intercepting the bombers. One light S.E. fighter gruppe was tactically subordinated to each T.E. fighter geschwader for protection against enemy fighters and was flying with them in battle formation. In Holland, two light gruppen had the task to tie up enemy escort fighters in the Dutch area. Industry fighters were flying their operations mostly in the form of scrambles. Nightfighters were put in action in element strength formations and were "Y"-controlled.

Comment: In September and October 1943 the defensive actions still took a successful course. With the beginning of the bad weather period, considerable losses through icing, dimming of cockpit windows, and in landing on days when the cloud base was low occurred in November and December.

Control by the Reichsjaegerwelle (Reich fighter frequency) alone was not sufficient. "Y" control with the majority of units worked only in rare cases. The most advanced gruppen in Holland, especially J.G.1, which at first would only contact the enemy in gruppen strength, suffered heavy, and irreplaceable losses by enemy fighters. When, at the end of November, enemy fighters flew as far as Emden and Muenster, much to the surprise of the German commands, even the Zerstoerer and the fighter geschwader farther back sustained greater losses through enemy fighters. Cooperation with L.Fl.Kdo.3 and with 7th Ftr. Div. was working only rarely in as much as fighters from northern France and Zerstoerer from southern Germany, when called in, would mostly be late in case of raids over northern Germany and would, therefore, not be able to engage the enemy.

The following demands were put up by the Ist Ftr. Corps and partly realized later (in spring 1944):

(a) Transfer of all fighter and Zerstoerer units of Ist Ftr. Corps father east, simultaneous withdrawal from Holland. This latter measure was taken because enemy fighters flying ahead of the bomber stream would attack our own fighters already in the process of starting and assembling.

(b) Forming geschwader combat units as battle formations, at least one third of the unit to be in readiness for fighting against enemy fighters.

(c) Increased supply of FuG 16 fit for "Y" operation.

(d) Organization of landing helps for bad weather. Speedup of supply and mounting of ZG 16 homing device (auxiliary apparatus working in connection with FuG 16) as a landing help.

(e) Providing installation for directing cold or hot air currents against the window panes in order to avoid icing or dimming of the cockpit windows.

(f) Reinforcing dayfighters in northern Germany by 2 geschwader.

(g) Arming Zerstoerer aircraft with 4–6 centrally controlled guns instead of mortars.

(h) Supply of extra tanks for all one-seater fighters in order to increase endurance.

Last of all, I tried, on 12 December 1943, to deepen the method of conducting operations in a tactical demonstration on maps (Planspiel) at Zeist (Holland), with all the COs of geschwaders and gruppen taking part.

(d) Second Period

Directions of Ob.d.L. had, on the whole, remained the same as during the first period, excepting the following change: about one third of the geschwaders were by tying up the enemy fighters to enable the remaining German fighters to attack the bombers. The Zerstoerer and nightfighters were to conduct their attacks upon the bombers out of range of the fighters or to attack otherwise unprotected elements of bombers. The 1st Me-163 P. staffel had to undertake the protection of Leuna.

Organization and Distribution of Units

3rd Ftr. Div.:	I/J.G.1—Twente
	HQ and II/J.G.1—Rheine
	III/J.G.1 (high altitude ftrs.)—Munich Gladbach
2nd Ftr. Div.:	I/J.G.11—Oldenburg
	II/J.G.11 (high altitude ftrs.)—Wunsdorf
	HQ and III/J.G.11—Rotenburg
	III/J.G.54—Lueneburg
	Sturmstaffel—Langenhagen
1st Ftr. Div.:	I/J.G.3 (high altitude ftrs.)—Burg Cottbus
	II/J.G.3—Gerdelegen
	III/J.G.3—Stendal
	HQ and IV/J.G.3—Magdeburg
	I/Z.G. 26—Voelkenrode
	II/Z.G. 26—Hildesheim
	I/J.G. 400 (Me 163 staffel)—Brandis

7th Ftr. Div. and Jafue Ostmark, as well as nightfighters and industry fighters (Industriejaeger), as during the first period.

Total number of aircraft ready for operation on an average about the same as in the first period.

Aircraft Equipment and Armament

Light high altitude fighters:

Me-109G6 and G5 with GM 1: one engine cannon central, 2 MG 131 (with little ammunition to save weight)

Heavy Fighters:

Me 109 (S): 3 MG 151, 2 MG 131

Fw 190 (S): 4 MG 151, 2 MG 131

S.E. fighters about 50% equipped with FuG 16 fit for "Y" operation.

Manner of Operation   Combat units, consisting of one high altitude gruppe and two heavy fighter gruppen each, or of one high altitude and 1 or 2 zerstoerer gruppen each, were assembled in close formation at operational height over landmarks, and on principle led to the enemy by "Y" procedure. For this, the

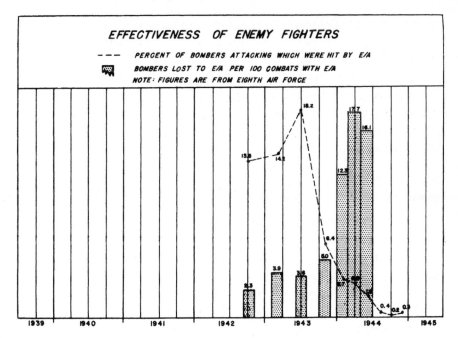

heavy gruppen assembled in gruppen V formation (gruppenkeil), one behind another, at sighting distance at about 6,000 m. Above them there was the high altitude group at 7,500 m, with the battle formation leader in loose gruppen V formation.

Battle formation leader and his deputy were monitoring "Y" frequency and had the possibility of keeping up communications with the gruppen on a geschwader frequency. Besides, the high altitude fighters had frequency of their own, so as not to interfere with the heavy gruppen during battle.

For the second start against returning bombers, so called "Jaegereinsatzplaetze" or "Stammplaetze" (fighter operation 'dromes or regular 'dromes) were assigned. At these 'dromes ample stores of ammunition, oxygen, oil and fuel were being kept. All other airfields in the Reich which were not "Stamm," i.e. regular airfields, were keeping supplies of fuel only. When a fighter, after his first mission, landed on such an aerodrome, he just tanked up and started for the nearest regular fighter 'drome, flying at low level from there, to be sent out again on a second mission together with other pilots, regardless of the unit to which they belonged.

The following characteristics mark the second period:

(a) Distribution of the units over the whole Reich area.
(b) Fighting all enemy raids, even in difficult weather conditions and using only part of our forces.

(c) Staggered engaging of combat formations, i.e. a certain time is allowed to elapse between the operation of one formation and that of the next.

(d) Fighting enemy fighters not the main purpose, but only with part of the forces and out of necessity, in order to enable the bulk of our own forces actually to engage the bombers.

(e) Leading large and small combat units into battle even from the greatest distances (owing to distribution) for fighting approaching enemy aircraft (art of fighter control).

Comment   Beginning from early 1944, the enemy forces, in particular their fighters, became stronger. The units of the Reich Defense had to fight against odds many times stronger than there were. The tactics of fighting in combat formations proved successful. The "Y" control procedure had increasingly become familiar with the ft. divs. and the units. Losses owing to bad weather conditions went on decreasing considerably. Nearly all S.E. units were now equipped with extra tanks so that Fighter Command had greater liberty of movement.

Already in March, the numeric superiority of the enemy fighters had become so great that fighting became most difficult for our own units. J.G.1, the unit stationed farthest west, suffered considerable losses, the zerstoerer equally, who, at that time, only rarely encountered bomber formations unprotected by fighters any longer.

Whilst standards of training, leadership, and organization of combat were satisfactory with all units, the defensive strength of the whole Defense of the Reich was suffering from its great general weakness. It is true, S.E. nightfighters were also to be engaged in dayfighting, but the majority of them had not yet finished their training for dayfighting. In spite of heavy losses, the supply of personnel and aircraft continued to be very unsatisfactory for all the units of dayfighters in the Reich Defense, so that the alacrity or fighting spirit of the troop was generally below the average.

At the end of spring 1944, the Gen. Kdo. 1st Ftr. Corps put up three essential demands:

(a) Reinforcement of dayfighter units in the Reich Defense by any means.

(b) Concentration of the units within the Reich into 3 large forces into the areas Hannover–central Germany, Frankfurt basin, northern Bavaria, so as to obtain in each case local superiority against enemy planes with strong single groups.

(c) Operation only in case of favorable weather or fighting conditions.

(e) Third Period

Directions of Ob. d L. April–May 1944   After the reinforcement of the Reich Defense by one dayfighter and zerstoerer units engaged up to then, and the operation of S.E. nightfighters by day, air supremacy within the Reich was to be restored by several maximum efforts and heavy blows against the USAAF.

June–August 1944   During the invasion in France, the S.E. nightfighters, the sturmgruppen and the zerstoerergeschwader had to provide for the Defense of the Reich by day.

September–November 1944   After withdrawing four geschwader from France, these were merged with the remaining elements of S.E. nightfighters. They had orders to protect industries in central Germany and in the Berlin area, as well as the synthetic oil plants in central Germany, at Poelitz in Silesia, and in northern Bohemia. At the same time, a large scale undertaking had begun for refitting a total of 10 geschwader. It had been intended to win back air supremacy within the Reich before the end of 1944 by a mass operation of some 1,200 fighters, prepared into its minutest details.

December 1944–end of March   After withdrawing the bulk of dayfighter forces to the Western front in December 1944 and to the Eastern front in January 1945, app. 2 dayfighter geschwader and one J.P. gruppe were to protect the remaining part of Germany, in particular Leuna and Poelitz.

Organization and Distribution of Units

April–May 1944:

3rd Ftr. Div.:	Geschwader z.b.V of 3 Gruppen—Frankfurt Basin
2nd Ftr.Div.:	J.G.11
	Nightfighter Hannover–Bremen
1st Ftr. Div.:	J.G. 1—west of Berlin
	J.G. 300—Berlin area
	Z.G. 26—east of Berlin
	Nightfighters
	I./J.G.400 (Me-163)—Brandis
7th Ftr. Div.:	J.G.302
	Nightfighters Munich
8th Ftr. Div.:	J.G.27
	III/J.G.302—Vienna area
	Z.G.76

Total number of dayfighters ready for ops on an average (approx.)	500
S.E. fighters	120
T.E. fighters	70

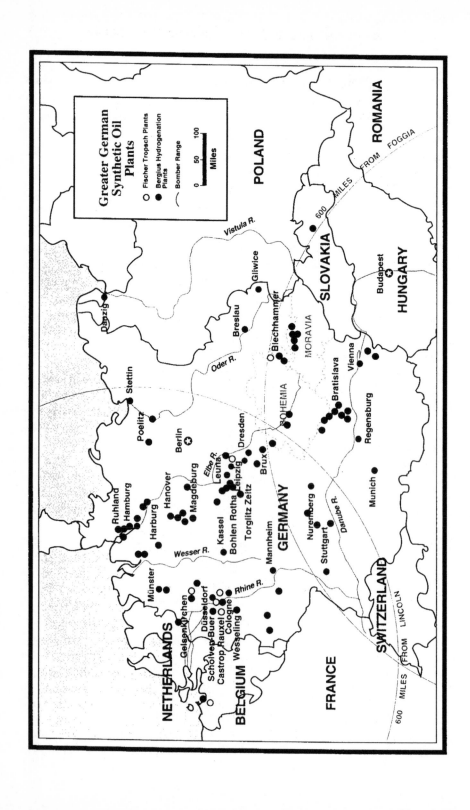

Greater German Synthetic Oil Plants

○ Fischer Tropsch Plants
● Bergius Hydrogenation Plants
⌒ Bomber Range

Miles
0   50   100

Zerstoerer	120
Industry fighters	50

June–August 1944:

3rd Ftr. Div.:	Geschwader z.b.V.—Frankfurt basin
2nd Ftr. Div.:	Nightfighters
1st Ftr. Div.:	I Sturmgruppe
	J.G.30—Berlin area
	Z.G.26—east of Berlin, J.G.400—Brandis
7th Ftr. Div.:	Geschwader 302
	Nightfighter Munich
8th Ftr. Div.:	IIII/J.G.302
	Z.G.76—Vienna area

Total number of S. E. fighters ready for ops on an average (approx.)	50
S.E. fighters	100
T.E. fighters	80
Zerstoerer	80
Industry fighters (no longer in operation)	0

September–November 1944:

3rd Ftr. Div.	–
2nd Ftr. Div.	–
1st Ftr. Div.	J.G.1—refitting west of Berlin
	J.G.11—refitting west of Berlin
	J.G.301—refitting west of Berlin
	J.G. 77—refitting north of Berlin
	J.G.6—refitting north of Berlin
	J.G.3—middle Germany
	J.G.300—middle Germany
	J.G.27—south of Berlin
	J.G. 4—south of Berlin
	Z.G.26—east of Berlin
	Unit Commander Training School
	J.G.400—Brandis
7th and 8th Ftr. Div.:	–

Total number of S.E. fighter reader for ops on an average (approx.)	200
Zerstoerer	40

| T.E. fighters | 50 |
| Me-163 | 10 |

Manner of Operation It was attempted to assemble each geschwader as a combat formation in such a way as to keep them out of the range of enemy fighters during assembly. The total strength of a geschwader formation was not to exceed 100 a/c. The average strength was about 50–60 a/c. "Y" control had proved extremely successftil.

Comment The distribution of dayfighter units in three large groups in the area: Hannover–Berlin, Frankfurt basin or Westphalia (according to choice), southern Germany (Nuremberg or Vienna, according to choice), had proved successful. It is true that reinforcements (3 gruppen) followed one another at more or less long intervals and too late.

A spell of fine weather, involving continual and current operations, had caused the Defense of the Reich to become a grinding mill for the dayfighter units, devouring a lot of their personnel and material. The authorities to which the Gen. Kdo. was subordinated did not possess the nerve to completely stop defensive action for a certain time, in order to reach out for heavier blows after a period of recovery and after concentration of strong forces. The first attempt to refit dayfighters on a large scale and to place them in readiness for a maximum

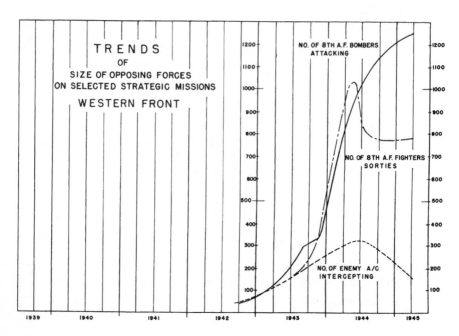

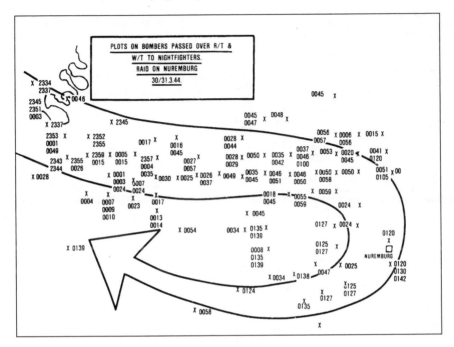

effort failed, owing to the fact that on the ninth of June the bulk of the aircraft were transferred to France for the purpose of repelling the invasion. In the Defense of the Reich, there remained widely distributed (Frankfurt–Berlin–Bavaria–Vienna) only the S.E. nightfighters, less two gruppen who had also transferred to France. For almost three months, the S.E. nightfighters waged a heroic battle against a strongly (about 20 times) superior enemy and, whilst winning splendid successes, were slowly using themselves up.

Thanks to the support of the General der Jagdflieger, in autumn 1944 two essential preusppositions for the prospect of a more successful continuation of the Reich Defense were acknowledged and granted by the Highest Command of the GAF:

(a) Concentration of all dayfighter forces in one area of the Reich.
(b) Systematic preparation of a large defensive blow by refitting the units.

This latter point was strongly delayed, owing to the operation of the units against the enemy airborne operation near Arnhem, owing to lack of fuel and to the dragging rate of aircraft supply. The whole refitting action could not be finished by October 1944, as had been planned, but was delayed until December 1944. Then the intended mass operation was no longer carried through, as the

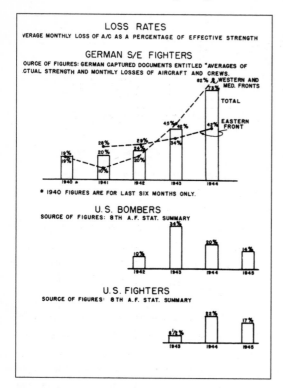

LOSS RATES
VERAGE MONTHLY LOSS OF A/C AS A PERCENTAGE OF EFFECTIVE STRENGTH

GERMAN S/E FIGHTERS
OURCE OF FIGURES: GERMAN CAPTURED DOCUMENTS ENTITLED "AVERAGES OF
CTUAL STRENGTH AND MONTHLY LOSSES OF AIRCRAFT AND CREWS.

* 1940 FIGURES ARE FOR LAST SIX MONTHS ONLY.

U.S. BOMBERS
SOURCE OF FIGURES: 8TH A.F. STAT. SUMMARY

U.S. FIGHTERS
SOURCE OF FIGURES: 8TH A.F. STAT. SUMMARY

units in the West were used for tasks of army co-operation in the winter offensive in the Eifel mountains. The intended great defensive operation had been, as regards problems of command, prepared by me very intensively by tactical exercises on maps (planspiel) and by ops room exercises at the 1st Ftr. Div. in October 1944. In doing so provision had been made for the first time for whole geschwaders to be engaged in fighting enemy fighters exclusively.

During the time from September to October 1944, in view of the intention of refitting the units, no reserve was shown in operations; on the contrary, all enemy raids had to be fought against, even in bad weather, so that the dayfighter forces who were in action were suffering heavy losses and achieving only little success in view of the strong enemy superiority, besides suffering great losses owing to bad weather conditions, as the still unsolved problem of cockpit window icing cropped up again. The last months of the war, during which the Defense of the Reich was carried out with a minimum of forces and only few J.P. planes, offered no new aspects of command.

PART THREE

DEVELOPING TECHNOLOGY TO DEFEND THE REICH

Fighter control, radar, radios, aircraft—these were the technologies that Germany had to develop and place in the hands of the Luftwaffe if she were to have any chance of countering the Allied bomber offensive that was growing both in numbers and technological sophistication. As 158-victory ace Johannes "Macky" Steinhoff, put it, "The war in the air is a technological war which cannot be won by a technologically inferior fighting force, however high its moral or dauntless its resolution."

Each of the authors writes about an area in which he had specialist knowledge. Galland writes about fighter control, how the Luftwaffe was able to vector fighters against threats by day or night. Martini and his OKL staff specialists discuss the "wizard war" of radar and electronic countermeasures that was vital to the outcome of the bomber offensive, especially at night. Finally, Willi Messerschmitt (the only non-Luftwaffe author) gives his account of developing the Me-262, the first operational jet fighter, for combat. However, as with many of of these accounts, the picture he presents of himself and his efforts has been reinterpreted in more recent studies: the Me 262 was never as mature as he says it was.

The problems the Luftwaffe had in fusing together information from different radars, passive sensors (including the "Y" Service) and visual observations are with us today. "Sensor fusion" for air (and missile) defense is a difficult task, even with the benefits of the microchip revolution. Indeed, the "single integrated air picture" (SIAP) is as much a desired (and unachieved) goal for the US military of 2002 as it was for the Luftwaffe of 1944.

To put this technology into action against the bombers required the full mobilization of German industry. In 1944, over 50 percent of all electronics, 33 percent of all optics, 30 percent of artillery tubes and 20 percent of heavy artillery ammunition produced went into the Air Defense of the Reich.

D.C.I.

Chapter 7

Fighter Control
Interrogation of Generalleutnant Adolf Galland
15 October 1945

1. Question: Why did the Germans put emphasis on fighter control from the ground at such a late stage of the war?

Answer: The peacetime GAF had made no provisions for fighter control from the ground. The solution of the problem of recognition, which simultaneously would have provided a possibility for fighter control, could not be solved, because of technical deficiencies. (Possibility of interception in the case of "Freya" apparatus).

In the Battle of Britain, battle participants and the staff recognized the advantages of fighter control as practiced by the RAF. In consequence thereof, the German demand for the possibilities of fighter control was amplified. The Technical Office and the Chief of Signals wanted to meet this demand as before, with the "Erstling" as airborne apparatus and with the "Freya" set from the ground. The British used regular R/T apparatus in conjunction with an automatic "Pip Squeak" D/F signal transmitter for airborne needs and a D/F organization on the ground. Since this solution of the British required very little time for construction and was quite simple, the GAF units demanded the same

As *General der Jagdflieger,* Adolf Galland (center) succeeded his friend and rival Werner Mölders (right) when the latter was killed in a plane crash. Here they are talking with General Erhard Milch. (US National Archives)

arrangement at the end of 1940/beginning of 1941 for the German fighter force in the West.

When no action was taken in this matter, the operational units took it upon themselves to have signal transmitters built, independently in a small plant in Dusseldorf, and installed same in fighter aircraft. In turn the Chief of Signals Communications supported these efforts and proceeded to establish the corresponding D/F organization in the Channel area. In this manner, it was possible to commence with the first attempt in ground fighter control in the West, about the middle of 1941.

The growing nightfighting force, under the command of the XII Fliegerkorps under General Kammhuber, tackled the problem of fighter control quite energetically right from the start. Already two systems had been tried in action:

(a) The "Freya-AN" system.
(b) The "Wurzburg" ("Himmelbett")system.

Both systems were specifically suited to direct individual a/c against individual enemy a/c and thus could not be used in dayfighting. But also the nightfighters needed a system with greater range, and if possible with greater accuracy. At that time, the "Y" system, in bomber operation already known, as developed by Oberstingenieur Plendel (he later became Staatsrat), was first tried and put into action in the Dutch area, in direct agreement and cooperation with the XII Fl. Korps. In the latter part of 1942, a final decision had to be made, as to which fighter control system should be adopted. At the time the following were under consideration:

(a) "Y" system.
(b) "Egon" system.
(c) Radioset (FuG) 16—D/F system.

As a result of an extensive demonstration of these systems in Rechlin, the XII Fl. Korps (Kammhuber) succeeded in obtaining the approval of their request for the "Y" system.

The dayfighter command, which was represented through me, held the opinion that the "Egon" system incorporated greater advantages in regard to its own needs. (Better overall control of the airspace, control of the whole formation to be directed as compared to the control of only one pilot aircraft in the case of the "Y" system, easier facilitation of transfer from one station to the next ground station, no taxation of the R/T frequency range, greater clearance (backlash) since there is no crowding because of frequency distribution and more promising possibilities for the development of this system.)

Yet one thing was clear: that only one system could be adopted for both day and nightfighting, because it was impossible to double the total expenditure in signal construction and personnel. The nightfighter command on the one side persisted on the "Y" system, because it provided the greater measuring accuracy necessary for night operation. The problem of recognition, which until then had not been solved, would have been eliminated as a matter of course, in the case of the "Egon" system. In the case of the "Y" system, on the other hand, it was necessary to find an entirely separate solution to the problem of recognition. But at the time General Kammhuber held the opinion that the entire output of "Freya" equipment was needed for enemy detection. Consequently the CinC of the GAF approved the recommendations of the Chief of Signals Communications, which were as follows:

(a) The introduction of the "Y" system as the primary fighter control system for day and nightfighting;
(b) The continuation of development of the "Egon" system as alternative system in case the enemy develops effective interference of the "Y" system; and
(c) Development of the URF Flying Safety system on the basis of the R/T–D/F system.

In the now following period of time, the areas of the individual fighter divisions were equipped with the necessary ground apparatus and signal communications for the "Y" system in accordance with specific plans. Hereby the area of the XII Flieger Korps (later I Fighter Corps) was always given priority.

During the years of 1943, '44 and '45, the "Y" system was successfully used in day and nightfighting, although its weaknesses and shortcomings in dayfighting became more and more evident. Particularly in regard to the "complete traverse" search equipment ("Panorama," "Jagdschloss," "Jagdhutte"), the advantages of the "Egon" system became more and more apparent. In actual construction, this was taken into consideration, as a steadily increasing expansion of the ground organization for the "Egon" system showed. So, for instance, the areas of the 7th and 8th Fighter Divisions were primarily and mainly equipped for "Freya" control and secondary for the "Y" system. By the end of the year, the "Egon" system had proven itself in all areas as the safest and least complicated method of control for dayfighters. In nightfighting the "Y" system and the "Egon" system were used side by side.

2. Question: What further development of control systems was planned for the defense of the Reich?

Answer: Already in the given situation, the simultaneous control of 10 fighter formations from one division C.P. (Operations) constituted a serious problem. But in future development of the Reich Defenses, 40–50 fighter formations were to be controlled concurrently, at short notice if the need should arise. This could only be solved by means of an "air-to-ground" D/F system contrary to the above named systems, which are all "ground-to-air" systems. With the aid of such systems ("Bernhardine," "Hermine," "Erika"), each individual a/c could determine its crossbearings independently in the air. If, in addition, the position, altitude and course of the enemy was given continuously, the fighters could easily solve the problem of interception point independently. Especially the introduction of He-162s (Volksjager), with their very limited flying time (time a/c can remain airborne), makes such a control system necessary. In bad weather operation, day and nightfighters would also have benefited by it considerably. A number of a/c were already fitted with this equipment. The most essential rotation radio beam transmitters were already in operation in the Reich territory.

3. Question: How would German R/T traffic have been affected by interference?

Answer: It is doubted whether the necessary energy would have been expended to cause complete jamming of the R/T traffic in the Reich territory. Whereas the complete jamming of the American fighter R/T traffic and fighter-to-bomber communication should have been possible much sooner and with less difficulty, yet I don't think these measures would promise a decisive

Intended to supplement the Me 262 in daylight operations, the Heinkel He 162 lightweight fighter had only a single jet engine and was mainly of plywood construction. (US National Archives)

success on one side or the other. Besides ,we (Germans) had provided an alternative in our fighter and nightfighter a/c on radio command transmission and reception. The nightfighters had the additional alternative to switch from R/T to W/T traffic. The radio teletype command transmission offered a third possibility.

4. Question: What would you have done had the Americans abandoned the idea of large successive bomber waves and instead would have flown in with many small formations at the same time?

Answer: We would have changed the dispersion of our fighters basically in such a way that nearly all concerned fighter divisions would have employed a number of fighter gruppen widely distributed over their entire respective areas. Independent operation of the fighter gruppen would have taken the place of the combat formation. In regard to control, it would have been the task of the fighter directing system to bring these fighter gruppen into contact with the enemy. The transfer of control from one division to another would have been difficult, when operations stretched over wide areas, because of the great number of formations and the heavy taxation of the means of control by own formations of the division which had to take over.

5. Question: Who decided which approaching enemy flight should be engaged?

Answer: The principle was, that only one flight should be engaged with all available power, if possible. In the case of simultaneous approach of two flights from the west, a simultaneous approach of one flight each from west and from south, the Fighter Corps decided which flight was to be attacked, in due consideration of weather conditions and distribution of forces. Hereby divisions simultaneously got clearance for take-off. Furthermore, the Corps had to assure the geographical and timely cooperation of neighboring divisions, as well as supervise the transfer of control from one divisional area to another. The "running commentary" on control and air situation facilitated uninterrupted cooperation between the divisions and assured the continuous possibility of intervention by the corps, Luftflotte Reich and—regrettably—by the CinC. This meant that, at the start of an interception operation, no long all-embracing orders were given, but that continuous directives were issued, as the development of the situation with regard to the approaching force demanded. This method is effective and correct.

6. Question: Could the delays which arose in the introduction of new equipment and new methods be traced back to the fact that the necessary requests on the part of the combat units were made too late?

Answer: It is not the task of the combat units to decide by what means (e.g. cm or mm technique) advancements or keeping up with the enemy must be achieved. These connections must be supervised by "development" and the Chief of Sig. Com. The combat units must simply ask for efficient equipment with which the enemy cannot interfere or otherwise make obsolete. Because of this, reproach that the combat units were at fault in this matter must be rejected most emphatically and energetically.

7. Question: What provisions were there, enabling a fighter pilot to switch over from one control system to another?

Answer: This possibility brought on the introduction of the 5-position spot-tune set (FuG 16Z-Y). This R/T set, which provides for automatic spot-tuning of 5 different bands and also for the possibility of "Y" control and for the possibility of target approach with the preliminary homing set (ZVG 16). The 5 different positions (frequencies) were arranged somewhat like this:

Position 1:   Reich fighter band (running commentary).
Position 2:   Frequency of the geschwader or combat formation ("Egon").
Position 3:   Short range flying safety (directed target approach).
Position 4:   Long range flying safety (directed target approach).
Position 5:   "Y" system.

From 1944 on, all fighter a/c were equipped in this manner, including radio set FuG 25A ("Erstling") for recognition and "Egon" control. In this manner it was possible to switch over from one control system to another and also to Flying Safety while in the air. In operational short and long range flying safety procedure, the D/F system, particularly when employed under bad weather conditions, had gained outstanding significance.

The possibility of directed target approach was a great innovation, the complete utilization of which fighter pilots excepted gratefully, after overcoming their initial hesitancy.

8. Question: Did the "Egon" control system meet the requirements of jet fighter formations?

Answer: In the beginning, correct compass readings in the Me 262 proved to be a difficulty, which was met by the introduction of a gyroscopically stabilized compass. This way, the previously occurring "tilting" of the compass dial was eliminated. Thus the control system could be used with the same success in the case of jet fighters, whereby of course prompt transmission of bearings and prompt interpretation (plotting) as well as quick measuring rhythm became most important because of the higher horizontal speeds of these a/c.

With particular regard to bad weather operation, bomber units have experimented with various control beam systems, which turned out to be just as ineffective as their employment of Me 262s for fighter escort. Here the point was missed, that the control of the formation is the main problem and not the control of individual a/c.

9. Question: How do you distinguish an actual approach flight from a deceptive approach flight?

Answer: This was the task of those responsible for the compilation of the air situation picture. It was compiled with the aid of findings of the radio interception service, radar detection service, findings of showing a/c and findings of the Flak Artillery. From 1944 on, the air situation picture was exclusively compiled by the fighter divisions for the purpose of directing active air defense. Up to that time, two pictures of the air situation were compiled: one by the Luftgaukommando in conjunction with the air reporting service, the other by the fighter divisions in conjunction with the radar detection service. The joining of the two organizations into one was an urgent necessity and has proven itself successful.

10. Question: What was the basic for estimating the fighter force which was to be employed?

Answer: Regrettably, every approaching flight had to be attacked with the greatest possible force, regardless whether the weather was favourable, or practically impossible, whether the formations were rested or whether they were completely worn out and totally shattered. Because of this, it was absolutely impossible to maintain a rational economy of forces with the purpose of maintaining a sound organization. So, in the case of a series of daily attacks in immediate succession, the available strength and striking power of the units dropped considerably. It would have been more successful, and more sensible, to refrain from engagement intentionally for one or more days, so as to reappear with doubled or tripled striking power. Seen as a whole, the latter system would have netted a greater number of enemy a/c brought down in the end. The time taken out for recuperation and formation of reserves for the "Great Push" would have been the only exception. In this connection, however, it must be taken into consideration that personnel of units not participating in the engagement were not on an alerted status.

Chapter 8

Luftwaffe Radars

Interrogation of
General der Flieger Wolfgang Martini

10 October 1945

1. Question: What decisions were made in reference to the radar and air reporting service at the time of Germany's change over to a defensive air war?

Answer: At the time when Germany turned its efforts toward active air defense, the radar and air reporting service underwent a special development. In peacetime we already ordered radar equipment for the Air Reporting Service. The equipments referred to here are the "Freya" and "Wurzburg" sets. We used "Freya" sets in the Air Reporting Service right from the beginning. For half a year, the Flak Artillery were given the "Wurzburg" sets, because the aiming and firing apparatus which was developed for the Flak Artillery did not work, and support had to be given to the Flak Artillery under all circumstances.

2. Question: What were your personal principles for the setting up of radar equipment?

Answer: The original idea was to combine the operation of one "Freya" set and 4 "Wurzburg" sets, so that they might supplement one another. The "Freya" set had a range of 80 km and the "Wurzburg" set had a range of 22–25 km. We wanted to use "Wurzburg" sets in the Air Reporting Service to provide us with accurate altitude measurements; this combination was introduced to supplement the total area, covered by the "Freya" set with the addition of 4 "Wurzburg" sets.

3. Question: What were, in your opinion, the phases in the development of the Air Reporting Service from the beginning of the war until the end?

Answer: In the beginning the Air Reporting Service in Germany itself was set up almost without any radar equipment. When radar equipment, the importance of which we recognized and of which there were 2 types, was introduced, I obtained a considerable number of sets: first 12 then 200 "Freya" sets and 80–100 "Wurzburg" sets for the Air Reporting Service. At the beginning of the war, a few "Freya" sets were just completed and were taken into service by the Air Reporting Service wherever they were needed—at first on the North Sea coast. The rest of the Air Reporting Service had as yet no radar

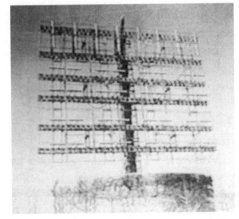

A "Freya" early-warning radar: a still from a German wartime training film. (US National Archives)

equipment. In the meantime, the "Wurzburg" sets were completed and a further delivery of 200 "Freya" sets was in progress. As they were delivered, they were installed in the most important places, and the respective organizations were set up accordingly. Because in the beginning equipment arrived singly on in small numbers of sets, it was installed at the principal and most important places—North Sea coast, and later on the Channel coast. Over the sea and water, the equipment brought good results, whereas operation over land had been bad. When the first "Wurzburg" equipment began to arrive, the great disappointment was that for the first half year we had to give it to the Flak Artillery, and only after that received it for our own use. On the Channel coast, fighter pilots complained more and more because British fighters received much more accurate data through radar equipment. From now on, the equipment came into the Air Reporting Service to the aid of the fighters. From that moment I could plan the organization. I combined three "Freya" sets with one "Wurzburg" set. In any case, the Air Reporting Service put forth its most concentrated effort in aid of the German fighters. We brought this company organization in close contact with the fighters. At first the plotting stations of one company, later of 3 companies (Abteilung), collaborated closely with the fighters. The plotting stations of the radio interception service were run from the same basis.

4. Question: If you had all the necessary apparatus at your disposal, what would your set-up have been like at the beginning of the war, or would the entire development have been step by step?

Answer: The "big plan" was the one dealing with 200 "Freya" and 800 "Wurzburg" sets.

5. Question: Were "Wurzburg" sets ever exclusively manufactured for the purpose of Air Reporting?

Answer: Originally yes; then, however, they were first put at the disposal of the Flak Artillery, because their accurate apparatus did not function properly.

6. Question: When did you decide to order these "Freya" and "Wurzburg" sets?

Answer: Before the war (cannot remember exact time). The first 12 "Freya" sets were already in operation at the outbreak of the war (the first big success in the air battle near Heligoland).

7. Question: How was it possible for you to obtain "Freya" equipment from the Navy?

Answer: The Navy was very cooperative and demonstrated the development of their equipment to us. Our own Technical Office had as yet not progressed this far. The (private) firm "Telefunken" was developing a similar device. In 1936–37 the Navy (Kriegsmarine) demonstrated the "Freya" equipment. This demonstration showed that over sea and water the apparatus worked well, while over land it had not as yet been proven and no good results had been attained so far. But it was hoped that it could be improved. From these facts, I concluded that this equipment (radar) could be well used for a multitude of purposes (Flying Safety—Radio Interception—and Air Reporting Service). Consequently, the Navy asked whether I was interested and if I wanted some of the equipment. The Navy was also interested in building up its own little experimental firm. I, of course, replied with the keenest interest, and asked them to supply me with 12 of these sets.

8. Question: You recognized the importance of this equipment for the Air Reporting Service. Was your opinion shared by the Chief of the General Staff? If so, why?

Answer: Of course it was recognized by the Chief of Staff, and considered to be very important. But, at the insistence of the Flak Artillery, the equipment was first given to them, because they had to be helped under all circumstances, since the "Lorenz" set, which was developed for the Flak Artillery, proved to be inferior to our "Wurzburg" set. For actual mobile fighter warfare, the equipment was not absolutely necessary, since the advance was very swift. The Flak Artillery wanted this equipment for the air defense of the home territory.

Concurrent with the permission for my use of these sets in dayfighting, arose the demand of the nightfighter. I knew that it would be a great help and obtained permission to put 3 or 6 air reporting companies with such equipment at the dispersal of nightfighters. After General Kammhuber, who thus far employed searchlights, became aware of the first successes of the new equipment, he came with the request for additional sets (for the nightfighters). The manufacturing of this equipment for dayfighting had to be cut down somewhat, since the Flak Artillery also had to be considered. As a result of this, the most concentrated effort of the entire organization of the Air Reporting Service was shaped by the nightfighters for some time. In my opinion, the regrettable fact was that, for the time being, General Kammhuber was only in command of the nightfighters and not of the dayfighters also. This also was the cause for various changes in our organization, because later on he also took over the command of the dayfighters (in his territory in Holland).

While, again, there was hardly any nightfighting in the sphere of the Luftflotte 3 (France), the entire radar operations were determined in consideration of the dayfighters (general Air Reporting Service and dayfighting). But since nightfighting gained great importance in the defense of the home territory, Luftflotte 3 had to take second place with its needs for dayfighters. From the beginning, Luftflotte 3 merged the eye-ear Air Reporting Service into this radar organization, which at first was made up of platoons and then of combined units. In nightfighting, it appeared, after some time, that this organization leaned solely on the radar service and was not very successful, but that in case of interference (jamming) of the equipment an eye-ear-service is needed. By this time, it had also become easier to make long term plans for the organization of the Air Reporting Service.

9. Question: Who decided the question, whether radar was to be used in the Reich?

Answer: The decision was made either by the Chief of the General Staff or by the Reichsmarshall personally.

10. Question: Who acted or advised on this matter?

Answer: From the technical and strategic point of view, I advised the Chief of the General Staff. The Chief of the General Staff was present when I put my case to the Reichsmarshall. From an operational point of view, it was the Commanding General of the nightfighters, the Commanding General of the fighters, and the Commanding General of the Flak Artillery who acted as advisors.

11. Question: Did the commanders of the fighter forces make their own requests?

Answer: The branch generals (Waffengenerale) did. These were General of the Fighter Forces, Molders (later Galland); General of Nightfighters, Kammhuber; and General of the Flak Artillery, Von Axthelm. They all stated their own requirements. In addition to these came the chiefs of the Luftflotten

(Sperrle, etc.), independent of the Waffengenerals, who said, "Seen from my point of view I need this and that."

12. Question: Did you have the intention of using directed fighter control at the outbreak of war?

Answer: Fighter control was intended in so far as we hoped to determine the place of interception with our recognition equipment. Ground directed fighter control was as yet not required. But it was already considered before the advance started. At present, I can't remember anything from pre-war times. From the technical standpoint, it was impossible to install this system any sooner, since it was entirely insufficient. We had the recognition apparatus which operated as counter part to the "Wurzburg" etc. It was possible to determine the approximate general direction from which the a/c approached, in azimuth.

13. Question: Was fighter control developed after you had gathered your experiences in the Battle of Britain?

Answer: The first encounter on the North Sea coast already led to the development of some sort of fighter control there, which was completely by and by, i.e. from platoon to platoon. As a result of individual successes on the North Sea coast, later on the Channel and in the Atlantic, fighters began flight by flight to recognize control from the ground. We, on the other hand, suggested and furthered this in nightfighting from the beginning. Mounting successes were now reported from the Channel.

Ever increasing emphasis was now put on control from the ground. But then came the disappointment, for the recognition apparatus of the "Wurzburg" set did not function. Now I made a great personal effort to obtain the introduction of the recognition apparatus for the "Freya" set. For this purpose, we had given this recognition apparatus different recognition signs.

14. Question: In your opinion, was the radar system adequate at the end of the war?

Answer: We got what we needed for fighter control. We had a picture of the situation, and we could carry out control. Unfortunately, we were not up to perfection in centimeter technique.

15. Question: If the war had continued, what would your demands have been? On the cm wave?

Answer: To continue work on the shortest waves with all urgency, although even in this field one can expect surprises. I had particularly stressed the need not only for cm, but also for mm waves. We even aimed not merely at being equal, but at getting the lead in developments. Consequently, I had also demanded that all electrical engineers be withdrawn from front line troops and all officers drawn into the scheme.

16. Question: You said that at the end of the war the radar reporting service arrangements were adequate. But supposing we had changed from massed to single aircraft attacks?

Answer: There were weaknesses, but we could overcome many of them because we had this large, highly experienced organization in which everyone worked with great enthusiasm. It compensated for backwardness in respect to the cm wave. On the other hand, our cm waves were well advanced in development.

17. Question: Was not the whole system somewhat too clumsy?

Answer: The system was not yet complete. It suffered from being an amalgamation of the following totally different organizations:

(a) The old a/c reporting service.
(b) The organization created specifically for nightfighting.
(c) The organization which was chiefly a radar organization for daylight fighting.
(d) The organization for Flak Artillery.

Because for a long time daylight fighting, nightfighting, and Flak Artillery were controlled by different command posts in the same area, the a/c Reporting Service was not a completely unified organization, from the start, although it belonged to the same branch of service. Only when the command became more highly concentrated was a final basis created for incorporating this into a completely unified organization and operational unification (January 1944). But this system never became fully operational, as the wire communications could not be readjusted quickly enough.

18. Question: You said the system proved successful during mass attacks. But how was it at the end of the war, when there were a great number of night attacks? Could everything be transmitted with sufficient speed at that time?

Answer: On the whole, it could be reported quickly enough. But, during the final period, many apparatuses were destroyed by enemy action and many communications cut, so that the transmission of messages was obviously rendered more difficult. I do believe that such single attacks were more difficult for us and certainly made the whole thing more confusing. Without the other effects of battle, we would have managed well enough for control. The system, as ordered in January 1944, proved very successful wherever it was completed.

19. Question: How great a part did the Navy play in supplying you with early information?

Answer: Not a very large one. When RAF bomber Group 100 and the other means of disturbance were troubling us so very much, we made an experiment with U-boats. We wanted to keep the U-boats near the British coast. But the Navy was against it. The experiment was never completed. Advance boats passed on reports of approaching aircraft which were intercepted on the coast, but they were of no great importance. The naval radar organization, on the other hand, cooperated extensively with us. But at harbor fortresses this somewhat separate organization sometimes caused minor frictions, which led to delays despite the best will for cooperation.

20. Question: What weaknesses did you discover in the Allied radar organization?

Answer:
(a) First of all, it was very easy for us to home in on your airborne high frequency apparatus. This was a great help to us in many respects.
(b) Sometimes we could recognize your running-in lanes.
(c) We could make quite good use of navigational aids (e.g. Gee).
(d) We could find out from certain signs in the signal traffic whether there would be an attack at night or not.

21. Question: Do you think there were further possibilities of making better use of radar than we did? Or had you any plans for developing and making wider use of radar?

Answer: The answer to both questions is about the same. It was inevitable that this device would be used more and more widely (e.g. for blind firing). For daylight fighting it could be developed so that the exact distance of a plane could be determined, even at very long range, and last but not least so that jamming would be entirely eliminated.

Chapter 9

Luftwaffe Radars and Radios
Interrogation of OKL Staff

1. Question: Give basic directions for radar operation by the Air Force for the defense of (a) a strategic point, (b) a strategic area. Who was competent to promulgate the above instructions? What errors and deficiencies have now become apparent?

Answer: The Commanding Signal Officer of the High Command of the Air Force was responsible for drawing up the instructions for the use of radar. The tactical directives for its use in the aircraft warning service and the fighter control service were issued by the Commanding Signal Officer of the Air Force, Department 1. The techno-tactical directives were issued by the Commanding Signal Officer of the Air Force, Department 6. Detailed descriptions of the various operational methods, proven at the front or suggested by new technological achievements were also contained in the (techno-tactical) directives.

Fundamental errors in radar operation in air defense cannot be detected, because it fully satisfied the demands made upon it till the end of the war (aerial position arrangement and fighter control).

Deficiencies were manifold and were also recognized at the time. They were caused by development and general situation and hardly to be remedied. For instance, insufficient training of officers. Cause: Continuous transfer of indispensable air signal officers to the parachute troops, making tactical instruction, which is absolutely necessary, impossible.

Installation of too many radar instruments, necessitated by the development of the air defense organization (belated amalgamation of radar orientation service with ocular-oral Air Warning Service, which in turn was caused by the time element necessary for night pursuit development and installation of the equipment for these purposes only. Lack of effective air defense organization: Fighter Corps—Air Force Administrative Command).

(a) Fundamental directions for installation of radar for the defense of a *strategic point* were not given, because they developed automatically in building

173

up for the main efforts, and because the objective of radar for air position arrangement must be overall coverage.

Only in exceptional cases (e.g. Ruhr Valley and hydrogenation plants) were special radar sets installed in the immediate neighborhood of the object to be guarded, in order to take air position more quickly and in a more specialized manner according to the problems and nature of the strategic point. In that case, the installation of radar depended upon the terrain, signal communication and incorporation into the aircraft warning service In regard to the use of radar, the installation service stations were given comparatively wide latitude.

Special instructions were given concerning the use of separate radar instruments for the protection of airfields near the front (airfield protective apparatus). They were meant primarily for airfields used by daylight fighters, in order to eliminate surprise attacks, made possible by delayed or inaccurate transmission of the aerial situation or by line disturbances.

Since the beginning of 1945, the command of the air maintained by the enemy in the entire western area of the Reich had made the use of radar necessary for all occupied airbases in that area; it proved to be very effective.

It was demanded that the installation be made in the immediate neighborhood

of the airbase, with the possibility of search in all directions and safe communication connection with the airbase, or the task forces shifted by it. As these apparatuses were not assigned to the general Aircraft Warning Organization, they could be used only for these purposes. The earlier assignment to the signal company of the bombardment wings was unsatisfactory, because the equipment was rather cumbersome, and could not be moved readily so as to keep pace with the faster shifting of the task forces; on arrival

Bomb damage, Nuremberg, April 1945. (US National; Archives)

at a new airfield, they found themselves without radar equipment. For that reason, these instruments were put under the command of the local aircraft warning units in the spring of 1944. . . .

(b) The following are the instructions concerning coverage by radar of a strategical area:

(1) Securing an outpost area, as extensive as possible (preferably on the coast) by the use of long range search equipment in dual emplacement.
(2) Securing a total coverage, i.e. continuous surveillance of the entire sky of a particular strategical area.
(3) Consideration of the conditions of the terrain with a view to including as much terrain as possible.
(4) Consideration of the existing signal communications, especially the junctions, with the view of bringing into easy reach all beneficiaries of the air position. . . .

2. Question: Describe the established methods of operation for every type of radio station in the airplane fighter control system.

Answer: Regarding the operation by radio, there are two types of communication to be distinguished in the airplane fighter control service.

(a) Ground to ground radio traffic.
(b) Ground to board radio traffic.

In order to meet the necessary requirements, of greatest possible speed and avoidance of delay, important for the fighter control service, we were forced, in general, to give up the idea of an effective coding system because it takes up time.

Ground to ground radio traffic: The ground to ground radio communications in the fighter control service served as a superimposition on the wire communications and were used only when these wire communications were interfered with by air attacks or through other causes. The coding of information relating to orders and messages which were effective only after some time was undertaken with air force codes, according to the methods of operation of the ground radio traffic or the air force. Code charts, especially those set up by the I Fighter Corps, were used for immediately effective information, and were, essentially, an abbreviation of the text in clear and were changed only from time to time.

Appropriate orders were supposed to prevent strategic information from being transmitted in this manner. Its use was permitted only for matters which were effective immediately.

Radio telephone traffic in place of CW transmissions was also partly used, which was abbreviated with the help of the customary code charts for the Reich Defense used otherwise only in the ground to board radio traffic.

In a similar manner, radio communications were installed as a superimposition on the aircraft warning wires, and the radio traffic was conducted by CW transmission with the help of the aircraft warning code chart.

Ground to board traffic: The ground to board radio traffic in daylight fighting was conducted only by radio telephone traffic because of the apparatus of the daylight fighter airplanes. The messages were abbreviated and camouflaged with the aid of the code chart for the Reich Defense. Lately, as a supplement to the code chart, a fighter airplane coding sheet, which changed daily, was published, with the aid of which the coding of place, time and altitude indication was possible.

Because of the interferences caused by the enemy, various methods of operation in the use of nightfighter airplanes were employed in order to avoid these interferences and yet guarantee adequate security in the operation and message transmission, namely:

(a) Radio telephone methods with the ultra short waves (radio set FuG 16) according to the methods of the daylight fighter airplanes with the aid of the Reich Defense code chart.

(b) Ultra short wave CW transmission with the aid of heavy ultra short wave transmitters on the ground for overcoming enemy interference. The CW transmission was abbreviated with the aid of the existing codes in the Reich Defense code chart or with the help of the code chart published by the first fighting corps.

(c) CW transmission by short wave was made as described under (b).

(d) Reporting by radio telephone over long wave transmitters was accomplished in the same manner as described under (a).

(e) Reporting over radio broadcasting stations was provided for, but was used only to a small extent. At times, it was attempted to transmit rough reports on the radio program by blending it with music in various ways.

The methods of operation for night fighting described above were used sometimes singly, and sometimes simultaneously (for overcoming enemy interference). At times, different reports or reports on other waves were carried on for the purpose of deception.

3. Question: How was contact with the airplanes maintained when they penetrated deep into enemy territory beyond the range of the usual ground apparatus?

Answer: Outside of the range of the radar orientation instrument, contact or communication with the daylight fighter airplanes in the depth of enemy territory was possible only within the limits of optical visibility. The service range could be increased by the erection of a powerful ground radio apparatus on an especially high elevation, and the control range could be extended by the erection of "Freya-Egon" apparatus on a high location, but only within the limits of optical visibility. Because we did not have air superiority, the fulfilment of this requirement was not necessary, and, apart from special equipment with short or long wave radio, no solution to this problem could be seen.

4. Question: What changes have been made in the fighter control system since 1937, including apparatus, frequencies, installations and equipment, and special apparatus? How was the system coordinated with changes, occurring in the tactical situation?

5. Question: What changes were made in the fighter control method when the offensive warfare changed to a defensive one?

Answers to 4 and 5:

Daylight fighting: Until the middle of 1940 (end of mobile warfare during the campaign in France), there was, with the exception in the German Bay, only one fighter control method used in the German Air Force, namely: *visual fighter control service with radio telephone communication* for location of enemy *at and above the fronts.*

This service was conducted by anti-aircraft companies (motorized). The anti-aircraft detachments had special radio squads.

Frequency range of the ground radio sets depended on the board radio set of the fighter airplanes. At first, short wave set (radio set X, ground) was used as counter station for radio set VII (airborne set), later radio set 16 (FuG 16) (ground) was used as counter station for radio set 16 (airborne). This method, tried out for the first time during the Spanish campaign, was perfected during the war and used successfully at mobile and stationary fronts until the end of the war. It corresponded to the ideas of strategic use of the Air Force and has proved excellent during the Polish and Western campaigns and on the Russian front during both advance and retreat.

In late fall of 1939, at the beginning of the British formation attacks, a *direction finding net for fighter control purposes* was established for the first time in the German Bay, using short wave at first because of the board radio set VII, and ultra short waves as soon as the daylight fighters were equipped with radio set 16, which was the middle of 1940.

At the end of mobile warfare in France, this direction finding organization was also used on the Channel and gradually on the entire coastal fronts (including Norway).

Direction finders were used for this purpose which transmitted their results to a direction finder central station at the headquarters of the commander of fighter units. Later on, the airborne radio set was provided with a switch clock, similar to the British "Pip Squeak," in order to obtain position reports at regular short intervals. But this switch clock was never used generally. It was made obsolete by introduction of other control methods, and the manufacturing plants were damaged by bombing.

From this method, the *direction finding call method* was developed, which was used for air defense in special cases until the end of the war (direction finding of the radio telephone traffic, of the formation leader, or of a leader of a two-ship element, especially selected therefore).

Along with the further extension of the direction finder net, the "Y" method was used generally after the autumn of 1941 for fighter control purposes, it having been tested successfully in the Heligoland Bight since the beginning of 1941. This method had the advantage, compared to the direction finding method, of greater accuracy and speedier position finding. The "Y" method meant considerable improvement in the German fighter control and proved very successful up to the end of the war.

For the control of single airplanes, no change in the method was necessary until the end of the war, except for improvement of accuracy of direction and range finding. For control of formations, the dependence of the method on the board radio telephone had certain disadvantages, especially on systematic jamming by the enemy; but these disadvantages could be eliminated by a special method of operation (Altrogge method, with special control airplanes). The entire territory of the Reich was organized for control by this method and used until the end of the war.

The possibility of interference when using the "Y" method made an alternate method necessary. This came with the introduction of the "Erstling." Through utilization of the extensive direction finding possibilities of the "Erstling," the "Egon" method was developed. By using "Freya" instruments with a wavelength of 2.40 m and disconnected reflection receiver, these instruments could be used in the air, similarly to the "Y" installation on the ground, and gave a satisfactory running picture of a particular situation. But because of the limited readability of the marker beam signal, the number of airplanes controlled by this method had to be relatively small, or else use of this signal had to be given up. This was easily possible during daylight fighting since only 2–3 airplanes of the tight formations switched on their marker beam signal. The advantage of this method was its increased security against interference. Not a single interference was reported up to the end of the war.

The strength of the control dependability of the German daylight fighters during air defense lay in the combined use of both of these methods. After development was finished at the end of 1944, many more daylight fighter formations could have been guided by these methods than were actually flown.

Nightfighting: Since nightfighting, except for long-range night pursuit, can only be used for air defense, only defensive control systems for nightfighters were necessary. The development of fighter controls was influenced by technical progress and enemy air invasion tactics. As early as at the end of 1938, an especially capable fighter control officer had invented the "AN" method for bad weather daylight invasion and had tested it during the first dark nightfighter penetration. It corresponded to the penetration tactics employed by the enemy at that time, i.e. use of single airplanes. This method (Relative method) cannot be surpassed as far as accuracy is concerned, but it requires a high level of training of the fighter control officer and the radar crew. Since it was necessary to develop the nightfighter control organization on a large scale, the "Seeburg-Tisch" method was devised using at first "Wurzburg" and, from 1942, "Wurzburg-Riese" apparatus. Both these methods corresponded absolutely to the enemy penetration tactics of invasion in width; they proved very successful during this entire period (formation nightfighting).

When, towards the fall of 1943, the enemy changed his penetration tactics fundamentally, these methods no longer met with the same success, since the flying time of the tight bomber formation was of short duration, relatively few nightfighter control stations were touched, and, consequently, only a relatively small number of nightfighters could be brought into action by control.

While retaining the best dark nightfighter regions, a new fighter control method for night pursuit became necessary. This was already at hand in the developments made for daylight fighting (fighter control station with "Y" ground installations and "Freya-Egon" apparatus), and could be used directly for nightfighting. Since the chances to succeed for nightfighters are considerably better when each individual nightfighter is controlled separately and guided into the bomber formation, several minor amplifications of apparatus at the fighter control stations had to be made.

Driven by the severe losses caused by this defense method, the enemy developed especially ingenious feints, flying evasive action during the approach run, dividing the bomber formation, etc. This made fighter control especially difficult since, the instance from the time evasive action in the bomber formation was recognized until actual change of course of the nightfighter, so much time elapsed that it was often impossible to locate the bomber formation. Therefore, a decentralization of nightfighter command and control was made necessary, so that orders to attack could be given the moment the correct enemy position was determined.

The nightfighter action control by the radar counter station of the first class with connected fighter control stations was most promising in this case. Lack of nightfighters and fuel, and the sudden end of the war, prevented this very promising method from being used.

Questions:

I

1. Give position of all air force and military radio, telephone, and radar stations within the Luftgau VI and XI.

   a. Purpose.
   b. Types and quantities of equipment necessary for this purpose.

II. Radar
2. Discuss ground installations for detection and warning, fighter control, bomber control, and air traffic safety control ("Wurzburg -Laude").
3. Discuss aircraft equipment for detection and for the support of bombing operations, firing weapons, altimeters, warning and signal equipment.
4. Discuss radar films (panoramic films).
5. Discuss radar countermeasures and radar jamming countermeasures.

Answers:

1. Preliminary remarks:
a. In the absense of all written data, the following exposition has been written from memory. They must therefore not be taken as being 100% reliable either quantitatively or qualitatively. The most important supplementary and comparative data are at the disposal of the intelligence service in the War diary

Documents with operational index cards and other appendices. These were dug up in May near Berchtesgaden by an officer on the Signals Officer General Staff.

b. In accordance with a second interview with the Intelligence Service, the expression "within the Luftgau VI and XI" is used only to determine a geographical area and not the extent of a command. As is well known, all radar stations, etc., of the Aircraft Warning Service and the Fighter Command were subordinate to the fighter division (who, in cooperation with the air force administrative command HQ, themselves supervised the installation of the stations), whereas the Radar Service of flak units was subordinate to the Luftgau, as were the flak units themselves.

2. Ground installations:

a. *Purpose and task:* The provision of radar data for the air situation picture for the Fighter Command and the Aircraft Warning Service in the approach sector opposite the east coast of England. This necessitated:

1. The location of as extensive as possible an apron above the sea by means of a connected chain of efficient radar stations along the coast.
2. Following on from these, a chessboard-like, internally overlapping radar system in the German antiaircraft defense area, to ensure unbroken control over the main land. Distinction must be made between radar stations of the

first order		for technical
second order	}	equipment
third order		see par. 3

b. *Location*

1. Radar positions of the first order in the coastal chain were located (from south to north) at:

Flushing (Walcheren) (Netherlands)
Birelu (Brielle) (Netherlands)
Zandvoort (Netherlands)
Den Helder (Netherlands)
Terschelling (Frisians) (Netherlands)
Schierimonnikogg (Frisians) (Netherlands)

Juist
Helgoland
Sinruin (southern part of Sylt)
Ribe (Denmark)
Blaavands Huk (Denmark)
Soenderrig (Denmark)
Thisted (Hanstholm) (Denmark)
Loekken (Denmark)
Skagen (Denmark)

c. Among the technically and tactically most important radar stations of the first order in the form of the interivew were the stations near:

Dusseldorf near Kylburg (southern Eifel)
Geilenkirchen
Harderwijk
Rheine (in Westphalia)
Cloppenburg
between Lüneburg and Buxtehude
Heiligenhaus near Mettonann (Ruhr)
Siegen
Korbach
Steinhuder Meer
between Brunswick and Peine
near Salzwedel
on the island of Fehmann
near Karow (Mecklenburg)

d. For fighter control a series of Freya instruments were established – according to the physical conditions usually on high ground.

1. "Egon" Control Station
   Because of their similarity of purpose and long range corresponding to physical location, "Egon" and "Benito" installations were often immediately contiguous and organizationally continued. Such stations were located, for instance, near Arnhem, Remscheid, Paderborn, Vever and Stade. The exact locations in the northwest and north of the German defense zone can be seen by reference to the operational index cards (cf. Preliminary remarks, par. 1).

2. In addition, all radar stations equipped with " 'Freya' instruments on original wavelength" were, of course, able to make use of the recognition system for distinguishing friendly from enemy planes and for fighter control.

3. "Egon" installations were intended to be suitable for bomber control as well. Whether "Egon" stations in northwest Germany or in the Dutch zone were used for the control of bomber operations against England, and later for the control of bombers and close support airplanes on the Western front, cannot be ascertained here and now.

4. The extent of and technical details concerning the operations of the radar air traffic control system ("Wurzburg-Laude" system) in the area under discussion cannot at present be ascertained.

e. Technical equipment. This usually included the instruments tabulated below:

Radar station	Type and number of instruments	Range*
1st order	1 long range search instrument (Wassermann)	250–300 km
	2 or 3 medium range search instruments ("Freya")	150–200 km
	2 instruments for precise height finding and short range enemy or friendly control ("Wurzburg-Reise")	
	1 Panorama (Jagdschloss)	100 km
	a large plotting center, with various facilities for fighter control and appropriate telephone, radio and other connections and installations (including radio beacons and beacon lights)	
2nd order	1 or 2 medium range search instruments ("Freya")	
	2 "Wurzburg-Riese" instruments	
	a smaller plotting and signals center	
3rd order	1 medium range search instrument ("Freya")	
	2 "Wurzburg-Riese" instruments	
	Seeburg plotting	

* The ranges indicated apply to formations at sufficient altitude or to four-engined single targets, in the absence of major interferences of all kinds.

The technical equipment of stations of the first order was sometimes supplemented by the following technical measures or additional instruments.

1. Additional switching gear on Wassermann instruments for the detection of planes at high altitudes and for height finding.
2. "Freya elevators" for long range height finding.
3. Long range search instruments, "Elefant," working on long wavelengths (used only on the coast).
4. Use of "Freya" instruments with a wave range lower and extended into the range of the Allied radio instruments, so that the "Flamme" system (reading of enemy recognition instruments) could be used.

f. Several stations, mostly of the first order, were, in addition, otherwise equipped, or in the process of being equipped, with radar search equipment. Details concerning this could be obtained from the senior Signals Officer General, Abteilung 3.

3. Aircraft equipment:

What has been said in "Preliminary Remarks II" is even more widely applicable to this field. The Luftgau had no immediate influence upon aircraft equipment. Only in the few cases, in which the operations of aircraft equipment were closely connected with ground operations in the Luftgau command area (e.g. cooperation of the "Freya" instruments of the flak division with the recognition instruments in an aircraft) could the Luftgau make certain demands concerning the equipment and its working. The control of the equipment of planes with radar instruments and the current supervision of their technical working condition was solely a matter for the flying units and their superior command posts. In the north and northwest area, the following radar aircraft instruments were to be found:

a. *Nightfighters*
   "Lichtenstein B/C" (going out of use)
   "Lichtenstein S/N2" with all its variants
   "Neptun V"
   "Naxos 2"
   "Flensburg"
   "Berlin" (experimental)

b. *Bombers*
Specific bomber radar instruments, comparable to the British H2S or to the American Meddo instruments, were not yet in use.

c. Radar firing equipment was, according to our knowledge, not yet in use.

d. *Height finders*
Low altitude finders, Siemens type, were installed in all planes. The stage to which the equipment of planes with radar height finders for high altitudes had developed is not known here.

e. *Warning instruments*
    "Lichtenstein R"
    "Neptun R"

f. *Recognition instruments (FF)*
Radio equipment FuG 25a in its original form. How far variants of radio equipment FuG 25a (several frequencies) were used in this connection is not known.

4. Displays—Films for Radar:
By the appropriate continuation of current photos of major target approaches, extremely instructive and revealing films had been made for several Jagdschloss tubes, e.g. at the Jagdschloss installations southwest of Darmstadt and near Hardenwijk. The most numerous and, from the point of view of being complete, most interesting films were made in the Berlin area where, as is well known, there were 3 Panorama instruments always kept at the latest stage of technical developoment (including long distance data transmission system to the central flak command post). A fairly large quantity of these films were still obtainable there in January of this year, partly through the Chief of Air Technical Equipment and partly through the following firms: Gemo, Lorenz, Siemens, Telefunken. Details should be obtainable from these firms and from the Chief of Air Technical Equipment.

   In addition, there were instructional films for training in the use of special instruments, e.g. "Lichtenstein SN 2," "Entdueppelung" (countermeasures for "Window" interference), etc.

5. Radar Countermeasures and Radar Interference Elimination Measures:
Under this heading the Germans include radar search and radar jamming service, radar deception and screening, as well as active and passive countermeasures against active and passive interference. Without data, it is impossible to take up a position beyond the making of general statements.

Chapter 10

The Me-262
Development, Experience, Success, and Prospects
by Dr Willi Messerschmitt

Attack planes or defense planes? This was the question on which the German Air Force High Command could not reach a definite decision throughout the war.

Professor Messerschmitt was of the opinion that Germany needed mainly defense planes, primarily fighters. Once military aircraft had to be built, his whole activities as a designer were concentrated on the light and fast fighter. The results of his work are well known—Me-109, Me-110 and Me-410.

At a very early date, it was clear to designers of fast aircraft that the use of air-propellers would be limited with increasing flying speeds, i.e., their efficiency would become less and their top speed would probably not exceed 700 km ph (420 mph). For great speed, other means of propulsion would have to be found.

Attempts were therefore made to develop new types of drive. Professor Messerschmitt took a very active part in this research, starting experimental work in his own plant. The methods of propulsion which he considered were the theoretically known, but undeveloped jet engine and rocket drive, both based on the recoil principle.

Both types were very quickly developed in Germany to the point of readiness for combat assignments. The Me-163—a rocket plane also created in the Messerschmitt plant—is universally known. While the Me-163 developed speeds of over 1,000 km ph (600 mph), its rockets afforded an operational time of from only 16 to 20 minutes. At the end of that period the machine had to rely on gliding.

Conditions were different in the jet or turbine-propelled planes. These had

Willi Messerschmitt and *Luftwaffe* General Erhard Milch, in 1937. (US National Archives)

Willi Messerschmitt (left) meets Hitler at a function in Augsburg, 25 May 1939. (US National Archives)

reached a stage of development as early as 1942 which enabled them to keep the air for about 40 to 50 minutes with the quantity of fuel (Diesel oil) that could be carried in a fighter.

The first jet-propelled fighters (Me-262) were completed and flight-tested in spring 1942. They were designed for speeds around 1,000 km ph (600 mph) and constructed with special consideration to the aerodynamic features involved. Two characteristics were high wing loading and sharply sweptback wings. As confirmed by foreign specialists after the war, this design embodied principles which were not generally known to aircraft experts in 1945.

Professor Messerschmitt and his staff were greatly disappointed in 1942 when this excellent high-speed plane, which seemed predestined for the role of a successful fighter, failed to capture the attention of the Air Ministry and the German Air Force Command. At that time they were interested solely in long-range fighters and bombers. The jet fighter prototypes were therefore shelved and left to rot.

However, when in 1943 Allied bombers became a growing menace to the existence and security of towns in the heart of Germany, the matter was reconsidered upon Professor Messerschmitt's untiring representations. The need for an efficient defense plane was recognized in the highest quarters, and the Me-262 jet fighter fulfilled requirements.

The Allied Mosquito fighter escorts were superior to the German Me-109 and FW-190 fighters. Moreover, Allied bomb raids were invariably preceded by daylight reconnaissance, and the Mosquitoes made the German skies their playground without fear of interference by the German Air Force. Realizing the situation, the Air Force High Command ordered preparations to be made for speedy serial construction of the Me-262 jet fighter. Discontinuation of the testing of the prototypes built in 1942 now proved to be a lamentable drawback. In consequence, it became necessary to conduct experimental work and flight-testing along with the preparations for serial construction, and this task was rendered all the more difficult since the Me-262 involved principles which lay in the extreme limits of technical and physical knowledge. There were other handicaps, such as the discovery that the runway of the plant airfield at Augsburg was too short for effective experimental work. As a result, although processing of results remained the responsibility of the Augsburg plant, flight testing had to be done on the Leipheim airfield (90 km west of Augsburg, near Ulm) and later at Lechfeld (25 km south of Augsburg) after the runway on that field had been extended.

Finally, on 26 February 1944, the Augsburg plant of the Messerschmitt A.G., including its experimental institute, was completely destroyed in an air raid. The experimental and testing department was transferred to Lechfeld, where it had to be completely rebuilt. Despite all these difficulties, the plane was developed into a reliable and efficient defense weapon in the course of a few months and certified ready for serial production.

To provide for early training of fighter pilots capable of handling the Me-262 in combat assignments, C-in-C German Air Force set up a training and test staffel in Leipheim. There, the Air Force personnel and the men of the Messerschmitt plant cooperated with mutual gain. The former had combat experience and could give the technicians many valuable hints on points of design.

The Air Force personnel soon familiarized themselves with the new plane and asked permission to fight enemy reconnaissance machines and bomber formations. This permission was granted. A radio control station ("Y" method) was soon set up at Lechfeld, and the planes were equipped with the necessary receiving sets. The task of the control station was to direct the fighters to within sight of the enemy as quickly as possible or to draw the enemy formation on.

An Me 262 single-seat day fighter in primer finish. (US National Archives)

While only a few Me 262B jet night-fighters saw operational service, they were able to inflict painful losses on the RAF's Mosquito Pathfinder and reconnaissance aircraft, which Bomber Command had come to rely on as integral parts of their tactics. The Me 262B reportedly achieved about 50 kills in 70 night attacks in the last six months of the war. (US National Archives)

It reported the approach of enemy planes and then guided the fighters towards them.

Up to that time, Mosquitoes had been free to scout almost daily over the Lechfeld area, and there was a well-planned bomber attack almost once a week. With all these disturbances, it was a most harassing experience to conduct experimental and development work, and in retrospect it appears almost unbelievable that it was nonetheless successful. Conditions changed abruptly when the Lechfeld fighter staffel commenced operations.

As the Me-262 did not carry nightfighting equipment, the staffel operated only by day. The results were convincing. When enemy planes were reported approaching from a distance of 200 to 300 km (120–180 miles), the Lechfeld staffel got ready for action. Almost all enemy reconnaissance planes reported were shot down. In one case, which is on record, a Mosquito pilot bailed out on the approach of an Me-262 before the latter opened fire. This testifies to the psychological effect of the Me-262, which appeared like a bolt in the sky and turned the Mosquitoes' "sightseeing" flights into very dangerous undertakings. There was but one possibility of escape, though a rather dubious one, viz., maneuvering. It is a well-known fact that a fast airplane is less quick on a turn than a slower machine. This is when the pilots had to use their judgment in estimating their opponent's next move.

The men of the test staffel were in high spirits, and justifiably so. For months, the area around Lechfeld remained free of enemy reconnaissance planes and bombers. The staffel also attacked and dispersed bomber formations, bringing down many planes. These successes, without a single jet fighter loss, kindled the pilots' ambition. This assumed such dimensions that Flight Captain Thierfelder pursued a large bomber formation single-handed. This was a very risky undertaking, and unfortunately the daring officer was shot down. C-in-C German Air Force reacted by flatly prohibiting the Lechfeld staffel from attacking the enemy. The consequences of this order for the Lechfeld staffel and the scattered Me-262 manufacturing plants were devastating. The reconnaissance planes came back and in their wake followed the bombers. Hardly a week— and by the end of 1944, hardly a day—went by without heavy attacks, or at least alerts, which interrupted the work for hours. Nonetheless, the Me-262 was developed to a high pitch of combat efficiency, and production was stepped up sufficiently to equip fighter geschwader with the new plane. These included the staffeln of 3rd Gruppe/Fighter Geschwader 7 at Brandenburg and Parchim.

Armament initially consisted of the conventional guns of 3.0 cm caliber. Later, 5 cm guns were experimentally installed. The effective range of these weapons was up to 250 meters (257 yards); in other words, the fighter pilot had to get within that distance of his opponent before opening fire. Due to the high speed of the Me-262, an engagement with a single enemy plane was not very dangerous, but—as mentioned before—for the very same reason "dog fights" were not a very easy matter. For this combat technique, special sighting equipment was developed, but the members of the Messerschmitt staff did not become acquainted with this as it was always installed in military establishments.

Conditions were different where jet fighters attacked compact bomber formations. The latter carried defense weapons of ever increasing caliber, number and range. The range finally amounted to 800 meters (880 yards). Before opening fire, the Me-262 had to approach to within 250 meters (257 yards). The most daredevil pilots went as close as 50 meters (55 yards). It is obvious that this led to high losses among the Me-262 fighters and the death of some of the best pilots.

Efforts were made to remedy this situation. The solution was a rocket projectile, type R4M, caliber 5.5 cm. This had a range of from 900 to 1,200 meters (990 to 1,300 yards). The missiles were carried on wooden lattice structures below the wings and fired at intervals of .4 seconds by means of a stepwise progressive switch ("Schrittschalter"). The staffel at Parchim was the first to be so equipped; this was early in 1945. When fired from a distance of

The twelve operational Me 262B-1a/l1 night-fighters were equipped with the improved FuG 218 "Neptun" V radar and the FuG 350 ZG "Naxos" radar detector (which homed in on H2S transmissions). (US National Archives)

850 to 900 meters (935 to 990 yards), some of these R4M missiles generally scored hits, and each hit brought down a B-17 bomber.

A combat assignment including 8 to 10 Me-262 fighters almost invariably resulted in the shooting down of 6 to 8 B-17 bombers without losses to the attacking fighters. In consequence, the bomber formations were almost always routed and deprived of their striking power. Dispersed formations were then disposed of by individual Me-262 planes without excessive risk to the latter.

The advent of the Me-262 was anticipated by the fighter geschwaders with considerable excitement, and, wherever planes of this type were allocated, they were enthusiastically received as a superior and reliable weapon. On the part of the enemy, they caused a feeling of uncertainty and dismay wherever they made their appearance.

Unfortunately, no attention was paid to them in Germany for nearly two years, otherwise they might have been available earlier and would at least have saved many towns from destruction.

An Me-262 formation from Fighter Geschwader 7 was transferred to Prague in March 1945 and utilized for ground strafing, but there are no records of its achievements.

In fall 1944, the Me-262 jet fighter reached a speed of 1,075 km ph (768 mph) in level flight. This speed was recorded by accurate instruments. The power plants for these planes were built by Junkers in Dessau.

At the instigation of the German Air Ministry, the possibilities of utilizing the Me-262 as a bomber were investigated in 1945. There were at that time no suitable bomb sights for such high speeds, and it was therefore decided to accommodate the bombardier in a prone position ahead of the cockpit. These investigations involved many interesting features and brought a maze of new problems to light. It appears that, originally designed for use as a fighter, the plane required complete reconstruction to make it suitable for bombing assignments.

To develop the Me-262 for nightfighting mission and to make it proof against enemy attempts at jamming radio communication, the Messerschmitt A.G. developed an acoustic direction finder. This equipment included acoustic "feelers" which responded to the noise of enemy planes and actuated the automatic pilot, directing the plane onto the enemy. This equipment was ready by the end of the war and had a response range of about 2,000 meters (2,200 yards). It came too late for use in combat assignments. The same basic type of equipment was designed for the control of guided missiles, such as the V-1 and V-8 projects and detailed designs were prepared both for small fighters with one jet and fast bombers with 4 or 6 jet engines. This development (which was not only intended for war purposes) was interrupted by the armistice.

The German research work in this field has become generally known and is most likely to have been continued in other countries. Unfortunately, news about such developments is always concerned with military application, never with civil aviation, although the propellerless power plant could certainly be successfully utilized for commercial purposes.

PART FOUR

APPLYING THE TECHNOLOGY: OPERATIONS AND TACTICS

These chapters are about defending the Reich from the sharp end, the operations and tactics of the fighter controllers and the fighter pilots. These chapters focus on the night battle, complementing the day-fighting emphasis seen in the earlier volume *The Luftwaffe Fighter Force: The View From the Cockpit*, also published by Greenhill.

The effectiveness of these tactics, for all their drawbacks, was demonstrated by their ability to inflict painful losses on Bomber Command by night long after the day fighter force had been defeated. They are a major reason why Bomber Command suffered 63 percent of its wartime losses to fighters (as compared with 44 percent of USAAF heavy bombers lost to fighters).

D.C.I.

Chapter 11

Commanding the Nightfighters

Interrogation of General der Flieger Josef Kammhuber

4, 22, 28 August 1945

A wartime German broadcast announced the promotion, with effect from 30th January, of Generalleutnant Kammhuber to the rank of General der Flieger. This is not in any way startling and has probably no special significance as his seniority as Generalleutnant dates from November 1941.

Kammhuber was born at Burgkirchen in Bavaria on 19 August 1896. He held a temporary commission in the infantry from 1914 to 1918. About 1933 he took an active part in sports flying, which was a cover for the nucleus of GAF activity. In 1936, after the official establishment of the GAF, he was in command of the Dortmund Fliegertruppe. In 1937 he was head of the organization section in the German Air Ministry and was described as "A small, insignificant looking man of about 40, of the type who does not drink or smoke much because he cannot stand it." He is also unmarried. In January 1939 he was promoted Oberst (Group Captain).

Soon after the outbreak of war he was given an operational command as the Kommodore of a bomber geschwader, KG 51, which was based at Lechfeld. On 3 June 1940 he was shot up in France and made a forced landing at Gocherel while piloting a Ju-88 in an attack in the area south of Paris. The morale of his crew was described in the French interrogation report as high, since they refused to bale out and leave their Kommodore in the aircraft. He himself was stated to be courteous and even affable, and representative of the southern German of the pre-Hitler period. He was released at the time of the armistice.

It was at the end of 1940 that his connection with nightfighters started; in October of that year he was promoted Generalmajor and given the command of a nightfighter division, which he built up as the need for such aircraft became more apparent. In November 1941, this nightfighter division was expanded into Fliegerkorps XII, and Kammhuber was given its command as a Generalleutnant. Like Fliegerkorps XI (the airborne corps), its function was limited to one field of operation only, whereas all other Fliegerkorps consisted of different types of units based essentially on a territorial organization. All nightfighter units were subordinate to Fliegerkorps XII, and also the aircraft

195

General Josef Kammhuber—described as a "Bavarian of the old school"—always had the respect of his aircrews. When his Ju 88 was shot down over France in 1940, his crew refused to bail out and leave him. Hermann Göring placed Kammhuber in charge of night air defenses in July of 1940. This extensive network of searchlights, radar and night-fighters was based in Occupied France, Belgium and Holland. A radar-controlled master searchlight introduced in 1941 made the "Kammhuber Line" even more effective, locking onto bombers automatically with a pale blue beam until the other searchlights picked it up. (US National Archives)

reporting services which were necessary for their operation. As a result of the increasing scope of nightfighter operations, it had now been found necessary to split up the area which had to be covered, into regions. The aircraft and nightfighter ground organization in each region were controlled by a nightfighter division, which, in turn, was subordinate to Fliegerkorps XII and thus to Kammhuber.

1. Question: Give a brief history of the organization and development of the German nightfighter system.

Answer: Nightfighting was organized in July 1940 with one night fighter division, which was reorganized on 1 August 1941 and became XII Fliegerkorps. This existed until 15 September 1943. On 1 August 1941 I was appointed General der Nachtjagd (Air Officer for Nightfighting) and became responsible for development, organization and setting up of nightfighting within OKL. The beginning was made in July 1940 at first with 1 night fighter squadron (nachtjagdgruppe) and 1 searchlight regiment. Gradually, these forces increased to 3 nightfighter groups (nachtjagdgeschwader), 3 searchlight regiments and 1 air reporting battalion (flugmeldabteilung). Upon the disbandment of XII Fliegerkorps, there were six nightfighter groups. XII Fliegerkorps was subordinate to Lufwaffenbefehlshaber Mitte (Generaloberst Weise). I, the Air Officer for Nightfighters, was subordinate to CinC GAF immediately. After the disbandment of XII Fliegerkorps, the authority "Air Officer for Nightfighters" was separated from the authority fighter corps (Jagdfliegerkorps), and was combined with the authority "Air Officer for Fighters" (General der Jagdflieger—Generalmajor Galland). Under him, an inspectorate for nightfighters was organized—at first Oberst Herrmann, finally Oberstleutnant Streib.

2. Question: Did the GAF have a night fighter organization prior to the invasion of Poland?

Answer: No.

3. Question: Who first attempted nightfighting?

Answer: I believe that during World War I there was some nightfighting, and some aircraft (about 7 or 8) were shot down. Colonel Udet on his own initiative tried to carry on nightfighting (about 1936 or 1939), together with Major Schoneneck, with searchlights. From these tests, no further conclusions were drawn. Then the Ar-68 (single-seat biplane) was employed. It was the predecessor of the Bf-109.

4. Question: Was the necessity of an aircraft designed primarily for nightfighters visualized by GAF authorities prior to invasion of Poland?

Answer: No. The proposal of constructing a nightfighter plane had been discussed, but had been rejected, in the light of fundamental tactical deliberations, since a war against England had not been taken into account.

5. Question: What was the GAF original nightfighter organization?

Answer: When the night attacks from England started in July 1940, Field Marshal Kesselring took up the idea of nightfighting and moved at OKL the setting up of the first nightfighter division a few days after a formation of RAF night bombers had flown directly over his (Kesselring's) headquarters. This was done on 19 July 1940. I was C/O of this first nightfighter division. At first, there was only 1 nightfighter group (NJG). Month by month, 1 squadron (gruppe) was added up to the final strength of 7 groups (geschwader), including 1 training group. I saw to it that the nightfighter division was set up. During the first year (July 1940), Me-110 and beside the Ju-88 (old type, A-4) as well as Do- 17C were flown. Aircraft radar equipment was not yet existing. It came into use only in winter 1941/1942. In 1941 (September and December) our nightfighter activity was increased (change of tactics). The enemy air attacks forced the development of German nightfighting.

6. Question: How large a nightfighter force would have been necessary to handle the mission of defence adequately?

Answer: In summer 1943, nightfighting forces ought to have been three times stronger in order to accomplish the tasks. I had six groups, but only with 18 groups the task could have been fulfilled. The ground apparatus was exceedingly great and the actual content was too small. The employment of 18 groups from the "Himmelbett" positions ("Himmelbett"—one kind of nightfighting tactics without searchlights when the nightfighters are concentrated in certain areas ("Himmelbett" positions) and then directed against enemy bombers by R/T—was possible since at the same time the SM 2 (a radar-apparatus) was being introduced, and by this we could proceed to the nightfighting by pursuit (Verfolgunanachtjagd) from these positions. When the enemy "Window"-jamming began, on 23 July 1943, the "Himmelbett" tactics were cut short at the same moment. Then the tactics called "Wilde Sau"—"wild boar"—were employed. A/c employed in this manner fought enemy a/c over the target. Jamming was not possible. These tactics were only improvised and were dropped again (too heavy losses).

7. Question: Were nightfighters attached to dayfighter organizations at any time during the war?

Answer: Sometimes nightfighters were employed at daytime. I always objected to this. The question whether nightfighters like to be employed at daytime must be answered in the negative:

1. Because the nightfighter had to sleep at daytime.
2. Because he had no suitable a/c for daytime employment.

8. Question: Did the size of the RAF raid on Cologne tend to accelerate the expansion of the GAF nightfighter system?

Answer: No, no influence. Attacks on Cologne had an indirect influence because thereupon requests for personnel and material were approved faster and better.

9. Question: What rank commanded: (a) geschwader? (b) gruppe? (c) staffel?

Answer: Ranks of commanding officers: (a) from Captain to Colonel (should be Colonel); (b) from 1st Lieutenant to Lt. Colonel (should be Major); (c) from Lieutenant to Major (should be Captain).

10. Question: What was the proportion of pilot officers to NCOs?

Answer: The proportion of pilot officers to pilot NCOs among the successful nightfighters with kills was 75% officers: 25% NCOs. In general, the proportion of the total was 30% officers: 70% NCOs.

11. Question: Who took over command of the GAF nightfighter organization after you left, and what was his rank?
  Answer: The following had their origin in XII Fliegerkorps:
  I. Jagdkorps/General Schmid (took over when I left)
  II. Jagdkorps/General Junck
  7. Jagddivision/General Huth

12. Question: What was your rank at the time you left the organization?
  Answer: General der Flieger (ranking as Lt. General or Air Marshal)

13. Question: How were awards and decorations made to night fighter crews?
  Answer: Awards were made only for a certain number of confirmed victories.
  The "killer," mostly the pilot, was specially favored.
  The Iron Cross 2nd Class was awarded in case of 2–3 enemy a/c shot down.
  The Iron Cross 1st Class was awarded in case of 6–8 enemy a/c shot down.
  The German Cross in Gold (Deutaches Krauz in Gold) in case of about 15
     a/c shot down.
  The Knight's Cross in case of about 25 a/c shot down.
  The Oak Leaves in the case of about 50 a/c shot down.

14. Question: Was there any naval nightfighter organization?
  Answer: No. Nothing special was set up for the Navy. Once there was a ship, "Togo," for the purpose of closing the gap between Skagen and Norway. There was a nightfighter radio position on this ship, but it was never operational.

15. Question: In the projected post-war GAF, what percentage of total fighter aircraft were to have been nightfighters?
  Answer: It would depend on the result of the war. Result Germany/England 1:1; dayfighter/nightfigher 1:1.

16. Question: What nightfighting was done on the Eastern front?
  Answer: Very little. 9 trains with "Himmelbett" radar positions were employed.

A Bf 110G night-fighter, showing the characteristic "Lichtenstein" SN 2 radar array and flame dampers: the aircraft now in the RAF Museum, Hendon. (US National Archives)

17. Question: Where is your best nightfighting school?

Answer: There was a nightfighter school at Schlmissheim which was later renamed Gruppe 101.

22 August Interrogation

1. Question: Do you believe that a force of ground attacking nightfighter bombers would have made it impossible for German armor and other units to move by night during the initial stages of the Normandy invasion?

Answer: In my opinion it is possible by employing a sufficient number of nightfighters as night ground attack aircraft to stop rail and motor traffic on the roads to an extent which would hamper units very considerably in their freedom of movement.

2. Question: Do you consider that the employment of nightfighter bomber forces operating in close support of ground troops is feasible and desirable?

Answer: Nightfighter aircraft could at any time, in suitable weather conditions, be called upon to act as night ground attack aircraft in support of the ground forces, such as occurred in Ardennes offensive.

3. Question: What are your reasons for choosing a good nightfighter defense rather than a good flak defense?

Answer: The reason that a good nightfighter defense is preferable to flak is backed up by the considerably greater number of enemy aircraft shot down in Germany by nightfighters as compared with flak. At the climax, the ratio was about 70–30 in favor of the nightfighters.

4. Question: What do you consider a proper ratio of nightfighters to dayfighters in a well balanced airforce?

Answer: That is dependent upon the military situation, but with the strategy the Allies used in the air during the war I believe the ratio should be one to one.

5. Question: What percentage of attacking nightbombers do you believe that nightfighters must shoot down in order to be considered successful?

Answer: If a steady 10% of the enemy aircraft are shot down by nightfighters, then the operational employment of the latter can be considered sufficiently successful to justify the expectation of a tactical success.

28 August Interrogation

1. Question: Name the major German nightfighting aircraft types with approximate dates on which each type became operational.

Answer: July 1940, Me-110, Do-17Z and Ju-88A-4. The Do-17Z was gradually eliminated and the Ju-88A-4 replaced by the Ju-88C. The next step was the improvement of the Me-110F and then the Me-110G. About mid 1943, the addition of the He-219, but only in very small numbers; at the same time, the employment of the FW-190 as a single seater nightfighter. At the end of the war, the Me-262 as a nightfighter without special additions (the fittings for the nightfighter versions were never completed); from the Ju-88A-4, the Ju-88G-6 was developed in late 1943. The Do-217J was also employed.

2. Question: What do you consider the correct camouflage for nightfighters?

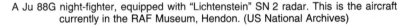

A Ju 88G night-fighter, equipped with "Lichtenstein" SN 2 radar. This is the aircraft currently in the RAF Museum, Hendon. (US National Archives)

Answer: A dirty greyish white on both upper and lower surfaces. Experience has shown that black is not suitable.

3. Question: Do you consider it worth while to sacrifice performance for the relative invisibility attained through the use of flame dampeners?

Answer: Nightfighting is not possible without exhaust flame dampeners. These must be built into the engine and not added afterwards.

4. Question: What type cockpit lighting system do you consider best?

Answer: Instruments with adjustable ultra violet lighting.

5. Question: Were night cameras used on your aircraft?

Answer: No. On one instance a camera was used that I know about, with good results. The picture of the exploding British bomber was widely circulated in all German newspapers.

6. Question: Were automatic pilots used in GAF nightfighters?

Answer: No. However, we had a rudder blocking mechanism which locked on aircraft on a steady heading, leaving the ailerons and elevator free, to be controlled by the pilot.

7. Question: What were the deficient qualities in your main nightfighter types?

Answer: Near the end of the war, the He-219 and Ju-88G-6 could no longer keep up, either in speed or altitude, with the Mosquitoes. On the other hand, we had the Me-262, which was faster than the Mosquito, and the Ju-388, with motors specially suited for high altitude. However, the Ju-388 was never operational.

8. Question: Explain in detail the characteristics and features you would incorporate in building the ideal nightfighter.

Answer: A margin of speed of at least 60 mph over the fastest enemy nightbomber. A ceiling at least 1,500 ft. above that of the highest flying enemy nightbomber. Note: if these two requirements cannot be combined, two separate types of nightfighter aircraft must be built, one for speed and the other for altitude. Twin engine for safety in flight at night. Two or more seater in order to be able to share out the work in the machine, as a number of instruments have to be watched at the same time. The pilot flies the plane, searches for the target and shoots; the airborne wireless and radar operator carries on the wireless traffic with the ground and also watches the radar search equipment; the flight engineer keeps a watch on the engine instruments and uses his eyes to look for aircraft (two pairs of eyes see more than one, three more than two). Equipping with an airborne radar set satisfying the requirement —range greater than altitude of the (nightfighter) aircraft. Tactical requirements for this radar set— range as great as possible, at least 5–6 miles, angle of reception 360°, separate image to 200 yds. Equipment with IFF (optical, not acoustical). Equipping with a warning device against the approach of enemy aircraft. This also fitted with IFF (optical, not acoustical). Armament—at least 6 guns arranged centrally round the nose of the aircraft: either six 3 cm or six 2 cm or four 3 cm and two 2 cm or two 3 cm and four 2 cm. Guns capable of being fired all at once or in any other desired combination. Good takeoff (if possible unassisted). Low landing speed (if possible, not over 115 mph). Good flying characteristics—high rate of climb and good maneuverability. If any characteristics are unattainable or incompatible, speed has priority over rate of climb. Complete blacking-out of the engines (exhaust flame dampers, which should not cause a loss of flying speed). Equipping with all navigational aids (automatic pilot, directional compass, D/G 6 or similar equipment, FuG 16 or similar equipment, radio telephony, "Y" lines or similar equipment). Blackout of dashboard lighting by using ultra violet illumination (and avoidance of all dazzling). Bullet-proof glass in front of the pilot and at the side (perhaps also above), with protective devices for removing oil or other dirt on the cockpit windows from burning enemy aircraft.

Chapter 12

Nightfighter Control

by Major Heinrich Ruppel

My Assignment in Nightfighters
from December 1940 to the End of March 1945.

Before being ordered at the end of November 1940 to a selected instruction course in the Nightfighter Squadron One (#1), I had been in charge of a munitions supply depot of the Air Force. Together with me there came about fifty (50) additional officers, all of whom had been, just as myself, former pilots or observers during the First World War, and who were to be put through a short course so as to test them for their qualifications to be appointed later on as squadron leaders of nightfighter echelons or of squadron groups.

Chief instructor was then Major and Squadron Commodore Falk. As his assistants and coinstructors he had three very capable and, in night flight especially, experienced officers of the service, namely, Captain Ehle, 2nd Lieutenant Woltersdorf, and 2nd Lieutenant Mueller, all of whom were killed later on during nightfighting. After completion of the course, four of the participants were given the post of attack leaders, presumably because of their suitability.

I was detailed to the Special Command of the second group of NFG 1 (Nightfighter Group 1), stationed at the Schiphol airfield near Amsterdam. This group consisted of 6 Bf-110, with the corresponding flying personnel (1 pilot and 1 radio man). The task of this Special Command was (1) to engage the enemy bombers crossing the "dark" area "Hering," and (2) to engage in "lighted" nightfight over Greater Amsterdam. The "dark" area "Hering" centered at Nedemblick (as the base), and extended over a radius of about 40 km.

The base position for the fighters for engagements over Greater Amsterdam was at Narkelen, northeast of Amsterdam, consequently beyond the range of the heavy flak batteries. Such areas were called "dark" where operations were undertaken only with the aid of radar ("Freya" and "Wurzburg" sets).

"Lighted" areas were those where batteries of searchlights were set up, which means nightfighting took place in illuminated areas. Because of the fact that the airfield Schiphol was distinctly a takeoff field for combat (bomber) planes, and because their then around the clock attacks interfered considerably with the use of nightfighters, the Special Command was transferred to the smaller airfield at Bergen am See (near Alkmar), after the latter landing field had been cleared for night landings; this took place in the middle of February 1941. While the defense positions (ops room) at Schiphol were located rather distant from the airfield, the new defense positions were set up on the airfield proper, which procedure proved to be advantageous from every angle.

Although the Special Command Bergen was subordinated to the NJG 1, and the latter again to the General Command of the XII Fleiger Korps, under the leadership of the then Major General Kammhuber, I was permitted to use my fighters according to my own judgment. The reason for that was that in the first place I was informed at least just as early and accurately about the most essential data (weather, takeoff and landing times of our own combat units, ship movements, flak range, enemy raids, etc.) as my superior commands; and in the second place, because the officers, noncommissioned officers and crews under my command for battle collaborated in a really exemplary manner, meaning that nothing could go wrong. The number of enemy planes downed over the "lighted" area (Greater Amsterdam) was comparatively low. This was due to:

1. Searchlight activity depended too much on weather conditions. At a cloudiness of more than 4/10 (four-tenth) below 1,000 meters, it was not permitted in 1940/41 to undertake "lighted" night flights because it didn't pay off.
2. During excursions of our combat planes out of the southern Dutch territory, with a course leading during the entire excursion in most cases past Amsterdam, it was not permitted to send up nightfighters over that territory.
3. In most cases, the enemy plane was "fixed" for too short a time in the beam of the searchlight, and, because of this fact, the nightfighter, who, as stated above, was waiting at a base outside of the flak range, started flying toward his objective after it had been "fixed" and usually arrived too late.

In contrast to "lighted" night-fighting, fighting operations in the "dark" area were very successful from the very onset. The use of the fighters in the "dark" area, later on called "Himmelbett," proceeded in the following manner:

"Himmelbett" GCI Tactics

As soon as the first enemy planes had been detected by the "Freya" of the "Hering" position—its radius covered originally 80 km and was later increased to 150 km—I gave to one of the readied crews the order to take off. After starting, the fighter reported his takeoff by radio signal on the frequency of the defense position and set his course directly towards the radio beacon "Hering." The radio beacon indicated the orbit position to the fighter, who circled it for the time being in a radius of 5 km. On his way toward the beacon, the first step was to establish radio communication with the ground position "Hering." Thereafter, the altimeters were checked and visibility as well as weather conditions were reported. By the time all this was taken care of and an altitude of 4-5,000 had been reached, the enemy bombers had usually arrived close to the periphery of the area, and the interception could be started. After a short orientation of the fighter by the controller with reference to the situation, beginning usually as follows: "Attention, attention, bombers coming from direction 10 toward 4 (face of clock), distance 50 km," the fighter approached still closer the radio beacon, while flying very sharp turns, so as to be able to intercept as accurately as possible.

After reception of the fighter's report "am over FF," all of which naturally was reported in code, whether by voice or Morse, the actual "takeoff" order was given. Assuming that the bombers had maintained the above-mentioned course, the "takeoff" order would have been as follows: "Vector 300°, altitude 4200." This meant for the pilot to set his compass for a heading of 300°, and that the calculated altitude of the bomber was 4,200 m. However, it was up to the fighter to decide whether to fly against the bomber at the same altitude or to assume a position 200–300 m below that of the bomber. The latter choice was the rule, because, as it is well known, even in the blackest night it is possible to see an object from below and to avoid, under all circumstances, a collision. Furthermore, it was possible for the pilot to assume immediately the correct position as soon as he had recognized the enemy or when going over to the attack, which was always undertaken from below and sidewise.

Whenever the bomber changed his course or altitude, the fighter received the corresponding corrections like "10° to the left" or "15° to the right," and "new altitude 4,500." As soon as the fighter had come sufficiently close to the bomber that he was at equal altitude, the fighter received the following order: "Attention, attention, steep turn to the left, reverse course." This meant that the fighter should fly a particularly sharp 180° turn, and that he should fly for a short interval at full throttle in order that he reduce the distance from his target which had been increased by the banking maneuver.

After the fighter had reversed his course, he was informed at short intervals regarding his distance from the bomber in kms. and given his orders regarding the speed to be maintained. As soon as the fighter had sighted the bomber, which fact he had to report immediately, and if possible with indication of the type, the controller did not give any further orders, so as not to disturb the pilot in his preparation for the attack. Ground guidance was again reestablished only when the fighter asked for it, which meant that he had lost his target. If the bomber had been shot down, the fighter returned without delay to the radio beacon in order to be directed against other oncoming planes. In order to find the radio beacon at the shortest possible delay, he was given the course and distance to that point.

The fact that the fighter plane had no possibility of engaging other targets from the time of the first encounter with an enemy until the return to the radio beacon, thus permitting a considerable number of the bombers to fly unmolested over the area, resulted, in May 1941, in the sending into battle two fighters simultaneously.

These fighters were guided as follows: A few minutes after the start of the first fighter, the second crew also took off. The latter, however, did not fly toward "FF Hering," but flew toward a specially marked point on the western coast of the Zuyder Zee. As the second fighter was tuned in on the same frequency as the first fighter, he could also hear all commands of the ground station, and consequently knew approximately when his turn would come.

As soon as that moment had arrived, he flew toward the beacon "Hering" and at the same time informed the ground station of that fact. As soon as the first fighter had reported "enemy plane afire and is crashing," or "lost target," the ground station took over the guidance of the second fighter. During the engagement of the second fighter, ground guidance was not continued whenever the report came "target lost," a fact which occurred rarely and only when the nightfighter had some new crew members. In such a case the nightfighter had, as a punishment, to locate all by himself the bomber, and if he could not do so within a few minutes, he had to return to the radio beacon at normal flight speed (in order the preserve the engines).

Apart from the fact that from now on there was no interruption in fighting enemy air raids, this method of fighting had the great advantage that in case the first fighter was suddenly eliminated (through engine trouble, radio failure, jamming of guns, crashing of plane, wounds, etc.), the controller still had another fighter at his disposal. In replacement of the crippled plane, the next crew held in readiness started at once, so that within a few minutes the area was again covered by two fighters.

Controlled Pursuit Tactics

As a result of the ever increasing bombing raids and the attacks over Hamburg in July 1943, new nightfighter control methods were introduced—controlled pursuit nightfighters and uncontrolled pursuit nightfighters. The controlled pursuit nightfighter method was controlled exclusively from divisions and proceeded as follows:

In the course of the nightly report on operations, the division commander indicated the number and state of readiness of aircraft and crews broken down into "Himmelbett," controlled pursuit nightfighters, and uncontrolled pursuit nightfighters. "Benito" operational frequencies were then assigned to the controlled pursuit nightfighters. After the first enemy plane had been detected, the sectional commander, after communicating with the divisional commander, issued the order to take off.

If the general flight direction of the bombers indicated, for instance, that my sectional area would be presumably penetrated, I ordered, at first, manning of the westernmost section. As soon as the crews assigned to this task ("Himmelbett" nightfighters) had started, the orders were given to the controlled pursuit nightfighters to proceed to a radio beacon, designated by the division commander. After the departure of the last controlled pursuit nightfighter, the uncontrolled pursuit nightfighters took off and assembled above the air field or an adjacent radio beacon.

When the air situation clearly denoted that the neighboring section would not be involved, the division commander would order the controlled nightfighters of the neighboring section to the radio beacon assigned to me. This was done so that I might direct them jointly and infiltrate them into the bomber stream by "Benito" control. In the bomber stream, the pursuit nightfighters under my control were controlled by me until they reached the border of my area. At that time they were either returned to my radio beacon or taken over by the neighboring division.

The uncontrolled nightfighters orbiting above the airfield and radio beacon, as before mentioned, were handled in the following manner:

If the raid occurred in their own section, the fighters tuned in to the division commentary and thus received further instructions.

Only the best crews were used for controlled pursuit nightfighting (they had to be not only good flyers, but men with quick and agile minds), since unquestionably, the most difficult tasks had to be undertaken by them.

If the bomber stream penetrated a neighboring section, my uncontrolled pursuit nightfighters, after communicating with the divisional commander, received the order either to proceed to a radio beacon in the neighboring section which was more inland, and then to tune in on the division commentary, or to proceed to a radio beacon of a radar station of the neighboring area and to await further instructions from the controller at the radar station.

Return flight engagements were chiefly handled by the "Himmelbett" fighters, because the latter, immediately after completion of their engagement, received landing orders in order to be assigned to new tasks.

If the sectional commander whose area was penetrated had too few "Himmelbett" fighters available, because the crews had been engaged in controlled pursuit nightfighting, or uncontrolled pursuit nightfighting, I requested the necessary fighters from the neighboring section commander if his "Himmelbett" crews had not been used.

Repeated attempts to use controlled pursuit nightfighters for the return flight engagements proved a failure, since usually there was not sufficient time to make the necessary preparations.

The "Wilde Sau" (single engine nightfighters), used in the fight above the city under attack, is basically only a continuation of the controlled pursuit nightfighters.

When the fighters had finally reached the target under attack, they tried to get the bomber which was illuminated by the beams of the surrounding searchlights or could be discerned in case of cloudiness, by fires and artificial illumination above the cloud surface.

The same procedure was followed by the "Wilde Sau" nightfighters, which were stationed chiefly close to important defense plants within the borders of the Reich. Their operations depended mostly upon weather conditions, preceded in such manner that they were assembled around radio beacons and directed to the targets by means of "Benito" control.

My duties and responsibilities covered the following:

1. Early occupation by nightfighters of the areas assumed to be penetrated, giving landing orders promptly, especially in case of deteriorating weather conditions in the respective areas, and directing aircraft to emergency fields.
2. Thorough knowledge of the air picture in my own area and reporting same to XII Flieger Korps as well as to my own controllers at positions further inland.
3. Giving orders to the controllers regarding the individual targets to be attacked.
4. Direction of flak while starting and landing at the field as well as in areas where marine batteries were employed.
5. Assisting all planes in distress, irrespective whether they are German or enemy aircraft, by directional lighting with searchlights pointing toward night landing fields.

Chapter 13

Nightfighter Direction
Interrogation of Major G. S. Sandmann
16 August 1945

1. Question: What was "Wilde Sau" nightfighting?

Answer: Once it was tried to strengthen single engined nightfighting by transferring a number of fighter squadrons (jagdgruppen) to nightfighting after a short retraining. Regarding the short time of special training, the results were very good, from the point of view of flying, but this kind of nightfighting showed no results from the point of view of kills.

Single engined nightfighting—according to my own views—will have successes in the future only, when it is limited to "Objektjagd" (fighting over the very target of the enemy bombers). "Objektjagd" will be successful in cooperation with searchlights under good weather conditions. When the sky is over-clouded, it will be necessary that the upper limit of clouds should be sufficiently lighted. This is dependent upon the extent of the layer of clouds. Therefore, there will always be weather conditions, under which "Objektnachtjagd" is not possible.

I am of the opinion that single-seated nightfighting was abandoned by the end of war above all on account of its small successes regarding the heavy losses. I attribute about 60% of the losses occurred in single engined nightfighting to the bad weather conditions (this figure represents my personal opinion). An exact investigation of losses by bad weather will be difficult, because losses occurring during single engined nightfighting will mostly be total losses. It, therefore, is always very difficult to ascertain subsequently the cause of the clash. I am inclined to attribute most of the remaining 40% to losses by action of enemy bombers. The percentage of a/c shot down by our own flak, however, is also rather high. The reasons for the abandonment of single engined nightfighting by the Germans will be, besides the high percentage of losses: the single engined nightfighter always is inferior to the twin engined nightfighter because:

(a) The W/T equipment of the single engined nightfighter can never be equivalent to that of a twin engined nightfighter. The insufficient W/T equipment makes it more difficult to direct the single engined nightfighter

GERMAN AIRCRAFT LOSSES 6 MO. PERIODS

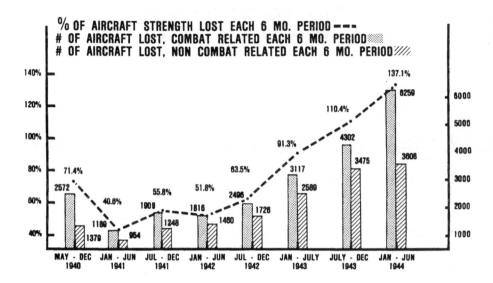

% OF AIRCRAFT STRENGTH LOST EACH 6 MO. PERIOD ---
# OF AIRCRAFT LOST, COMBAT RELATED EACH 6 MO. PERIOD
# OF AIRCRAFT LOST, NON COMBAT RELATED EACH 6 MO. PERIOD

against the enemy. In addition, it renders possible only a most insufficient navigation by W/T.

(b) The indispensable request of full ability to fly by instruments can never be covered by a single-seated nightfighter, regarding the present state of technology.

c) The tasks of a nightfighter crew are so multiple during flight and battle, that they cannot possibly be accomplished by one single man. A long and expensive training would be required for the accomplishment of the many tasks by one single man. This training would be out of all proportion to the extraordinary risks which the single engined nightfighter runs, in comparison with those of the twin engined nightfighter crew. There were no single engined two-seater nightfighter a/c in the GAF.

2. Question: Did the presence of enemy nightfighters in the air effect your decision to send aloft nightfighters, night intruders, or nightbombers?

Answer: The employment of enemy long range escorting nightfighters, noticed for the first time during the last year of the war, had no final effect on our own missions, except for a short (2 months) influence on the morale of the nightfighting crews. In order not to give themselves away, the crews abstained from employing the flares necessary for marking optically the enemy bomber stream.

3. Question: Did your nightfighters ever perform air to air bombing?
Answer: No.

4. Question: Did your nightfighters ever perform pathfinding?
Answer: No.

5. Question: Did your they ever perform bombing or strafing of ships?
Answer: No.

6. Question: Did GAF nightfighters monitor our Very High Frequency while airborne?
Answer: No, but bombers carrying special equipment and ground high frequency stations could.

7. Question: How closely was the nachtjagdgeschwader coordinated with the operations and command of the ground control unit in the same area?
Answer: The tactical unit in nightfighting was the single aircraft; the operational unit was the nachtjagdgruppe. The latter was immediately subordinate to the jagddivision for operational orders and to the geschwader for discipline and administration. Separate staffeln corresponded to the gruppen wherever they had their own means of operational direction (1 kW, short wave transmitter). When the Air Defence of the Reich was functioning normally, both tactical and technical commands were wielded exclusively by operational battle HQ. Operations were generally ordered by the Korps. The division passed these orders on to the gruppen. When the Air Reporting Service was reorganized to include the fighter division in the responsibility of providing a prompt and uniform picture of the air situation at any moment, and binding for all concerned, the main task of the fighter division altered. This resulted in a separating of the tactical from the technical command, i.e. the Korps or division gave orders as to who should take off, when and against whom, also when and where they should land. The gruppen, with the aid of a short-wave transmitter, then directed their aircraft onto the enemy, unless they were being directed from divisional battle HQ or from a 1st class station by the "Y" or "Egon" procedure. In this, the gruppen relied on the air situation reports which they received by wire or wireless from the division. The geschwader, therefore, except for the special position of No. 1 Nightfighter Geschwader in the last months of the war, was not embodied in the operational chain of command.

Apart from purely administrative and disciplinary functions, the geschwader staff were responsible for the uniform equipping of the geschwader for the offensive tactics proper to their particular type of aircraft. They were also responsible for the immediate evaluation of all operational experiences. Occasionally, however, individual geschwaders had a special geschwader wavelength at their disposal, on which the stabs-schwarm (HQ flight) of the geschwader usually flew, and in an emergency the gruppen of the geschwader also, that is if their own gruppe control broke down.

8. Question: How many nightfighters could be controlled from one ground station simultaneously?

Answer: Any number of nightfighters could be controlled by one divisional battle HQ; about 40–60 aircraft per division could be controlled individually ("Y" and "Egon" procedure); any number could make use of the "reportage" control (freelance) and find their way to the enemy with the enemy positions which it gave them.

9. Question: Was the pilot ever empowered to disregard orders of the military when he felt that he had a better solution to a given problem?

Answer: In the "Himmelbett" ("four-poster") nightfighting procedure and in the "led and unled tame sow," the crew were strictly under orders from the ground until direct contact with the enemy was obtained. An indication on the radar searching equipment counted as direct contact. Naturally, the free initiative of the pilot was never eliminated, i.e. the pilot was trained to a critical attitude with regard to all orders from the ground in order to counter possible errors in the reporting of the air situation (time-lag, confusion of friendly with enemy aircraft, etc.). In principle, the more accurate the method of control the more strictly the pilot was bound to the orders given him from the ground. The less accurate the method of control, the more reliance was put on the initiative and experience of the pilot. The more efficient and reliable the airborne radar equipment, the greater the freedom allowed to the pilot in choosing his target and attack. These principles explain the method adopted in practice of controlling junior crews mostly by the "Y" and "Egon" procedures, while directing more experienced crews on to the enemy by the "reportage" method.

10. Question: Give an example of the dialogue between the controller and nightfighter crew.

Answer: I am not in a position to give an example of that kind as there were considerable differences between the various control methods ("Y," "Egon," "Four-poster," "Bernhardine," "Bear" transmission, "reportage," etc.). Extracts from the wireless traffic logbooks of that period are doubtless in the hands of the Allies, apart from the fact that the wireless traffic was listened-in to in England and, as far as I know, written down. A pilot under "Y" or "Egon" control flew on course and altitudes worked out and ordered from the ground. In the case of "led and unled tame sow," the pilots used wireless or visual beacons or courses chosen by themselves ("self-navigation") to exploit an enemy's position communicated to them from the ground. The methods overlapped according to the range and reliability of the airborne radar equipment.

11. Question: Did German control attempt to segregate fast and slow flying targets?

Answer: Yes, and the faster nightfighters were put on to the fast targets.

12. Question: How close could ground control bring the fighter to the target?

Answer: As a working approximation, I would say 2 km, subject, however, to considerable variations in both directions. It depends upon the method of control, the distance of the aircraft from the ground station, altitude, climatic influences, time-lag in the air situation report of the division, degree of training of the fighter control officer, the degree of enemy jamming, etc. The accuracy of ground control was in every case what it was required to be. It was well within the range of the airborne radar equipment. In my opinion, the demand of the future is not so much "more accurate ground control" as "elimination of 'Window' interference, and reduction of minimum range to the point of visual contact."

13. Question: Were extremely slow flying bombers encountered on the Eastern Front?

Answer: Yes, and they were shot down, either by freelance nightfighters cooperating with searchlights, or by "four-poster" methods (movable railway positions).

14. Question: Were nightfighters patrolled between two or more given points, orbited around a single point, or constantly controlled from the ground?

Answer: All three possibilities mentioned in the question were used. The method of flying backwards and forwards between two or more given points was not employed in the early days of nightfighting, particularly in conjunction with searchlights (Scheinwerferriegel).

The method of waiting at a single point is the special characteristic of the "four-poster" procedure. Continuous direction from the ground if the fundamental method of control in nightfighting in pursuit (Verfolgennachtjagd).

15. Question: At what altitude above the ground were patrols normally made?

Answer: 3,000–4,000 m average altitude. The altitude at which they waited was the expected altitude of the enemy, provided weather conditions were suitable. Waiting at low altitude was deliberately avoided because of many intruders . . . to disturb the smooth running of local flying at the night-flying stations.

16. Question: Were nightfighters ordered to concentrate on low-flying bombers?

Answer: No, not when they were set onto the huge enemy aircraft. If the enemy incursion consisted of two or more separate formations at different heights, the attack was naturally made in such numbers as limited the height of the target to be attacked at that particular time.

17. Question: How did weather or cloud situations affect your attack approaches to enemy targets?

Answer: The type of attack was varied to perform the most practical use of the cloud formation.

18. Question: What system was employed to prevent your nightfighters from being shot down by friendly nightfighters and friendly flak?

Answer: High Command provided for the danger of flak to German nightfighters by having the individual aircraft guided round or over flak barrage areas, or by causing fire to cease while the aircraft flew over the area in cases where this could not be avoided. (Direct communication between Fighter and Flak Battle Headquarters.) There was nothing to guarantee that nightfighters could not be shot down by another German nightfighter. As ordinary nightfighters attacked neither Mosquitoes nor long-range enemy nightfighters, no safety measures, in organization or technique, were required. Enemy aircraft were attacked only when definitely recognized as four-engined.

19. Question: Was positive visual identification required before firing?

Answer: In the "four-poster" procedure the crew attacked on the orders of the fighter control officer. Identification of the enemy aircraft on the part of the crew themselves was not required. In the pursuit procedure (in which the bomber stream is approached from behind) and the objective procedure (in which the nightfighters operated over the bomber's target), the definite identification of a four-engined aircraft was required before attacking.

20. Question: Did the increasing efficiency of RAF nightbombers hurt the morale of GAF nightfighter crews?

Answer: Yes.

21. Question: Were your nightfighters ever used for escort of night bombers?

Answer: As far as I know, nightfighters of the nachtjagd had never been employed as escort for German bomber attacks. Upon the revival of the air attacks against England, complete nightfighter units sometimes were employed as dummy attack formations (diversionary maneuver of Nightfighter Group NJG 2).

Chapter 14

Night Fighter Operations
Interrogation of Major G. S. Sandmann
1 August 1945

1. Question: Briefly outline the operational objectives as established by the GAF Staff for the organization and employment of the GAF in the nightfighter defence of Germany.

Answer: The operational objective of the German nightfighter force was to maintain air superiority over Germany and its occupied territories by night. Its main mission was to protect the German people, their living spaces, their industry, and their transportation facilities from enemy bomber attacks.

After lengthy consideration of the question as whether to place the emphasis on knocking down as many enemy aircraft as possible, or on preventing concentrated and orderly bombing raids, the question was decided for the first time in September 1944.

The decision was published in a series of instructional pamphlets, "Air Defence of the Reich," by the GAF Operations Staff, presumably in recognition of the long argued theory that in view of the steadily increasing Allied air operational strength, the latter (bomb carpet) was, in general, impossible to achieve.

This was accomplished by incorporating the mass of nightfighter forces into the Luftflotte Reich. A few units operated in other Luftflotte areas, in conjunction with the ground forces, in which all primary GAF defence principles and methods, though sometimes slightly altered, were applied.

The I Fighter Corps issued the operational orders. The operational control was handled by the fighter divisions. Training directives were passed down from the C.G. of the Fighter Arm thru' Nightfighter Inspector Section, which section was also delegated the responsibility of recruiting cadets. This latter function was later handed down to the Nightfighter Corps. The responsibility for technical improvements and development of equipment was the function of the C.G. of the Fighter Corps advised by the Nightfighter Inspectorate.

2. Question: Give an outline of the tactics and techniques employed by nightfighters throughout the war and the reasons for, and effectiveness of, the changes.

217

Answer: Information concerning operational tactics by nightfighters will be furnished by the Nightfighter Inspector. He is in a position to name all the individuals concerned and outstanding unit commanders.

3. Question: What aircraft types were employed and why were they selected?

Answer: Twin engined nightfighter types: Me-110, Ju-88, He-219. Single engined nightfighter types: Bf-109, FW-190. Jet aircraft: Me-262.

The Me-110 owes its use as a nightfighter to the fact that as a twin engined dayfighter it would not keep pace with modern fighters. It was being mass produced and there were many available. As a nightfighter, it proved its value in the first few operations. During the development period of the nightfighter, it became more and more apparent that a special radio operator was required. It was difficult for a third man to find accommodation in the Me-110.

Thus came about the selection of the Ju-88. A special series production of the Ju-88 was effected as a modification of the bomber type, since the endurance of the Me-110 under the circumstances was too limited. Sufficient Ju-88s were available. Also, during the Battle of Britain, the Ju-88 had proved its value as a nightfighter.

The He-219, the first German special nightfighter of its kind, primarily owes its development and realization to the enthusiasm of General Kammhuber, who demanded a nightfighter with increased capacity and greater speed, to enable it to meet the increasing demands of nightfighting.

Unfortunately, by the time the He-219 was finally introduced, the "Himmelbett" (GCI control) system was no longer used. When this aircraft made its first appearance, there were only eight airfields with runways long enough to accommodate it. Shortly thereafter, the aircraft was released from production. Only one gruppe, I/NJG 1 at Venlo, was equipped with the He-219.

The demand for a single engined fighter especially constructed for use with searchlights was repeated time and again, even after the He-112 had failed at the beginning of the war.

Following the use of "Window" (metallic strips for use against radar) by the Allies, which caused the complete collapse of the twin engined nightfighter system, a system employing single engined fighters (Bf-109) and referred to as "Wilde Sau" (Wild Boar) was introduced. Another suspension of single engined nightfighting would certainly have happened if the appearance of the Mosquito had not forced the employment of single engined nightfighters into an attack from the rear. This was true because all twin engined types at this time could not even be considered for the job of tackling the faster and higher flying Mosquito, so, as in the case of dayfighting, the Bf-109 was replaced by the FW-190, and later by the Me-262, in nightfighting tactics.

The single seat nightfighting system using the Me-262 got no further than a small experimental enterprise (Kommando Welter), with five aircraft. The initial successes of the Me-262, with its increased range, promised great things, even in the nightfighting field. The suitability of the Me-262 as a nightfighter even with its one man crew must be considered proved.

4. Question: What types of missions were your nightfighters assigned?

Answer: Nightfighters were used in coordinated night missions in the following systems: Control and non-control pursuit fighting; objective nightfighting ("Wilde Sau").

Single engined nightfighting was chiefly intended for objective nightfighting. It was a costly mistake to send inexperienced dayfighter pilots unacquainted with nightfighter tactics and instrument flying out on these "Wild Boar" missions, and this subjected them to pressure of Allied feint and diversionary maneuvers before they had had a chance to receive the required training.

Night flying instruments, radio apparatus and radar equipment in single engined aircraft are only aids in determining the question of range. Consequently,

The Heinkel He 219, the only purpose-built German night-fighter, was designed for the vectored ground control intercept missions associated with General Kammhuber's tactics. The first version produced in quantity was the He 219A-5, with two 30 mm and two 20 mm cannon. At the end of 1943, the He 219 was officially abandoned on the grounds that the Ju 88G was capable of catching the Lancaster and Halifax, but, as the aircraft was the only one able to deal with the Mosquito, production conmtinued. (US National Archives)

An Me 262 filmed in action with an enemy fighter. (US National Archives)

the single engined aircraft must temporarily be regarded as unsuitable for pursuit nightfighting.

Towards the end of the war, a twin engined geschwader (NJG/1, Ruhr District) was employed in objective nightfighting since the single engined nightfighters, because of their limited scope caused by lack of forward area, aircraft warning service stations, could no longer provide an adequate defence. Moreover, the single engined nightfighters had already at this time been given over to bad weather dayfighter operations, since they were especially suited for this and since the emphasis on air defence was leaning more and more toward day raids.

5. Question: How mobile were your nightfighter units?

Answer: The mobility of nightfighter units was unusually great. Fundamentally, each gruppe occupied several airfields, with the idea that a freedom of choice would always exist in the event of bad weather conditions or of unserviceability of the field due to bombing. In addition to this, personnel of one gruppe were immediately available to help service aircraft of another gruppe. This was true because each unit had to take care of taking its defence party (ops room) personnel along in transport aircraft in the event of a move.

6. Question: What navigational aids were employed with your methods of control?

Answer: "Y" procedure and "Egon" procedure; occasionally used "Bernhardine" or a directional beam transmitter (controlled "Wild Boar"). Navigation in the nightfighter sectors was carried out with the aid of radio or light beacon. Running commentary control, and control aided by directional beam transmitter, were supported by "dead reckoning navigation," or by means of radio or visual locators (1—"Tame Boar" and 2—"Wild Boar").

7. Question: What demands are made on your homing and warning equipment?

Answer: The following primary demands are made on this equipment: Complete 360° coverage, small antenna (wind resistance), clear indication until close visual dissolution, independence of altitude, light weight, easily adjustable, resistance to cold weather and total immunity to disturbances.

Only a few of these requirements of the German equipment were fulfilled. The realization was still a matter of research and development.

8. Question: How effective were Allied countermeasures to your nightfighter tactics, and what methods did you use to counteract them?

Answer: The effectiveness of Allied countermeasures (air and ground jamming, bluff tactics, and "Window") was considered, on homing and warning equipment, very good. Germany, nevertheless, always managed to counteract a new measure by developing new methods of defense. For example, the aircraft carrying the very dangerous jamming equipment could be easily approached and shot down in many cases, because of our development of an instrument to home on these jamming devices. In like manner, "Window" was easily recognized as belonging to, and being in, the area of the enemy stream. In this way, the location of any bombing stream was simplified.

As regards the jamming of ground equipment, the effect was considerably less and very temporary. The effect of "Window" when used against ground equipment assumed dangerous forms, because of the employment of experienced air signals troops as front line combat personnel and the replacement of those specialists by new, feminine, and less capable personnel. In comparison with air jamming, ground interference was far less dangerous, and always was susceptible to evasion. For instance, the same running commentary ("reportage") was given simultaneously over different wavelengths and on several frequencies.

It was not until forward area AWS stations were captured that these deception maneuvers became really dangerous.

9. Question: How did our nightfighters and intruders effect your night operations?

Answer: The general effect of Allied nightfighters was little. Takeoff and landing casualties, even in the case of the 3rd Fighter Division, which was often visited by Allied nightfighters, were never serious. I know of only two incidents during an eighteen month period where Allied nightfighters might have shot something down. This caused crews of all Me-110s to become more careful, in contrast to the Ju-88 crews, who had a fourth man aboard in order to observe enemy fighter tactics more closely. Up until this time, it had been the exclusive function of this man, who was selected for his unusual night vision, to offset disturbances caused by "Window" by visually searching for the target.

Bomber attacks by your nightfighters and intruders had an initial shock effect. Occasionally, because of this, the German nightfighters were delayed in their takeoff. In so far as I know, only once was a unit, which was based in its entirety at the same field, completely knocked out. The effect of three to five medium bombs could be easily neutralized where the proper precautionary measures are taken.

The effect of single Allied intruders against active German air defence was nil: they were usually recognized, and in keeping with the SOP these were not engaged.

10. Question: How would you evaluate the comparative quality of your nightfighter pilots?

Answer: The quality of nightfighter pilots, especially the commanders, compared favorably to that of the dayfighter pilots. Nightfighter pilot quality deteriorated with the length of the war. The reason for this could be traced to the extremely high casualty figures.

It was proved by experience to use as nightfighters only those pilots that had at least one year's nightfighting experience before employing them in combat. Pilots who became operationally fatigued were too impatient after waiting this long time, or those who had little success were ruthlessly removed from the formation by the commanders. A nightfighting unit (gruppe) averaged from five to seven experienced combat pilots and three to four times as many beginners.

Towards the end of the war, only experienced pilots were employed, because of the fuel shortage. In January 1945, the nightfighter forces were reduced to one-fifth of their regular strength, because of the transfer of personnel into the infantry or to the Eastern front, where little nightfighting was carried out.

11. Question: Did your nightfighters ever use rockets offensively?

Answer: Employment of rocket shells from nightfighters never took place to my knowledge, and was not even proposed.

12. Question: How extensive were your nightfighter losses?

Answer: I can answer this only to a limited extent. In the area of the 3rd Fighter Division (Holland, Ruhr District), on the average, the nightfighter losses were far below the confirmed successes. The larger picture shows that the percentage of losses among nightfighters was decidedly smaller than that of any other branch of the Fliegertruppe. An exception is to be found in the case of the single engined nightfighters, in which the net result showed that the losses far exceeded the successes, particularly after they departed from the policy of pure objective nightfighting due to lack of material. I can make no numerical estimates.

13. Question: What developments were planned for the future?

Answer: To the best of my knowledge, plans called for a general intensification of performance on the TL basis (PTL), the development of jam-proof aircraft, search and warning equipment, blind apparatus, and also the development of the basic requirements mentioned under Question 7.

Chapter 15

Nightfighter Tactics

Interrogation of Major Heinz-Wolfgang Schnaufer (and two
NJG 4 Gruppenkommandeure)
21 May 1945

Method of Search and Attack

Major Schnaufer said that jamming and concentrated bomber streams rendered AI useless. He would fly to a position where jamming was greatest and then search visually. He was convinced that the majority of the inexperienced pilots had little success, and that most claims were made by the experienced pilots. He considered that after eight victories a pilot was good for a long life. The majority of those shot down were at their 4th to 6th victory stage.

On a dark night, once the stream was intercepted the number of bombers seen by each fighter averaged 1 to 3. This number increased with better visibility, and on a bright moonlight night would be anything up to 25. The experienced pilot would attack an average of 3 on a dark night, the inexperienced 1 or none. Schnaufer claimed 9 in 24 hours on 21 February 1945 (a 5 Group raid on Munster), two in the early morning and 7 in the evening.

Pilots and crews always searched upward, and the type of attack favored was to approach from below, fly a little ahead of the bomber, climb and drop back until guns came on, fire and break away down. Firing range on a dark night was 100 meters or less, sometimes as close as 30 meters, and on a light night 200 meters or less. The same approach was used for an attack with upward firing guns. The pilots of this NJG had not been briefed on "Fishpond" cover, and no approaches were made from above or level dropping below cover and no approaches were made from above or level dropping below the bomber inside "Fishpond" minimum range.

Schnaufer considered that, in the later stages of the war, 50% of the attacks were carried out with upward firing guns. With the less experienced pilots, the tendency was towards using upward firing guns. One reason for this was the little difference in the speeds of the Ju-88 and the Me-110 compared with the Lancaster and Halifax. When approaching from astern and below for an attack with forward firing guns, if the bomber corkscrewed, it was most difficult for the fighter to gather speed quickly enough to follow it down in the initial dive.

Major Heinz Schnaufer (center), his radar operator, Friedrich Rumpelhardt (left), and another Luftwaffe aircrewman. Schnaufer had 121 kills at night and commanded *NJG 4* at the end of the war. (Gordon Permasnn)

Schnaufer had attacked 20 to 30 bombers with his upward firing guns at about 80 yards range, and of these only 10% saw him, at a range of approximately 150 to 200 meters, and corkscrewed before he could open fire. This pilot claimed to have shot three bombers down with his upward firing guns while they were actually corkscrewing, and Krause claimed 6 corkscrewing bombers with his upward firing guns, but all three pilots admitted that it was most difficult to shoot down corkscrewing bombers with this type of armament. They said it was possible for a fighter to remain under the bomber and corkscrew with it, but only if the maneuver was not violent. The fighter would fire when the bomber changed direction, usually at the top.

Pilots would usually aim to hit the bomber between the two nacelles on either side, or if the rear turret became troublesome they would aim at that.

Pilots had the greatest respect for the mid-upper turret at the commencement of the corkscrew. They said that as they approached from below and the bomber commenced to corkscrew with a dive in their direction, it gave the mid-upper gunner a perfect view and a good chance to fire. This would normally be at fairly close range.

On the approach, if the bomber commenced corkscrewing, or opened fire at the fighter at a reasonable range, the fighter pilots would usually break away and either leave the bomber and look for another target or sit off in a position where they would not be seen by the bomber, and come in again in approximately 5 minutes, even to the second and third time. If they were about to open fire when seen or fired at, they would press the attack. The less experienced pilots would usually press the attack anyway; Schnaufer thought the reason for this was probably lack of confidence in finding another target and their keenness to get a kill.

Schnaufer and other experienced pilots usually carried flares to drop when they found the stream. These flares were of great assistance to the less experienced pilots, enabling them to find the stream and its direction.

In a brilliantly lit target area, when single engined fighters would be carrying out target interception, Schnaufer said the twins would also go in and attack over the target. He could not be sure how many would do this, and he thought that it was a matter of courage and keenness on the twin-engined pilots' part. He personally would attack in the target area rather than follow a bomber out into the darkness.

In NJG 4, no coordinated night attacks were ever carried out, and Schnaufer thought that if a bomber was attacked by two aircraft at the same time it was merely coincidence. He pointed out that it was most difficult to formate with another fighter at night, and they would invariably lose contact with each other.

Of the bombers shot down by NJG 4 pilots, approximately 40% did not fire or maneuver, 50% fired or maneuvered after the fighter had opened fire, and 10 to 20% fired or maneuvered first. About 98% were flamers. Pilots always carried a maximum ammunition load and used their maximum fire power; there was a certain amount of competition in the staffel as to who could shoot down the most bombers with the least ammunition.

The Corkscrew

All pilots considered the corkscrew a most effective evasive maneuver, but they were of the opinion that a corkscrewing Halifax was an easier target than the Lancaster, although the Lancaster caught fire, when hit, more easily. Their idea of the Halifax was a robust but slower aircraft than the Lancaster, less maneuverable and with a poorer search.

The pilots could not distinguish between different types of corkscrews, and usually followed the target aircraft through one complete movement of the corkscrew, which enabled them to anticipate change of direction at the top. If the bomber was not shot down at this stage, the experienced pilots would break away altogether, or sit off for a time, as they thought that to attempt a second attack on the aircraft straight away would be suicidal. Pilots did not hold off from a corkscrewing bomber and fire on the changes of direction, as they considered it was too difficult to anticipate the position of these changes.

Schnaufer said the more violent corkscrew, starting with a really steep dive and turn, was usually most successful, as the nightfighters hadn't the speed to follow. He added that the general maneuverability of the Lancaster, and the most violent maneuvers carried out by some Lancasters he had attacked, amazed him. On the other hand, he said that he'd never lost a corkscrewing bomber, but he thought that the less experienced pilots may do so.

The majority of bombers tended to corkscrew to port, but all three pilots maintained that they could not base their attack on this. However, Schnaufer stated repeatedly that he preferred to attack on the starboard side, and break away to starboard, as he thought there was less chance of collision with the bomber.

Banking Search

The banking search was considered most successful, as the pilots could not tell whether they had been seen or not; it definitely put them off.

All three pilots considered that the bomber's tracer or gun flash did not give away the bomber's position, and Schnaufer remembers only two or three cases when bombers have been shot down due to this. He said he rarely saw the bomber's tracer, and, therefore, it did not worry him unduly while aiming. He was of the opinion that the bomber gunners did not fire nearly enough or soon enough. He was convinced that had the bombers fired more and used much brighter tracer, many of the pilots, the less experienced especially, would not have attacked. Asked if bright tracer fired from the fighter interfered with his aiming, he said it did, and appreciated that it would be the same for the bomber gunner.

Schnaufer had been surprised twice by fire from a bomber which he had not seen, and in each case the fire was accurate; these bombers he did not attack. He said that, generally, the bomber's fire was accurate, but once again emphasized that we did not fire enough or open up soon enough.

He had been hit seriously twice, and on numerous other occasions had arrived at his base to find his aircraft damaged. He thought that the most dangerous range for the fighter was from 300 to 100 meters, and considered ranges of less than 100 meters were less dangerous due to the fact that he would have either surprised the bomber or be breaking away at this range. Most of the fire from bombers was at about 150 to 200 meters' range. On one occasion, Schnaufer was shot at at 800 to 1,000 meters' range, and he said that the fire was so accurate that he could not approach the bomber.

The bomber gunners invariably fired once they were in the corkscrew maneuver, but rarely during the initial stages. It was thought that they were either afraid of disclosing their position, or the "G" was too great. In some cases they continued firing accurately even when the bomber was in flames and going down.

Identification

Schnaufer said he could usually recognize each bomber he attacked, as he invariably came in close enough to see the guns. The first indications would be the silhouette, then on the Halifax the exhausts could be seen faintly at four to five hundred meters from below. With the Lancaster, the exhausts can only been seen when the fighter is flying directly astern and in line with it; on a dark night these would sometimes be visible at a range of 800 meters but usually less. Night glasses were not worn.

Schnaufer said that he attacked a Fortress on a Frankfurt raid at night in 1943, and made three attacks before being seen, but on the 4th attack the bomber fired and shot him down. The Fortress also went down.

Under Guns

Schnaufer said that in 1942 they were told that the heavies were carrying a .5 under gun. He was very worried about this until he found that very few bombers were in fact carrying it.

Contrails

The pilots always took advantage of contrails. They were able to estimate the approximate distance of the bombers ahead by the density of the contrails which they followed, and as the end of the contrail was approached would weave from side to side in search of a bomber. Also, contrails gave fighters the true direction of the bomber stream. Schnaufer added that he found it most difficult to see the bomber which was creating the contrail and he also realised that it was difficult for the gunner of the bomber to see the fighter.

Searchlights

Searchlight crews were instructed not to cone a bomber with more than 6 searchlights when working with the fighters; pilots were able to see their targets satisfactorily with this number. Usually much larger cones were formed which would blind the fighter pilot just as much as they did the bomber gunner; this was due to the ground crews all wishing to take part in the victory.

Fighter Losses

Losses in NJG 4 during the last seven months of the war were 50. Of these, 30 were shot down by Mosquitoes, 5 by heavy bombers, and 15 due to reasons unknown. It was estimated that each pilot flew 30 to 40 sorties in that time, and the number of aircraft available was at first 50 and latterly down to 15. In addition to these losses, a number of aircraft would crash on landing, or be compelled to belly land due to damage caused in combat. Schnaufer said that the maximum nightfighter effort put up against any one of our raids was 150 to 200 aircraft.

General

Pilots had not been told that some bombers were carrying .5 armament in the tail turret, but said this would not have worried them.

Pilots were told in July 1944 that AGLT ("Village Inn")existed, but it did not worry them unduly as, with their type of attack, when they were at close range they were out of AGLT and rear turret cover until the last moment.

To Schnaufer's knowledge, no Allied type of aircraft were employed at night at any time; he thought that if bomber crews had reported this, it was probably due to friendly aircraft shooting at each other. On one occasion when about to attack a Lancaster, another Lancaster shot at it and he sat off and watched both Lancasters shoot each other down. (It was omitted to ask him if he claimed these two as destroyed.)

Pilots were familiar with the fields of fire of bombers, and based their tactical approach on this.

The pilots had no knowledge of any rocket projectiles of the type reported by crews in late '44/early '45. They said that they would definitely have been briefed to this effect had such weapons been used. Schnaufer added that if something of that type was used, it would be fired by flak personnel and probably in an area where fighters were not operating.

Schnaufer considered the lane of flares as used in the Berlin raids to assist the fighters to intercept was the best tactic developed by the German nightfighter force. He said it was being planned to use this method on all targets.

It was said that in 1942–43 some bombers when being attacked fired off a white flash which blinded the fighter pilots and caused them to lose their target. They thought the idea most effective and could not understand why it was not continued.

Chapter 16

Nightfighter Tactics (NJG 6)
by Major Josef Scholls

The operations order for all nightfighter units is telephoned from the fighter division. The units are connected to one another and to the division by a hot-loop. Over this they receive a running report on any changes in the air situation, or any order concerning an alert or an operation. In this way, each unit (gruppe or independent staffel) can follow the picture of enemy air penetration as well as their own operations as they develop. Announcement within the unit of both the air situation and the orders is accomplished by the operations officer at the gruppe CP by means of a loudspeaker system to all plane crews, whether in quarters, in ready rooms, or at the hard-stands. Each day, after darkness has fallen, the division sends out its order indicating the degree of readiness to be maintained by all crews. This is regulated by the following conditions:

1. The probability of enemy air penetration (weather or moon).
2. The possibility of friendly flying operations (weather); distinction is made among the following degrees of readiness:
   (a) 60 minute readiness: Operations are not expected. Crews are to remain in their quarters; may remove their clothes and sleep.
   (b) 30 minute readiness: Crews must stay in their quarters, dressed and ready for flight. There is possibility of a takeoff within 30 minutes.
   (c) 15 minute readiness: Crews must stay in the ready-rooms (near the hardstands), dressed and ready for flight. There is possibility of a takeoff within 15 minutes.
   (d) Seated readiness: Crews sit in the planes, ready for flight. There is possibility of a takeoff within 5 minutes.
   (e) Takeoff order

The unit (NJG 6) was equipped with Ju-88G6 and Me-110 and was employed primarily against penetrations by four-engine bombers. Because of the enemy's deceptive measures (intruder aircraft and mixed flights of Mosquitoes and four-engine bombers) it was difficult for operations to recognize clearly, and early enough, the penetration of the four-engine planes. Because of this, false takeoffs and false sorties frequently occurred, and in one case it led to losses on our part, because our own formations got mixed up with some Mosquitoes (long-distance nightfighters).

Execution of the Operation

The operation order, which is transmitted verbally and hence without loss of time as described above, comes directly from the division to the crews, and would read like the following example:

"Takeoff order for 706 (the code number for the airfield at Schleissheim); rendezvous over the field (or over radio beacon 'A') at 5,000 meters."

The radio beacon in the order is situated usually from 50 to 1200 km from the home station in the direction of the approaching enemy formation. If a more distant one is selected, the choice is based on the degree of favorability of the location for committing our own planes by the shortest route, even if the enemy machines veer off in another direction. Altitude for the rendezvous is usually ordered at the same level as that which has been gauged, or is thought probable, for the enemy formation. Nevertheless, for better protection against enemy long-distance nightfighters, and to obtain the best results with the "Naxos," the crews usually flew lower (as low as 1,000 meters above the ground).

From September 1944 to spring 1945, the "Zahme Sau" ("Tame Boar") was flown almost exclusively, since this procedure still promised the greatest success. The attempt was made to bring a nightfighter gruppe of approximately 30 aircraft in as close a formation as possible (without visual communication from plane to plane) into the bomber stream and its path of approach, to such a distance from the enemy planes as would enable the crews to carry out their final approach to the target independently with their own search apparatus. In order to keep the scattered formation together during the approach flight, a formation leader was designated to reveal his position to the other crews by firing off flare signals at regular intervals. This measure was seriously hindered by alert enemy nightfighter activity. If the aircraft were successfully guided into the bomber stream in closed formation (the choice was made by the crew of the leading plane), then the possibility of success was greatly heightened. By this means, young crews were greatly assisted in finding their way into the bomber stream.

The primary requisite for a successful operation is the greatest possible accuracy in directing the nightfighters into the bomber stream and its course of approach. This should be carried out in the following manner:

1. Through course orders from the rendezvous point and course directions straight to the target. It is essential that the course, in accordance with the flight order, be strictly adhered to. This will be determined by the a/c safety control officer at the gruppe CP.
2. By means of running account of the air situation. The crew themselves plot their course to the target.

   e.g. "Course 270 degrees, fifty four-engine bombers from RP to CP." Give also the locations and numbers of other enemy planes in the formation, as well as the locations of enemy nightfighters, so as to warn our own aircraft.

A great help in locating the bombers was the "Naxos" apparatus installed in many of our airplanes, which enabled the crews to pick up the H2S ("Rotterdam Geraet") in the four-engine bombers at great distances (more than 100 km). With this device it was possible to find the way to the target, even at the shortest distance. The last part of the approach flight to the target could be made with the additional assistance of the SN 2.

The transmission of orders and air situation reports during the entire approach and return flight was carried out by radio alone on all available wavelengths. Air situation reports were occasionally also transmitted in code form over long, medium, and short waves. Enemy interferences necessitated making use of the entire frequency band. Radio traffic was employed only in the neighborhood of the home station for flight security. During the operation, R/T traffic was impracticable due to powerful interference.

Final Stage of Target Approach

I. Approach flight with SM 2 (Saw Mill 2)

Once the aircraft has been directed from a ground station or with the aid of "Naxos" into the immediate vicinity of the bomber stream, the radar operator, having switched on his apparatus, tries to obtain contacts. Although the enemy's use of "Window" complicated matters, it did not prevent the SM 2 from picking up a target. The "flash" produced in the cathode X-ray tube of the SM 2 appears considerably larger than the interference flash caused by "Window." Other disturbing phenomena on the screen of the SM 2 led to the assumption that the enemy was emphasizing yet other mediums of interference. In this case, it was not possible to carry out an approach flight with SM 2. The radar operator orders the pilot to make every necessary change of direction. The pilot, however, remains in charge of the aircraft and is responsible for it.

II. Approach Flight with "Naxos"

The approach flight is made in accordance with the effect of the "Rotterdam" apparatus (H2S), which transmits impulses downwards from the carrier aircraft in a cone-shaped area of radiation. It is only possible to pick up a target with "Naxos" in the area of the cone beneath the enemy aircraft. The farther the attacker is from his target, the lower he must fly to get a quick contact.

The contact shows the attacker the direction of his target only (sideways). By constantly gaining altitude, he flies to the extreme limit of the cone-shaped radiation area of the "Rotterdam" apparatus, and is finally successful, although somewhat less so than when using the SM 2, in reaching his target. The SM 2 can be used as a supplementary measure in the last stage of the approach flight. The disadvantage of this procedure is that one is, to a large extent, dependent on the frequency and duration of the use of the "Rotterdam" apparatus by the enemy.

Advantage: It cannot be interfered with because it is only a receiving apparatus.

The "Kill"

In the main, there are only three ways of shooting an aircraft down.

(a) Attack directly from the rear.
(b) Attack from below (with oblique or horizontal armament).
(c) Attack made obliquely from below the aircraft (more to the side than beneath).

During the approach flight to the target using the radar apparatus, the pilot must adapt his speed to the decreasing distance between the two aircraft, so that, at the moment of pickup (this depends on the clearness of the night), attacker and target are flying at approximately the same speed. If the attacker has definitely identified his target (basic principle: no attack should be made until attacker obtains visual recognition), he pulls away to the side of the target from which he is going to make the actual attack and takes up his position as far from it as the limit of his visual range will allow. Having thus taken up his position for the attack, he attacks with full throttle as follows:

To (a): Method not very often used. Attack should be made as quickly as possible after recognition.
Advantage: Aeronautically simple, good chance of strikes.
Disadvantage: Easily noticed by the enemy (warning apparatus). Enemy aircraft have heavy rear armament.

After the attack a vertical or oblique dive should be made.

To (b) A frequently used method of attack. Approach should be made with oblique armament from directly beneath the enemy aircraft. Climb to within 70 to 50 meters of the target, level off, fix the target in the gunsight, fire and dive away obliquely.

> Advantage: The possibility of approaching unobserved is good. It is possible to prepare the attack carefully and there is a good chance of scoring hits.

> Disadvantage: If the target takes evasive action, approach and aim are made difficult.

> To attack from the same position with horizontal armament: Pull-up, fix the gunsight on the leading edge of the fuselage, open fire, and let the full length of the target pass through the sight. Draw back sharply and dive away obliquely.

To (c) Frequently used method of attack. Take up a lateral position of attack. Vigorously manipulate the lateral controls and fix the edge of the aircraft wing facing the attacker in the sight (lead factor). Open fire at a distance of 100 to 150 meters. The aircraft must be kept as horizontal as possible. Pull away in the direction of the burning aircraft, but, in any case, down and away.

> Advantage: Good possibility for surprise; defense is difficult.

> Disadvantage: This tactic is difficult to carry out and necessitates much practice.

Causes for Failures of Missions Against Mass Attacks
I. Interference with ground controls.

1. Jamming of ground radar sets by jamming aircraft flying in advance of the main force.

2. Concealment of the attack purpose by mixing the units (fast bombers, long range nightfighters, and four-engine bombers) on different approaches and simulating several attack purposes.

> Because of the above two reasons, a clear cut use of the crews was not possible. The approach of the four-engine bombers was recognized too late. Orders for attack are issued too late; missions against fast units are not successful; they result, rather, in our own losses.

3. Jamming of ground–air communication and issuance of orders on all wavelengths.

In spite of our own camouflage, the jamming was sometimes so effective that our airplanes remained in the hangars and obtained no information about the air situation or further orders. Because of this type of jamming, the formerly used V-system or "Himmelbett" system became impractical. The "Himmelbett" system could not only be used for radio keying traffic.

II. Disturbance of the Air Crew

1. As in I.3.
2. By long-range nightfighters:
   (a) Flying in advance to airfields and radio beacons.
   (b) Accompanying the bomber formation.

The crews were forced to maneuver continuously and take constant evasive action during the three to four hour mission. This made it difficult to find the target and to attack. Our own losses caused by long-range nightfighters were very disturbing.

III. Countermeasures

To 1 and 2 (I): In order to determine the intentions of the enemy more quickly, one observer aircraft was dispatched over the most important

A Ju 88 night-fighter caught by a USAAF fighter in daylight. It has the characteristic mottled camouflage of late-war German night-fighters. (US National Archives)

targets (Munich, Augsburg, Stuttgart, Nuremberg, etc.). This airplane was to radio in to the division at once all visual observations made over the target assigned to it (dropping of flares and demolition bombs). An experienced crew must be selected.

To I.3: Experiments with strong ultra-high frequency transmitters had better success.

To II.1: Radio discipline of the crews.

To II.2: Rendezvous points were located at 60 to 80 km from the radio beacons; operational orders were given in code. Locations of long-range fighters were passed on. Evasive action.

Because of the fuel shortage, there were no more missions against single aircraft in my time. I have no knowledge of experiences in this respect. Occasional failures in the enemy jamming equipment brought greater success at once.

Chapter 17

Nightfighter Missions
Interrogation of Major Josef Scholls
16 August 1945

1. Question: In the later stages of the war, was there any ambiguity of command between day and nightfighters in the staff?

Answer: Yes, there was in the jadgdivision under General Huth. Command of NJG 6 from September of 1944 to June 1945 was split three ways. Each sector commander had command of both day and nightfighters.

2. Question: Did the presence of enemy nightfighters in your area effect your operational efficiency?

Answer: Yes. It forced us to take evasive action often while actually tracking a target.

3. Question: What was duty schedule for your nightfighter crews?

Answer: We were all on duty every night. Each crew had to be available to fly, even though operations were not actually conducted.

4. Question: Were special diets given to your nightfighter crews?

Answer: No. Although black pills were provided to be taken, these were not often taken.

5. Question: Were nightfighters ever a hazard to one another?

Answer: No. The only confusion resulted from nightfighters orbiting the area beacon. However, that was no hazard as we orbited to the left at different altitudes, often as many as 30 aircraft orbiting the same beacon at one time.

6. Question: What were the conditions which were considered prohibitive to nightfighter operations?

Answer: Our weather minimums were a 300 ft ceiling and 1½ miles visibility.

7. Question: Did your unit use night binoculars?

Answer: No.

8. Question: Were general orders such as "shoot anything down with four engines" adopted?

Answer: Yes, but visual identification was always required.

9. Question: Was your unit ever used for night close support?

Answer: Yes, I believe all nightfighters were assembled for night attack during the Ardennes offensive. These missions were commanded by the Luftwaffe.

10. Question: Have you ever used rockets for these close support missions?
Answer: No.

11. Question: Was ground control used to assist your night close support missions?

Answer: No.

12. Question: Do you believe that an observer should be carried for the primary purpose of visual searching for the target?

Answer: Emphatically yes.

13. Question: What method do radar observers use to overcome "Window"?

Answer: It was possible to change frequencies of the SN 2 (AI) radar.

14. Question: What was the range of SN 2?

Answer: The range could not exceed the altitude of the aircraft above the terrain, and was therefore worthless at low altitudes.

15. Question: What is your estimation of the British nightfighter system?

Answer: I believe that both the British nightfighter system and the British radar are better than ours.

16. Question: What procedure was used to ensure night adaptation of crews on alert status?

Answer: Red glasses were issued to my crews, but they were seldom used.

17. Question: How close would ground control bring the nightfighter to the target?

Answer: From 4 to 6 kilometers.

Chapter 18

Fighting the P-61
Interrogation of Major Heinrich Ruppel

P/W was asked as to activity of P-61 Black Widow. He stated that it had been known since 16 December by his Group, and he had been informed that Black Widows would be operational in August and September, but Black Widows were not identified until December and January in von Rundstedt's offensive.

Three combats with Black Widows were reported in December. From questioning of the crews the following tactics were arrived at.

The three crews stated that in their opinion the Ju-88 nightfighter and the Me-110 could easily out-turn the Black Widow. They were not definite as to the tactics used by our nightfighters, and there was no information as to our tactics. There were two schools of thought on the tactics of the Black Widow. One school believed in a stern chase followed by attack; another school believed in a stern chase followed by a diving procedure with an up shoot.

A formation of Ninth Air Force Northrop P-61A Black Widow night-fighters. These aircraft encountered German night-fighters on many occasions in 1944–45. (US National Archives)

One crew reported that a Ju-88 had got on the tail of a Black Widow and out-turned him when the Black Widow broke contact. This contact was 20 km west of Luxembourg.

P/W was questioned as to how his pilots were divided for standby for night operations. His pilots were divided into two categories—the type that could get up in three minutes and the type that could get off in five minutes.

When asked as to the procedure used for night operations in case intruders were in the area, lights on a dummy airfield nearby were turned on and a decoy with wing lights representing an aeroplane was dragged across the runway in the approximate direction of takeoff. The field lights were then left on for approximately 3 minutes. The plane that was to take off was led to the end of the takeoff strip, a searchlight was placed along the ground at an angle of about 40 degrees, and the pilot took off by means of the searchlight.

P/W stated that, on 7 or 8 January, a famous German nightfighter, Herman Mueller, flying a Ju-88, was shot down by a Black Widow near the Frankfurt/Rhein area flying approximately 480 meters high. The crew escaped. However, they were so badly shaken up that it was necessary to send them to a rest camp for quite a length of time.

In mid-January, a report was sent to all German nightfighters to not fear the Black Widow. This was reputedly on reports of crews who had been in combat with the Black Widow.

P/W was asked concerning possible use of Ju-87s as decoys flying in pairs in December and January. To his knowledge, Ju-87s were not used as decoys, and no reports of combat were reported.

When asked if airborne radar of the Black Widow caused interference with the airborne radar of the German nightfighters, P/W stated that to the best of his knowledge it caused no interference. No warning was given by that means that we were in the area.

When asked concerning visual lighting system for pilots landing at German bases, P/W stated that lights were turned on only before landing, and when identification was positive. Further aids to the German nightfighter warning against intruders was a system of lights, a green light representing "No intruder aircraft about" and a red light indicating that an intruder was about. If the red light was showing when the German nightfighter reported to base, he was immediately sent to a different base. The antiaircraft and searchlights then stood by and engaged the intruder when he came over the airdrome.

P/W was asked where American intruders made their biggest mistake in intruding on aerodromes in Germany. He stated that flying at extremely low altitudes definitely identified US as hostile. German aircraft were under orders in his area to fly between 800 and 1,000 meters. Anything under that was considered hostile. He recommended that if we were to intrude on a definite target, to go in at an altitude of from 4,500 to 5,000 meters. He also recommended that if we intrude over an airport, we do not orbit in the nearby vicinity because it was a dead giveaway. He also recommended that on intruding a definite target, we go in high and orbit down very fast, hit our target, and then go back, not on the same route that we came in.

P/W stated that no attempts had been made by his nightfighters to follow our nightfighters back to base.

P/W was questioned if our position was disclosed by R/T at night. He said yes, that Americans normally talked too much on the air. He quoted an incident in the latter part of December. Monitoring our VHF nightfighter channels, an American pilot on a chase was heard to tell his ground control that he was about to shoot down a Ju-88. The German operations officer upon hearing this immediately warned all German nightfighters in his area to take hard evasive action.

P/W did not have information as to the number of P-61s in our area and very little information was known as to the speed and range.

P/W stated that they were not aware of our nightfighter tests in the afternoon.

A P-61A Black Widow night-fighter in flight. The USAAF was anxious to learn about the effectivenes of its tactics against German night-fighters, in order to improve its tactics in the Pacific Theater, where the P-61 was startinbg to encounter radar-equipped night-fighters. (US National Archives)

When asked for specific information on our intruder missions across the Rhine, P/W stated American Black Widows were identified over airdromes every night from December until the middle of February.

When asked if a definite route was known by intruders, he pointed out entries along the Rhine River where we navigated as a checkpoint for the start of an intruder mission. He stated that they became very alarmed over repeated intruder missions every night. Twin-engined German nightfighters (Me-110 and Ju-88) were not used to stop these intruder missions because they thought the Black Widow was too fast.

Finally, a situation was arrived at to send a Me-109 piloted by an ace German nightfighter, Hptm. Mueller, up against us at the entry of our intruder route. This was not followed because of a shortage of petrol.

When asked about what the main results of our intruder missions were, he told us that he could remember a number of locomotives that we had destroyed in the Giessen, Main-Rhein, and Wesboden area. He also stated that German nightfighter pilots training in the Giessen area were restricted, and instructed to land immediately, and it was impossible for him to train pilots in that area at night.

P/W was asked for information concerning Do-217s flying on 21 March. He stated that they were used as intruder aircraft against specific targets and were not nightfighters.

P/W stated that he did not know the location of our GCI in December or January. However, he knew that it must be located close by, because of R/T and the nature of traffic. He had no idea of the range of our GCI, but his personal guess was that we had very short range because of hills and mountains in that vicinity.

When asked the best range of his GCI, he stated that it was 200 km at 25,000 feet. This was a 20 kilowatt set; the normal set was 200 watts.

He also stated that their GCI located at Giessen was frequently attacked at night. When asked if it was located in a barracks area he replied, "Yes."

The German nightfighter Ju-88 in his Group carried a crew of four—pilot, flight engineer, and two W/T operators. The spare W/T operator acted as navigator, and also as observer for hostile aircraft. This was not good practice because the small size of the Ju-88 limited moving inside the plane and prevented the pilot from getting out.

No claims were made by German nightfighters of P-61s shot down over Germany by nightfighters, and to the best of his knowledge no planes had crashed or been shot down.

When asked why the single nightfighter intruders were not fired at by antiaircraft, P/W stated that it was a waste of ammunition.

When asked concerning the navigation lights on German nightfighters, P/W stated that they were always the same colour—red and green. However, identification lights located under the fuselage changed from night to night, and the colours varied from one area to the other.

When asked if jetplanes were to be used as nightfighters, P/W stated that to the best of his knowledge jets were never used as nightfighters. However, training flights were done by jetplanes, and possibly freelance contacts with Black Widows were made in bright moonlight periods.

However, as a method of combating high-flying Mosquitoes, an ace German nightfighter was given a squadron of Me-109s. However, this did not prove successful, so this pilot was to be equipped with the Ar-234 jetplane; radar and search equipment was to be installed in the aircraft. At the time of P/W's capture the plane was not in use.

PART FIVE

SUMMING UP

The von Rohden-compiled document reproduced here reprises some of the themes from the initial chapter, looking at the causes of the Luftwaffe's—and Germany's—ultimate defeat.

This chapter, like the previous essays by the same author and that from Willi Messerschmitt, dates from 1946–47; the remaining chapters, even when not specifically dated, came from the same 1945 interrogations that were included in the earlier Greenhill volume *The Luftwaffe Fighter Force: The View From the Cockpit* .

Over a five-month period, from October 1943 to March 1944, the Luftwaffe succeeded in defeating both the US and British bomber offensives against Germany, effectively to halting the deep-penetration attacks that the two Allies considered vital for their strategic impact. The German military of World War II was good at securing operational success—winning a major battle or campaign—but could not convert this to a lasting solution to Germany's fundamentally insoluble strategic problem of fighting a multifront war against enemies with much greater resources and, in the air war, generally better technology. This is seen in the focus of the preceding chapters. Von Rohden, trained as both a historian and a staff officer, tries to provide some context.

While conventional wisdom that the bomber offensive could not reduce German industrial production nor crack civilian morale, and that its impact was limited to keeping German fighters and flak at home rather than in Normandy, has been largely contradicted by more recent writing, the historical reassessment of the bomber offensive and how the Germans fought against it will continue on.

D.C.I.

Chapter 19

Looking Back

by Generalmajor Hans-Detlef Herhuth von Rohden

The defeat of the German Reich's Air Defense—which was slowly coming about—and its sudden collapse, had laid the foundation for the Reich's defeat during the Second World War. The reasons for the Allied victory as far as the military sectors of the air war are concerned are quoted here briefly:

1. *The German Armed Forces* basically thought only in an offensive vein in all three branches of the overall conduct of the war.
   The Allies, who had been thrust on the defensive until the year 1941, had learned the value of defense.
2. *The "Luftwaffe"* was employed only for offensive purposes.
   The Allies gave their air forces a strong defensive task.
3. *The German Armed Forces* employed and used up their offensive and defensive Air Force powers mainly in the Army's battles for fighting their way to victory in individual war theaters.
   The Allies, after heavy battles, originally gave the air superiority to the Germans in these war theaters, then strove to insure decisive bases for strategic defensive air supremacy for the future.
4. *Germany* underestimated her aerial enemy, and learned nothing by her own mistakes.
   The Allies had realized the harm inflicted by initial German air superiority, and calmly strengthened their offensive and defensive air power by utilizing their experiences which were illustrated by Germany.
5. *The German defensive air force* became too weakened in material and personnel by the splitting of the overall war strategy to be able to withstand an intercontinental (global) air war for any long period of time, both in numbers and material.
   The Allies had the material and personnel of almost the entire world for building a strong air force at their disposal.
6. *Germany* had essentially tried until the end of the war to manage the aerial defense, both numerically and qualitatively, in personnel and materials, by

makeshift and improvisation, and had adopted new types of aircraft too late.

The Allies had placed the main effort of general armament on the planned and far-seeing armament of their Air Force.

7. *The German Air Force High Command* did not interfere with England's rebuilding of power because it was tied down with its offensives on all fronts, and because the High Command believed it could lay the foundation for the last battle against the British bases here.

The Allies had begun to undermine the German air defenses during this rest period in the air war on the West by an ever perfecting plan of continually building up of their strategic attack command.

8. *The German High Command* had actually secured its northern flank against an air envelopment through the conquest of Denmark and Norway; however, despite the addition of sufficient forces, the weakness of the southern flank did not change on account of the war against Russia.

The Allies recognized these weaknesses and looked for their advantages here in a "mass."

9. *Germany's envelopment* from the air developed from this; the air force was now unable to oppose this less than ever.

Bomb damage, Leipzig, 1945. (US National Archives)

The Allies fully exploited the advantages which a strong and a far reaching air force had on the external lines.

10. *The German Air Force* had ended the war with almost the same types of aircraft, weapons, and equipment with which it had begun. In any case, however, technical defensive developments were not adapted to the developments of the offensive weapons.

    The Allies employed new types, etc., for their defensive and offensive air supremacy, which had far better results.

11. *The German leaders* did not realize the importance of the US long range fighter plane, and again and again demanded combat with the enemy bombers, until at last it was too late.

    The Allies thoroughly developed their escort fighters and saw in them the backbone of offensive air supremacy before it was too late. By doing this, they laid the foundations for final victory of the aerial war and for the overall conduct of the war.

12. *The Luftwaffe* was inferior in the radar warfare.

    The Allies were able to use the radar system for defensive combat in 1940 already.

13. *The Luftwaffe* had used the more or less space-limited "radar controlled area-fixed nightfighter defense system" during night operations, and had developed no new methods in proper time—neither materially nor from a command point of view—to effectively counter the nightbomber stream system.

    The Allies employed new methods in good time, assuring them of superiority from both a technical and command point of view.

14. *The Luftwaffe* had split up its daytime fighter strength.

    The Allies had held their strength closely together.

15. *The German leaders* neglected to transfer sufficient power to the Reich's interior.

    The Allies could therefore tie the German fighters down to the advance bases, and undertake effective penetrations into the Reich by 1943. Mosquito attacks were also part of these successful penetrations.

16. *The German Air Force* either did not carry out the long range fight during the day and night at all, or had neglected it severely.

    The Allies therefore had a secure base, which made the battle for defensive and offensive air supremacy easier for them.

There can be no doubt that the practical utilization of experiences which the Germans also could have gathered in the battle against England in 1940—aside from the correct estimation of the opponents' war potential—should have led the German High Command to other interpretations, methods, and to improved defensive armament.

The good tactical results of all branches of the Reich's Air Defense could not make up for the actual mistakes of the German High Command, and the deficiencies of its responsible personalities.

Thus it happened that the Reich's Air Defense had to succumb.

Glossary

AA Antiaircraft.

Abschittsführer Section leader.

a/c Aircraft.

AGLT Automatic Gun Laying Turret.

AN- Beam-radio range navigation/homing method.

ARS Air Reporting Service.

"Benito" Fighter direction based on tracking by ground radars, first introduced in 1941. Unlike the "Egon" system, it did not require the fighters to transmit a signal. Used by night fighters and bombers (with FuG-17Z) as well.

"Bernhardine" Radar system based on ground transmissions and receivers onboard night fighters (especially Ju 88Gs).

BF Bayerische Flugzeugwerke (later Messerschmitt).

Black Widow The Northrop P-61, the standard USAAF night fighter in the European Theater of Operations in 1944-45, replacing the Beaufighter.

CinC GAF Goering.

CinC Sigs Comm Martini (see authors' biographies, p. 9).

CO Commanding Officer.

Commentary The *Reichsjägerwelle* (lit., Reich Fighter Pilots' Waveband)—a running commentary on the tactical situation in the Defense of the Reich. Rather than vectoring specific formations, it allowed formations to navigate towards the enemy and be warned of major threats. Other formations, notably I. Jagdfliegerkorps, had their own commentary as well.

Dark nightfighting Night-fighter tactics carried out independently from searchlights. For details see Kammhuber's and Schmid's chapters.

Deckungsschwarm Cover flight.

D/F Direction-finder/finding.

E/A Enemy aircraft

E(N)JG Reserve/Replacement (Night) Fighter *Geschwader*.

"Egon" A navigation system, similar to the British "Oboe" system.

Elfe Radar blind-firing device for cannon. Not used operationally.

"Epsilon" Codename for *Y-Gerät* (q.v.) ground and air stations.

Erganzung Reserve/replacement unit.

"Erstling"   Codename for FuG 25—an IFF transponder.

Erpobung   Test or evaluation.

f.i.   for instance

Fighter Command   *Jagdkorps*; the Luftwaffe fighter force.

"Fishpond"   Codename for RAF "Monica" bomber tail warning radar.

"Flensburg"   Codename for Telefunken FuG 227 passive sensor intended to detect RAF "Monica" tail warning radars.

Fliegerführer   The air officer commanding a specific operation—usually also a commander of one of the units involved.

Fliegerdivision   Air division. A *"Jagd"* prefix indicates one mainly of fighter units.

Fliegerkorps   Air corps.   An operational formation composed of an unspecified number of units, but usually multiple Geschwader, several hundred aircraft strong. Could be under a *Luftflotte* command or, as in the case of von Kammhuber's *I. FliegerkorpsXII*, independent.

Freya   German radar and radio beacon, with a range of about 120 km.

FuG 16ZY   Standard German VHF fighter radio system, 39–47 MHz. Used for R/T, W/T, it provided "Y control". In addition to standard air–air and air–ground frequencies, it would also receive the *Reichsjägerwelle*. FuG-16 = radio alone.

FuG 25   IFF equipment, codenamed "Zwilling"(Twin) and using a characteristic loop antenna.

FuG 125   Lorenz VHF signal beacon receiver, codenamed "Hermine."

Führungsstab   Operations staff of the OKL (q.v.).

FW   Focke-Wulf

G 1   A mechanical turbo supercharger.

GAF   German Air Force (i.e., the *Luftwaffe*).

General der Jagdflieger   Inspector of Fighters, a *Waffengeneral* (q.v.); not a rank. Had responsibitity for readiness, training, and tactics rather than an operational command. This was Galland's post from November 1941 to January 1945.

General Staff Officer   A member of the German General Staff, a small body whose members received extensive training and provided almost all the Army's general officers.

Generalfeldmarshall   A German rank equivalent to General of the Army (US) or Marshal of the Royal Air Force(British).

Generalleutnant   A German rank equivalent to Major General (US) or Air Vice Marshal (British).

Generalmajor   A German rank equivalent to Brigadier General (US) or Air Commodore (British).

Generaloberst   A German rank equivalent to General (US) or Air Chief Marshal (British).

Gen. Kdo.   *Generalkommando.* The general officer commanding, or headquarters, followed by the formation. Thus, "Gen. Kdo. I Fighter Corps" was Schmid or his headquarters.

Gefechtsverband Combat formation. The standard tactical formation could range from a few fighters to multiple *Gruppen* formations of about 100 aircraft. Formations grew larger to meet large daylight bomber raids.

Geschwader A *Luftwaffe* unit equivalent to a wing, and usually composed of three or more *Gruppen*.

Geschwader Z.b.V. Wing-sized force of miscellaneous units.

GM 1 Nitrous oxide.

Gruppe A *Luftwaffe* unit which, in the fighter force, was composed of between 40 and 80 aircraft; three or more made up a *Geschwader* (q.v.). Identified by a roman numeral and the designation of its parent *Geschwader* (e.g., I./NJG 6), or, if independent, by arabic numerals.

Gruppenkommandeur CO of a *Gruppe*.

Hauptmann German rank equivalent to a Captain (US) or a Flight Lieutenant (British).

Helle Nachtjagd Light nightfighting (q.v.)

"Hermine" Codename for FuG 125 VHF beacon receiver (q.v.).

"Himmelblatt" The original system of ground-controlled interception by night fighters directed by ground-mounted radars and fighter-specific voice commands (lit., Four-Poster Bed). See the Kammhuber chapters for details.

Hptm *Hauptmann* (q.v.)

HQ headquarters

H2S British bomber radar used for navigation and bombing through overcast. Known as *"Rotterdam Gerät"* to the Germans, from the location of first one recovered.

H2X US-built version of H2S.

i.G. On General Staff duties (*im Generalsstabdienst*).

Industry fighters Independent flights of fighters kept at aircraft factories in the early stages of the bomber offensive. Manned by test pilots during air attacks.

Jafu *Jagdführer.* Area fighter leader.

Jagddivisionen Fighter division.

Jagdfliegerführer Fighter leader.

Jagdkorps Fighter corps.

Jagdwaffe *Luftwaffe* Fighter Force.

Jagdstab Staff of the *General der Jagdflieger.*

JG *Jagdgeschwader.* Fighter wing.

JK *Jagdkorps* (q.v.)

JLO *Jägerleitoffizier.* Fighter Control Officer.

j.p. jet powered.

Kdre See *Kommodore.*

Kette   Three-plane tactical formation, usually flown in a "v."

Kommando   Independent detachment, often named for its commander or base.

Kommodore   Commanding Officer of a *Geschwader*.

Kommandeur   Commanding Officer of a *Gruppe*.

Kompanie   Company or squadron.

Lehr   Instructional.

L.Fl.K.   *Luftflotte* HQ.

Lichtenstein B/C   Telefunken-designed FuG 202, the first German AI radar. Four large nose-mounted antennas. Used by the Nachtjagd.

Lichtenstein C   Telefunken-designed FuG 212. Simplified version of FuG 202.

"Light" Night-Fighting   Night-fighting tactics carried out in cooperation with searchlights. See the chapters by Kammhuber and Schmid for details.

Luftflotte   A formation of *Fliegerkorps* or multiple *Geschwader* of different types. Roughly equivalent to a USAAF numbered air force.

MG 131   13mm machine gun.

MG 151   15mm (later 20mm) cannon.

"Mickey"   Codename for the USAAF H2X radar, a version of the RAF's H2S. Used for radar-aimed bombing and navigation.

Milch   *Generalfeldmarschall* Erhard Milch, Director General of Equipment for the *Luftwaffe* from November 1941 to May 1944. Sentenced to 15 years' imprisonment for war crimes involving use of slave labor.

Mölders   Oberst Werner Mölders, an ace with 115 victories and a keen tactician. Served as *General der Jagdflieger*. Killed in a crash in November 1941.

Mosquito   De Havilland Mosquito, an RAF twin-engine light bomber, fighter, and reconnaissance aircraft. Used for Pathfinder and diversionary attacks over Germany.

MW50   Methanol-water injection.

Luftgau   Air zone. Used as an administrative and support command echelon pre-war.

LW   *Luftwaffe*, i.e., the German Air Force.

Nachrichten   Signals (including radar).

Nafu   Signals unit.

"Naxos"   Codename for Telefunken FuG 350 passive sensor intended to detect RAF H2S bombing and navigation radars.

NJG   *Nachtjagdgeschwader*. Night-Fighter Wing.

NVG   Martini, signal and radar chief, OKL (q.v.).

Ob.d.L.   OKL (q.v.)

Oberleutnant   German rank equivalent to First Lieutenant (US) or Flying Officer (British).

Oberst   German rank equivalent to Colonel (US) or Group Captain (British).

OKL   *Oberkommando der Luftwaffe.* Air Force High Command.

OKW   *Oberkommando der Wehrmacht.* Armed Force High Command.

Ops   Operations

"Pip Squeak"   RAF radio system used in 1940 to track airborne fighters in areas not covered by radar. Ground stations triangulated short transmissions.

Planspiel   Map wargame to test out alternative plans.

P/W   Prisoner of war.

QMG   Quartermaster General. Much broader staff function than US Quartermaster.

RAF   Royal Air Force.

Reich   Greater Germany, including both the post-Versailles borders and territory annexed from neighboring countries, but not areas only under military occupation.

Reichsjägerwelle   See Commentary.

Rotte   Two-plane tactical formation, usually flown by a leader and wingman.

"Rotterdam Gerät"   German codename for H2S radar (q.v.).

RP   rocket projectile

R/T   radio (voice) telephone

RTU   Replacement Training Unit

RU   rendezvous.

"Saw Mill"   Allied codename for SN-2 (q.v.). Also SM-2.

Scanner   AI radar.

Schwarm   Four-plane tactical formation, usually flown as a "finger four."

SE   single-engine(d).

Seeburg Tisch   Seeburg Table. Plotting board showing radar plots of both friendly and enemy aircraft. See Kammhuber's chapters for details.

SN 2   FuG 220. Improved Telefunken Lichtenstein radar.

"Spanner"   AEG-designed experimental IR detector.

Sperrle   General Hugo Sperrle, commander of *Luftflotte Reich,* 1944–45.

"Spoof Service"   Allied designation for German camouflage and diversionary efforts. Included both the construction of dummy targets on the ground and the use of misleading and jamming transmissions.

Stab   Staff (of a unit).

Stab-   Prefix of a unit or formation size, indicating the staff of a unit or a subunit of aircraft flown by that staff.

Staffel   Unit of about 9–16 aircraft. Three or more usually made up a *Gruppe* (q.v.).

Staka   *Staffel kapitän.* Commanding officer of a *Staffel.*

Sturmgruppe   Fighter group dedicated to the antibomber mission, comprising fighters with additional armament, usually external.

Sturmjäger   Single-engine, antibomber fighter unit, usually equipped with uparmed and uparmored FW 190s.

TAF   Tactical Air Force.

"Tame Boar"   Night-fighter operations with ground control but without the precise GCI of the "Himmelblatt" (q.v.).

TE   twin-engine(d)

T/O   table of organization

TOE   Table of Organization and Equipment. A unit's war establishment, indicating the personnel, equipment, and subordinate units it is supposed to have under its command.

USAAF   US Army Air Forces. Became US Air Force (USAF) in 1947.

Verteidigungszone   Air defense zone.

Waffengeneral   A position such as *General der Jagdflieger* (and its counterparts for the nightfighter, bomber and ground attack forces), concerned with a specific force rather than a particular operational unit. Could be held by a colonel.

Water-methanol injection   See MW50.

"Wild Boar"   Night-fighter operations without ground control.

Wilde Sau   "Wild Boar" (q.v.).

"Window"   Original wartime name for chaff—strips of metal dropped from aircraft to create spurious radar reflections.

W/L   Wireless.

W/T   Wireless telegraphy (Morse).

Würzburg   Short-range ground radar, used for fire control.

"Y"   Standard method of fighter guidance by VHF radio, using direction-finding from the ground on signals transmitted by an aircraft (the aircraft would receive signals transmitted from the ground). Capable of providing both range and bearing.

Y-Gerät   Equipment for using "Y" guidance on German aircraft.

"Y" Service   Allied designation for the monitoring of enemy radio transmissions.

Zahme Sau   "Tame Boar" (q.v.)

z.b.V.   *zur besonderen Verwendung* (for special duties).

Zerstörer   Twin-engine day fighter.

ZG   *Zerstörergeschwader* (twin-engine day-fighter wing).

Ia   Operations officer or section on a German staff, equivalent to a USAAF A-3 or S-3.

Ic   Intelligence officer or section on a German staff, equivalent to a USAAF A-2 or S-2.